Studies of Bactrian Legal Documents

By

Hossein Sheikh

BRILL

LEIDEN | BOSTON

Cover illustration: Document Uv written 726 CE in Khesh (a city between Bamiyan and Kabul), private collection, permission for use granted by the owner.

The Library of Congress Cataloging-in-Publication Data is available online at https://catalog.loc.gov
LC record available at https://lccn.loc.gov/2022050168

Typeface for the Latin, Greek, and Cyrillic scripts: "Brill". See and download: brill.com/brill-typeface.

ISSN 2667-2871
ISBN 978-90-04-51997-8 (hardback)
ISBN 978-90-04-51998-5 (e-book)

This book is printed on acid-free paper and produced in a sustainable manner.

Printed by Printforce, the Netherlands

To the memory of my parents

Ma'sumeh Ashrafi
(1942–1991)

Ali Sheikh
(1940–2013)

וָאֶקְנֶה אֶת-הַשָּׂדֶה מֵאֵת חֲנַמְאֵל בֶּן-דֹּדִי אֲשֶׁר בַּעֲנָתוֹת וָאֶשְׁקְלָה-לּוֹ אֶת-הַכֶּסֶף
שִׁבְעָה שְׁקָלִים וַעֲשָׂרָה הַכָּסֶף. וָאֶכְתֹּב בַּסֵּפֶר וָאֶחְתֹּם, וָאָעֵד עֵדִים וָאֶשְׁקֹל הַכֶּסֶף
בְּמֹאזְנָיִם. וָאֶקַּח אֶת-סֵפֶר הַמִּקְנָה אֶת-הֶחָתוּם הַמִּצְוָה וְהַחֻקִּים וְאֶת-הַגָּלוּי. וָאֶתֵּן
אֶת-הַסֵּפֶר הַמִּקְנָה אֶל-בָּרוּךְ בֶּן-נֵרִיָּה בֶּן-מַחְסֵיָה לְעֵינֵי חֲנַמְאֵל דֹּדִי וּלְעֵינֵי הָעֵדִים
הַכֹּתְבִים בְּסֵפֶר הַמִּקְנָה—לְעֵינֵי כָּל-הַיְּהוּדִים הַיֹּשְׁבִים בַּחֲצַר הַמַּטָּרָה.

And I bought the field at Anathoth from my cousin Hanamel, and weighed out the money to him, seventeen shekels of silver. I signed the deed, sealed it, got witnesses, and weighed the money on scales. Then I took the sealed deed of purchase, containing the terms and conditions, and the open copy; and I gave the deed of purchase to Baruch son of Neriah son of Mahseiah, in the presence of my cousin Hanamel, in the presence of the witnesses who signed the deed of purchase, and in the presence of all the Judeans who were sitting in the court of the guard.*

JEREMIAH, 32.9–12

∴

* Translation of Coogan et al., 2010, 1111f.

Contents

Preface

Bactrian[1] was an Iranian language spoken and written in a vast region of northern Afghanistan but ceased in writing by the end of the 9th-century CE. Before the 1990s, our textual evidence for this language was minimal, comprising one complete inscription[2] among damaged ones and coin legends.[3] However, since the 1990s, the situation has dramatically changed, and the volume of textual evidence has considerably increased.[4] Discoveries containing inscriptions,[5] legal and economic documents,[6] letters, etc.,[7] have been deciphered, edited, and published by Nicholas Sims-Williams. He has also written excellent philological and historical commentaries.[8] For example, in the first edition of Bactrian legal and economic texts, he states:

> Ideally, a commentary might have been added in which these documents would be compared with similar documents from earlier cultures (Babylonian, Aramaic, Greek, etc.) and those of neighboring countries (Middle Persian, Parthian, Sogdian, Khotanese, Uighur Turkish, Tibetan, and so on).[9]

My work partly addresses this desideratum by writing a commentary on the legal formulary and historical background of Bactria during late antiquity. To that aim, I have used Sims-Williams's elaborate translation of the documents because his literal translation enables me to consult each legal or technical point in the same way, each time it occurs. For the remaining documents, I have used those translated into English. Otherwise, I have translated the texts from the originals. The originals and translations have been included in this work.

Currently, there are only two articles on legal practices in Bactria, one by B. Waghmar, where he analyses "Bactrian diplomatics" and compares it with

1 For Bactrian grammar, see Sims-Williams, 2007, 38–49; Gholami, 2014.

2 This inscription is named for its findspot in Surkh Kotal, 1953. For an edition of the inscriptions see Davari Djilani, 1982, 53–64. For the new translation, see Sims-Williams, 2012a, 78f.

3 For all evidence before 1990, see Sims-Williams, 1988, 345ff; 1989, 230ff.

4 Sims-Williams, 1997 (2012).

5 For the inscriptions, see Sims-Williams and Falk and Sims-Williams and Cribb, 1996–97; Sims-Williams and Lee, 2003; Sims-Williams, 1998a; 2004 (2008); 2015a.

6 Sims-Williams, 2000 (revised edition 2012).

7 Ibid., 2007.

8 Ibid., 1998b; 1997 (2000); 2001 (2005); 2003 (2007); 2005 (2009).

9 Ibid., 2000, 7.

documents from various regions of Central Asia such as Gandhara, Tibet, etc.[10] The other writing by J. Cheung is a philological discussion of two words in Bactrian deeds, which he compares with an Arabic document from 11th-century CE Egypt. My study examines another topic by placing the Bactrian legal formulary within the context of Near Eastern legal practice.[11] Nevertheless, I recognize that my text is a first step in studying Bactrian legal culture, and I hope it will further advance the field.

10 Waghmar, 2010.

11 Chueng, 2009.

Acknowledgments

This text is a revised and expanded version of my PhD dissertation, which would not have been possible without the generous guidance and support received from many people over the years. I wish to offer my heartfelt thanks to the following individuals.

I would like to thank my thesis advisor, Prof. Dr Philip Kreyenbroek, for guiding and advising me through the research process. His strong support for my ideas and confidence in my abilities encouraged me to pursue research topics for which I am truly passionate.

Gratitude is also extended to Prof. Dr Michael Job, a talented teacher and passionate scientist. I am indebted and thankful for the help he offered. As a student, what I learned from him about linguistics and languages encouraged me to write this thesis.

Thankfulness is also extended to Prof. Dr Klaus Röhrborn for helping me read and understand documents in Old Uyghur. He also drew my attention to some works in Chinese. Several times, he generously lent me the books I needed from his personal library.

I would like to thank Prof. Dr Nicholas Sims-Williams for sending his publications, feedback, and suggestions. This dissertation could not have been written without his masterly and elaborate translation and commentaries on the Bactrian corpus. It would not have been possible to obtain permission from the owner of the document Uv for the book cover without his assistance.

I would like to express my sincere gratitude to Shervin Farridnejad, a former classmate and dear friend, for his unselfish assistance and accepting the publication of this work in the *Ancient Iran Series*. My thanks also go to the people who sent me their research papers, especially Jan Dušek (Praha), Andrew Gross (Washington), and Eleonora Cussini (Venice).

Thanks are due to the text editor, Dr Gregory Bilotto. He not only polished my English, making it clear and comprehensible, but also saved me from many mistakes in the text and offered invaluable suggestions for improving the content. I am thankful for the help of Maryam Ghanei who proofread and formatted my entire work. Her sharp eyes and care saved me from many errors and unclarities. However, I am the only person responsible for errors in this thesis. I'd also like to thank Abdurraouf Oueslati, Acquisitions Editor Middle Eastern and Islamic Studies at Brill, and Pieter te Velde, for their perseverance in getting this book published as soon as possible.

Finally, I would like to give special thanks to my amazing family, particularly my sisters Fatemeh, Tahereh, Hamideh, and Leyla, for their love, support, and constant encouragement throughout my studies.

Abbreviations

AfO	*Archiv für Orientforschung*
ArOr	*Archiv Orientální*
ASJ	*Acta Sumerologica*
BAI	*Bulletin of the Asia Institute*
BaM	*Baghdader Mitteilungen*
BiOr	*Bibliotheca Orientalis*
BSOAS	*Bulletin of the School of Oriental and African Studies*
CAD	*Chicago Assyrian Dictionary* (see Gelb et al., 1956–2010).
EIr	*Encyclopedia Iranica* (Yarshater (ed.), 1982–)
EW	*East & West*
JA	*Journal Asiatique*
JAOS	*Journal of the American Oriental Society*
JCS	*Journal of Cuneiform Studies*
JHS	*The Journal of Hellenic Studies*
JJP	*Journal of Juristic Papyrology*
JJS	*Journal of Jewish Studies*
JNES	*Journal of Near Eastern Studies*
JRAS	*Journal of the Royal Asiatic Society*
JSAI	*Jerusalem Studies in Arabic and Islam*
KTU3	*Keilalphabetischen Texte aus Ugarit* (see Dietrich et al., 2013)
MDP	*Mémoires de la Délégation en Perse* (see Scheil, 1930–33)
MHD	*Mādayān ī Hazār Dādestān* (Macuch, 1993 and Perikhanian, 1997)
MHDA	*Mādayān ī Hazār Dādestān* (see Macuch, 1981 and Perikhanian, 1997)
Or	*Orientalia*
PAT	*Palmyrene Aramaic Texts* (see Hillers and Cussini 1996)
RA	*Revue d'Assyriologie et d'archéologie orientale*
RlA	*Reallexikon der Assyriologie und vorderasiatischen Archäologie* (see Ebeling and Meissner, 1928–2018)
SRAA	*Silk Road Art and Archaeology*
TAD	*Textbook of Aramaic Documents from Ancient Egypt* (see Porten and Yardeni, 1986–1999)
TB	*Talmud Bavili* (see Goldschmidt, 1929–1935)
TDOT	*Theological Dictionary of the Old Testament* (see Botterweck and Ringgren (eds.), 1977–2004)
TY	*Talmud Yerushalmi* (see Heinrich W. Guggenheimer, 2000–)
UF	*Ugarit-Forschungen*
ZA	*Zeitschrift für Assyriologie*
ZAR	*Zeitschrift für Altorientalische und Biblische Rechtsgeschichte*
ZSSR	*Zeitschrift der Savigny-Stiftung für Rechtsgeschichte*

Historical Timeline

Date*	Cuneiform corpora		Aramaic corpora	Greek corpora	Iranian documents	Islamic documents
	Mesopotamia	Syria and Levant				
2900 BCE	The Early Dynastic period (2900–2334)					
	The Sargonic Empire (2334–2193)					
2000 BCE	Ur III Period = Neo-Sumerian period (2193–2004)	Mari Alalakh VII				
	Old Babylonian Period (2004–1595)	Ḫana				
	Old Assyrian Period (1950–1740)	Alalakh IV				
1500 BCE	Middle Babylonian Period (1595–1155)	Ekalte				
	Middle Assyrian Empire (1363–912)	Ugarit Emar				
1000 BCE						
	Neo-Assyrian Empire (972–612)					
625 BCE						
	Neo Babylonian Empire (612–539)					
550 BCE	Achaemenid Empire (550–330)					
			Elephantine papyri			
			Wadi Al-Daliyah papyri			
311 BCE	Hellenistic Period (323–31)					
	Seleucid Empire (312–63)					

(*cont.*)

Date	Cuneiform corpora		Aramaic corpora	Greek corpora	Iranian documents	Islamic documents
	Mesopotamia	Syria and Levant				
250 BCE						
	Parthian Empire (247 BCE–224 CE)					
100 CE	Roman Empire (27 BCE–395 CE)					
	Kushan Empire (the 1st–3rd-centuries CE)		Mada'in Salih and Palmyrene inscriptions	Avroman Parchments		
				Judean Desert papyri		
			Judean Desert papyri			
				Dura Europos		
250 CE			Dura-Europos			
	Sasanian Empire (223–652)			Euphrates		
			Euphrates			
				Parchments		
			Mishna and Tosefta			
					Bactrian	
	Byzantine Empire (395–1453)					
600 CE			Palestinian			
	Early Islamic Period (622–1000)		Babylonian		MHD	
			Talmuds			
750 CE					Sogdian	
					Pahlavi	Egypt
					Khotanese	Khurasan
1000 CE						Bamyan
	Early Medieval Era = before mogul invasion (1000–1220)					Yarkand
						Ghur
						Balkh
1200 CE						Azerbaijan

* These dates are approximate.

Maps

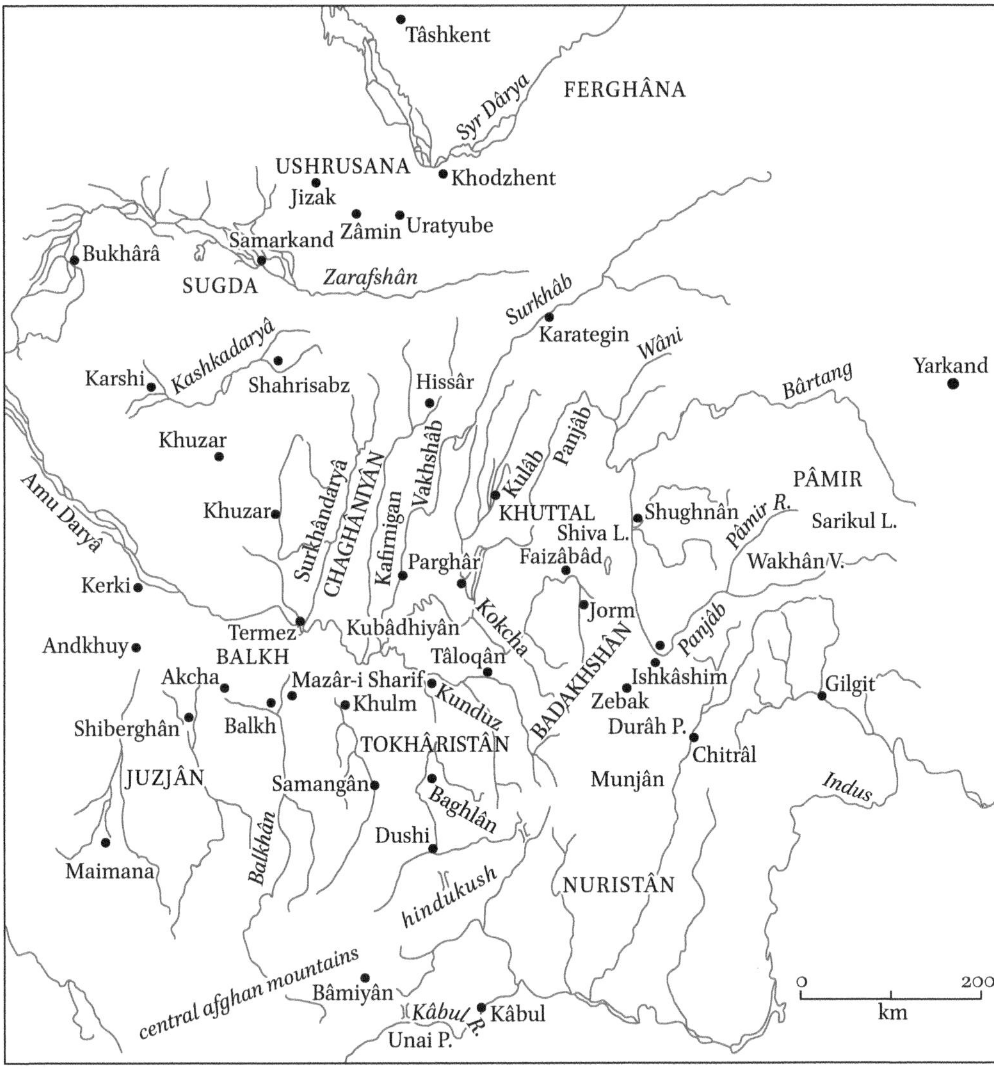

MAP 1 Bactria and adjacent areas
VOGELSANG, 1992, 53

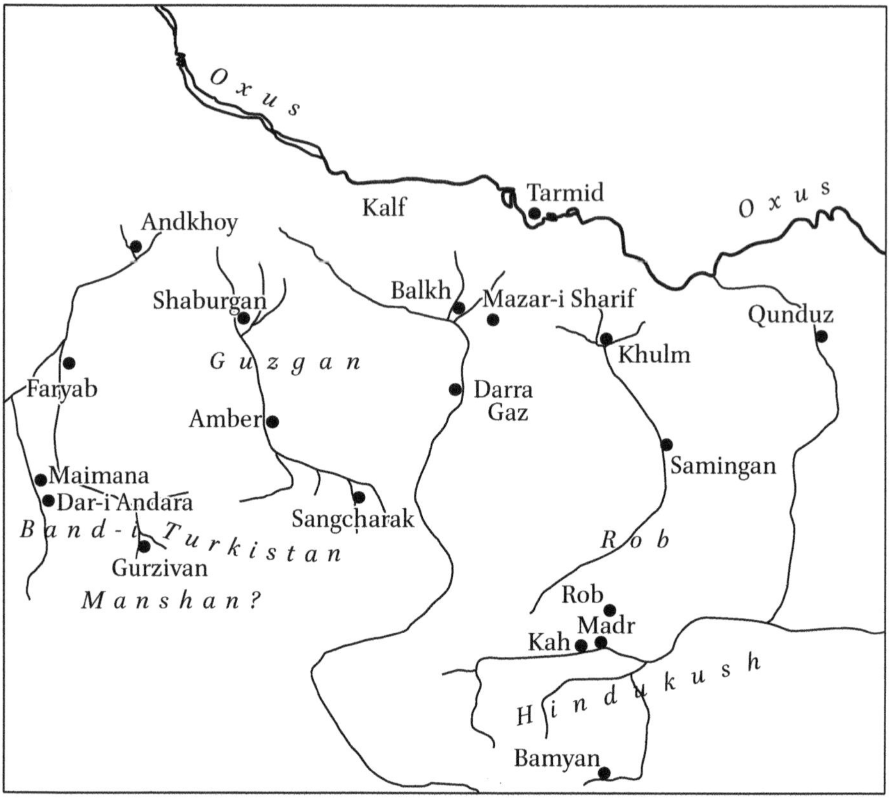

MAP 2 Northern Afghanistan
SIMS-WILLIAMS, 2006–2007

Introduction

1 Geography of Bactria

Bactria is located in Afghanistan, north of the Hindu Kush, and extends roughly to the Oxus (Amu-Darya). Dariush I (522–486 BCE) in the Behistun inscription, where he enumerates the lands under his rule, is the oldest attestation of the name Bactria.[1] Bāxtriš is one of these lands.[2] The Roman writer Ptolemy, in his book, *The Geography*, describes the land of Bactria in the following manner:

> Baktrianē is bounded from the West by Marginē, (the boundary running) along its side-line described above [from the corner at 103° 44° to the SW corner at 109° 39°]. From the North and the East (it is bounded) by the Sogdianoi, boundary running) along the remaining part of the River Ōxos (1) [from the corner by the NE corner to the SE corner]. From the South (it is bounded) by the remaining part of Areia from the boundary-point adjoining Margianē [SW corner] to a point (2) at 111° 39°, thereupon by the Paropanisadai, (the boundary) following the parallel line (from that point) along the bend of the Paropanisos mountain (3) [at 111°30′ 39°] to the sources of the Ōxos [SE corner] (4) at 119° 30′ 39°.[3]

In classical sources, Bactria was famous for its wealth. The lapis lazuli from Badakhshan in Bactria was very popular in Mesopotamia, and agricultural wealth generated by the great oases of pre-Achaemenid Bactria, served by vast irrigation networks, has been discovered by surveys in the basin of the Upper Oxus.[4] Archeologists have revealed that Bactria was developed well before the Achaemenid period, implying that state structures existed in Bactria as early as the end of the second millennium BCE.[5] In the Avesta, Bactria is only mentioned in a list of countries in the first chapter of the Vendīdād as Bâxδî with adjectives srīra. ərəδβō.drafša (beautiful, with uplifted banners).[6]

1 DB, 12–17 for more evidence in Old Persian, see Schmitt, 2014, 87; 153.
2 About the name and its etymology, see Humbach and Feiss, 2012, 35f; De Blois, 2013; Sims-Williams, 2016; Witzel, 1980.
3 Ptolemy, 6.11.1; text and translation in Humbach and Ziegler, 1998, 152f.
4 Briant, 2000, 39.
5 Leriche, 2007, 125ff.
6 Vendīdād 1.6 and 7. See Vogelsang, 2000, 52; Vogelsang, 1992, 53; Witzel, 2000, 294ff; Grenet, 2005, 30f.

 | DOI:10.1163/9789004519985_002

2 Administrative Languages in Bactria

Our knowledge of Bacteria's history suffers from a paucity of information. What we know originates from external sources or documentary evidence, including numismatic and archeological finds.[7] Among these discoveries are texts in various languages that are important and necessary for studying administrative languages in this region from the Achaemenid period to the Muslim conquests. Administrative languages in this region can be divided into three chronological phases: Aramaic, Greek, and Bactrian. Aramaic became the lingua franca in the Achaemenid Empire until Alexander the Great defeated Darius III (336–30 BCE) and conquered his territories.[8] Evidence from Bactria indicates that when it was part of the Achaemenid Empire, Aramaic, like other satrapies, was the official language, regardless of local preferences,[9] which was most likely an Iranian language. After Alexander conquered Bactria, Aramaic remained the official language. Eventually, it was succeeded by the Greek language in the Hellenistic period, enduring until the rise of the Kushan Empire. If we believe Kanishka I (first half of 1st-century CE),[10] he pushed Greek aside, and the local language, Bactrian, became the official, although the Greek script was integrated. From the Kushan Empire to the Islamic conquest of Central Asia, this region experienced numerous political shifts and events, but one element remained constant: Bactrian continued as the administrative language in this region. In addition, the neighboring languages and religions of this region played a significant role in social life. For example, we find Indian elements in Bactrian legal texts, which likely date to the Maurya period and its dominance of political and religious policies in Central Asia.[11] Contact and relationships between middle Iranian languages in this region are other determining factors. Numerous parallels exist between middle Iranian legal terminologies, even though there is no single explanation for these parallels. For example, similarities between Pahlavi and Bactrian terms, such as the word for valid (wābar in Pahlavi and οαοαρο in Bactrian) are understandable since Bactria was part of the Sasanian Empire for a long time. In contrast, the full

7 For more information on the political history of Bactria, see Grenet et Leriche, 1988; Mairs, 2021; Benjamin, 2018; Rezakhani, 2017.

8 For more on Aramaic as lingua franca, see Follmer, 2020.

9 See Naveh and Shaked, 2012.

10 Kanishka declares that he issued an edict in Greek and then a Bactrian version: Οτηια ι ιωναγγο οασο οαζοαστο ταδηια αριαο ωσταδο and he issued a Greek edict (and) then he put it into Aryan (Sims-Williams, 2004 (2008)); for more about this inscription and the word Aryan, see Gnoli, 2002.

11 For further details on the Maurya Empire, see Ray, 2021, 198ff.

price element (see Chapter 2) in three languages (Bactrian, Khotanese, and Sogdian) has its origins in the imperial formulary.[12] Nevertheless, one thing is certain—Buddhism, the majority religion in Central Asia, played an essential role in the relationships between peoples, and its role in our study within the context of legal terminology is obviously significant.[13]

3 Legal Formulary in Bactria: Language

During the Achaemenid period, the Bactrian people spoke a language other than Aramaic, most likely an Iranian language (Bactrian), as noted above. For example, they contain personal names with Wakhsh, a god in Bactria,[14] whose name reappears in Bactrian documents.[15] Before Kanishka declared Bactrian the Kushan Empire's administrative language in the early centuries CE, it appears that people in Bactria continued to speak in their mother tongue during the Hellenistic period.

For this study, similarities between Aramaic and Greek legal formularies with Bactrian are important for the manner that previous terminologies transitioned into the Bactrian language. An example might be a contract where an oral agreement was made between two parties. The content of these documents was first translated orally into the respective language of either party, thereby ensuring that the agreed terms had been recorded in the contract, particularly the legal jargon of the documents. Accordingly, in the Achaemenid period, Aramaic legal terms were translated into the local language, probably Bactrian.

After Alexander the Great (356–23 BCE) conquered the region, the official language was changed to Greek, and new elements were added to the legal formulary and terminology, but it was not completely transformed. More specifically, the changes did not reshape the documents, rather new elements or alterations were added, making the text more precise and exact to avoid future legal disputes. Therefore, it seems that Greek scribes relied on the previous agreement schema, Aramaic, common in Bactria, and translated it into Greek.

As scribes translated the content of documents from Greek into the vernacular language they gave special attention to new elements, much like in

12 Sheikh, 2021.

13 For more information on Buddhism in Central Asia, see Heirman & Bumbacher, 2007.

14 Naveh and Shaked, 2012, Glossary. For example, whwḥšw (Vauvaxš) or wḥšwbndk (Vaxšbandaka).

15 Sims-Williams, 2010, no. 321–25.

the past. Thus, when Greek faded as the official language in Bactria and had been replaced by the Bactrian language, the legal terminology was already well-known to the locals. In other words, before Bactrian became the official language, its position as the local language necessitated that Aramaic and Greek legal terminologies had already been translated and incorporated. Remarkably, despite migrations of various ethnic groups over time, Bactrians used a stable legal terminology originally established in the Achaemenid period. The absence of significant changes in Bactrian deeds written throughout the 4th–8th-centuries CE demonstrates the stability of legal practice and terminology.

4 Methodological Approach

My study has two goals: an in-depth examination of how Bactrian legal conveyances are structured and a comprehensive investigation of its historical context. For the first, I will thoroughly examine the terms and clauses in the documents to determine how Bactrians wrote a legal document. For the second, I will investigate the Bactrian legal formulary in three contexts: ancient Near Eastern legal practice, imperial legal formulary, and legal formularies in Iran and Central Asia. For the first context, I will examine cuneiform legal traditions to identify where terms and clauses originated. In the second, I will compare this legal formulary to others from the Achaemenid period to the rise of Islam in the Near East. After Aramaic became the lingua franca during the early Achaemenid period, the central power issued a template legal formulary for all of its satrapies to follow. I have labelled this template, the imperial formulary. It begins with the date and ends with the names of the witnesses. The investiture clause, surviving centuries after the Achaemenid Empire, is the main part of the formulary. Although the order of elements in the formulary did not change during the Hellenistic period, some new elements for the future waiver of charges were added. The validity clause and double copies are two of these elements. Later, in Iran and Central Asia, the imperial legal formulary was recorded in various local languages, including Bactrian. In the third phase, I will look for pre-Islamic elements in the legal documents of Central Asia until the Mongol invasion. In summation, I will trace the evolution of clauses and terms in Bactrian deeds and examine their context within ancient Near Eastern legal practices and in the later traditions of Central Asia following their extinction.

5 Discovery of Documents

In the 1990s, Bactrian documents and texts were discovered, and their deciphering was presented through a lecture by Sims-Williams in 1997. Further texts have been discovered, and with the number increasing, Sims-Williams published them in three volumes: vol. I, economic and legal documents,[16] vol. II, letters, vol. III, plates. Additionally, he has treated legal and economic documents separately in several articles, each with extensive philological commentary.[17] Rather than restating what Sims-Williams and others have noted about these discoveries, this work will only focus on legal deeds, their structure, and historical context.

6 Typology of the Sources

The legal sources of Bactria may be divided into two main categories: primary sources, including legal texts, and secondary sources, comprising inscriptions, letters, and seals, which can provide information on legal practices and systems in Bactria. Legal texts are written records of legal agreements, e.g., loans, marriages, peace agreements, receipts, releases, and sales. These attest to the application of the law and are contemporaneous with the transactions recorded. However, these documents were indirect evidence of the law and reflect a shadowy presence behind the transactions described. Hence, this study primarily focuses on legal terminology to shed light on legal formulary in Bactria during late antiquity. These documents, spanning nearly 400 years and the majority either completely preserved or incurring only minor damage,[18] have two main characteristics: continuity and conservatism. Both are consistent with other legal traditions in the ancient Near East.[19] Unfortunately, we do not have evidence from earlier eras to show the historical evolution of legal practice in Bactria over time, but there are additional documents written in Aramaic, Greek, and other languages throughout the Near East comparable to

16 First edition of Bactrian documents was published 2000, second edition 2012.

17 Humbach admires the work as "a philological and linguistic masterpiece" Humbach, 2002, 418.

18 See description of Bactrian documents in Sims-Williams, 2012b, 10ff.

19 For more details on this theme, see Westbrook and Wells, 2009, 23.

the Bactrian documents, which clarify their structure and development. Below is a table categorizing a list of legal texts.

7 The List of the Contracts and the Receipts

TABLE 1

Doc	Type	Doc	Type
A	Marriage contract	P	Contract for the purchase of slave
Aa	Receipt	Q	Contract for a monetary loan
B	Receipt	R	Undertaking to keep the peace
C	Deed for gifting an estate	S	Undertaking to keep the peace
D	Report-receipt	Ss	Contract for a monetary loan
E	Receipt	T	Deed for gifting an estate and female slave
F	Deed of manumission	Tt	Deed of gift
G	Receipt	U	Contract for the release of a vineyard
H	Receipt	Uu	Undertaking to keep the peace
I	Contract	Uv	Familial contract
Ii	Contract	V	Contract for the purchase of an estate
J	Contract for the purchase of an estate	W	Contract for the purchase of an estate
K	Contract for a loan of grain and wine	X	Undertaking to keep the peace
L	Contract for the purchase of an estate	aa	Contract for the purchase of an estate
M	Receipt	ab	Contract for the purchase of an estate
m	Contract	ac	Loan contract
N	Undertaking to keep the peace	ad	Unclear
Nn	Contract for the purchase of an estate	an	Receipt for a sum of money
O	Undertaking to keep the peace		

8 The Classification of Bactrian Deeds

The documents can be classified according to two criteria: the legal nature of the contract (donation, lease, sale, etc.), or the type of property involved (immobile property, mobile or personal property, etc.) see Table 2:

TABLE 2

Family law	**Immobile property**	**Moveable property**	**Procedure (settlement)**
Marriage contract Doc. ***A***	Sales or leases of land or vineyard Doc. ***I, Ii, J, L, m, Nn, U, V, W, aa, ab, ae***	purchase of slave Doc. ***P***	Undertaking to keep the peace Doc. ***N, O, R, S, Uu, X***
Familial contract Doc. **Uv**	Donation of a land Doc. ***C, Tt***	Receipt for money, flour, etc. Doc. ***Aa, B, E, G, H, M, an***	
	Lease of a vineyard Doc. ***U***	Loan of grain, wine, etc. Doc. ***K, Ss, ac***	
		Manumission Doc. ***F***	
	Donation of an estate and female slave Doc. ***T***		

9 The Structure of the Bactrian Deed of Conveyance

A contract is a protocol of oral proceedings usually performed before witnesses. Each legal system has criteria for what it recognizes as a legally binding agreement, the conditions of enforcement under its terms, and the extent of enforcement. Bactrian legal documents begin with the date and location of the deed's execution and end with the signatures and names of witnesses. Let us begin with a summary of the main elements in the Bactrian legal formulary, and a brief explanation of each element.

10 The Opening Section

The opening section in a Bactrian deed refers to the origin, and the opening section begins with the date and ends with the issuer's declaration. The section comprises the following elements—known as outer elements:

10.1 *Date*

Bactrian deeds start with a date from a local calendar. This calendar begins in the early–3rd-century CE, between 223–4 and 227–9.[20]

10.2 *Title*

Every document has a title because of the agreement type. The word μολραγο, which means a sealed document, appears frequently in the title. The act of sealing implied that the deed was authorized and valid.

10.3 *Location*

After the title, the precise location of the deed would be given. A location is always a public place, such as a market, or an official one, namely the royal court.

10.4 *Authorities and Witnesses*

Agreements are typically drafted before a government official, king, or ruler, and with freemen serving as witnesses. The presence of an official makes the agreement legitimate and authorized. The witnesses are exclusively male and free, while women and slaves have no place. However, in Bactria, there is a phenomenon called the mass witness, when a large number of people from a city or district gathered as witnesses in the location where the agreement was drafted.

10.5 *Operative Section*

The operative part of a Bactrian deed begins with an introduction, establishing the facts of a transaction and revealing its purpose and nature. Since the document is primarily concerned with repeated facts, stereotypical phrases are used.

---

20 For information on the calendar, see Sims-Williams and de Blois, 2005; Schindel, 2011; de Blois, 2006; Sims-Williams, 2011 (2012); Sims-Williams et al., 2018.

11 Declaration and Introduction of Parties

Bactrian deeds of conveyance are formulated as first-person declarations (subjective style), and the issuer introduces himself, his partner/s, and his opponent/s (addressee).

11.1 *Volition Term*

The issuer declares that he is performing the agreement freely and willingly, meaning it's voluntarily and not under duress.

11.2 *Cause of Agreement*

The reason for entering into the agreement is stated by the issuer, although the reason changes depending on the subject of the agreement. Normally, the reason for a sale deed is debt, when the owner is forced to sell property to pay taxes he cannot otherwise afford.

11.3 *Property Description*

The seller describes the property in a deed if it's a sale contract. In land sale deeds, the property description typically consists of two parts: (1) a boundary description listing each of the neighboring lots, (2) an itemization of the property's constituent parts. The issuer does not give an exact size of the property in the description because he wants to avoid any future claims concerning the size.

11.4 *Sale Price*

The seller is always paid in full for the sale, and the quality and quantity of coins are specified in the text. Receiving the full price implies that the addressee has completely spent the price and the two parties have agreed on the price amount before the contract is written.

12 Acknowledgment of Receipt and Satisfaction Clause

The issuer declares that he has received the price and is satisfied. These two elements are not only combined in sale deeds, but also in any agreement with a subject paying money, and an issuer declaring satisfaction. Additionally, these two terms are applicable for gift deeds, when satisfaction with the service received must be declared.

13 Investiture Clause and Final Clauses

13.1 *Entitlement Phrase*

In this clause, the issuer acknowledges the addressee's rights in perpetuity and declares that the addressee has full control over the property.

13.2 *Contingency Clauses*

The issuer (the seller or donor) promises to uphold and defend the new owner's ownership rights against any future contingencies in these clauses. This includes challenges from either the issuer or third parties.

13.3 *No-Contest Clause*

He and his family will not pursue any legal action against the addressee.

13.4 *Warranty Clause*

Third-party challenges are also covered by another clause referred to here as the defense clause.

13.5 *Penalty*

The penalty term, part of the warranty clause, is when the issuer promises that if he, his family, or descendants bring a charge against the addressee in the future, he will pay the addressee and the state the same amount. Furthermore, the issuer must pay a fine if he fails to defend the addressee against a third party. Usually, the fine is double the value of the property.

13.6 *Validity Clause*

This clause brings the contract's clauses to a close. In fact, it is the closing formula, and nothing can be added to the text without rendering the deed null and void.

14 Seals and Signature

The witnesses sign their names and place seals on the documents. Regarding double copy documents, their names are written transversely on the reverse, and with simple documents, it's written inside of the document.

15 Settlements

Settlements are the result of making peace after a quarrel, which is typically made between two families. Their structure differs from that of a sale or gift contract in terms of content, with the distinction occurring after the cause clause is declared. In peace agreements, the clause is inserted directly after the warranty, while in a quarrel, it's added once the two parties (plaintiff and defendant) reach an agreement, and the issuer (defendant) assures the plaintiff that he and his family will not file a claim in the future. In some settlements, the peace clause is triggered after the payment of a fine (monetary).

16 Manumission

Document F describes the release of a debt slave who was sold by two people (presumably his creditors) to pay off their debt. Actually, he had initially been enslaved for his debt, and then was sold to cover the debt of his creditors. His creditor would manumit him once he had paid the full amount. This contract is the result and aftermath of two sale agreements, which means that the slave sold himself into bondage, likely to two brothers, who then sold him to a new creditor. Similarly, to sale and gift deeds, the new creditor declares that he has received the money in full and is satisfied.

17 Marriage Contract

Only one marriage contract from Bactria has been discovered, and it's the oldest example of a legal text written in Bactrian. Following the opening section, the fathers of the bride and the bridegrooms introduce themselves, and then the father of the bridegrooms requests the marriage of his sons to the daughter of the bride's father. Interestingly, the warranty clause in this contract includes three parties: the father of the bridegrooms, the bridegrooms, and the master of the bridegrooms. The request of the bridegrooms' father is not a legal requirement, but rather a custom. The bridegrooms and their master, on the other hand, promise to pay a fine if they fail to perform their duties and obligations. The document's closing is damaged, but it once contained a dowry list. There wasn't a divorce clause in the contract.

18 Other Corpora

Regarding the above-mentioned history of the official Bactrian language, it is obvious that at least two linguistic traditions in Bactria played an important role in shaping legal practices: Aramaic and Greek. I studied Aramaic and Greek legal corpora from the Achaemenid and Hellenistic periods to understand better the origins of legal formulary in Bactria, and I investigated the Akkadian corpus, which influenced Aramaic legal formulary.

Furthermore, I explored other contemporaneous corpora from Bactria's neighbors, and probed the similarities between Bactrian and other middle Iranian languages, particularly Pahlavi. Undoubtedly, this language was influenced by Aramaic. Khotanese, Sogdian are two other middle Iranian languages.

19 Akkadian and Ugaritic Corpora

For this study, the largest sources originate from cuneiform writings on clay tablets. Sumerians in south Mesopotamia created the cuneiform writing system in the late–4th millennium BCE. It was adopted by the Akkadians, another Mesopotamian people, who spoke the Semitic language, Akkadian. This language is best known in two dialects: Babylonian and Assyrian. The Sumerian language had faded by the end of the 3rd millennium BCE, but Sumerian culture and learning, as well as their script, were preserved by Akkadian-speaking inhabitants of Mesopotamia for another 2,000 years. In the 2nd millennium BCE, Akkadian became the lingua franca for international relations, and was the language of law and administration in Syria-Palestine and Anatolia. It was replaced by languages written in alphabetical scripts during the 1st millennium BCE, even though the influence of Mesopotamian culture was maintained further west through conquests of the Assyrian and Babylonian Empires. Extant documents in Akkadian are rich and numerous. This is partly due to the chance circumstances of preservation and also the pattern of ancient cultural dispersion. While most materials used to keep records, e.g., parchment, papyrus, or wood, deteriorate, clay tablets, once baked or sun-dried, are virtually indestructible. The majority of the tablets are from Mesopotamia, but an increasing number of discoveries occurred in Syria and Anatolia. The cuneiform legal record dates from the 26th–2nd-centuries BCE. The largest number of tablets has been found in Babylonia, and during the Old Babylonian (ca. 20th–16th-centuries BCE) and Neo-Babylonian-Persian periods (ca. the 7th–4th-centuries BCE),[21] they numbered in the tens of thousands. Several

21 For the number of Akkadian tablets, see Streck, 2014, 4.

thousand documents in Akkadian come from 15th-century archives of Nuzi,[22] a Hurrian-speaking province of the Mittannian Empire situated on the Tigris.

In Anatolia, significant archives have been found at Kanesh, an Assyrian merchant colony in Anatolia flourishing during the 18th-century BCE.[23] Cuneiform archives found in Syria date to the late Bronze Age, with the most important from Ekalte[24] and Emar,[25] on the Euphrates; Alalaḫ[26] on the Orontes; and Ugarit,[27] a seaport on the Syrian coast. Despite the legal documents having been written in Akkadian, the residents of those cities all spoke northwestern Semitic languages. Indeed, a cuneiform alphabetical script was developed at Ugarit, but the majority of Ugaritic writings are literary in nature, with only a few legal documents discovered.[28]

Akkadian texts from Mesopotamia and Syria form a massive corpus covering a wide range of subjects and themes. During more than two-thousand-year period, the form and rules of legal texts changed due to factors of time and location. In south Mesopotamia, for example, the satisfaction clause vanishes in the middle Babylonian period, but it can still be found in legal deeds from Emar in the 12th-century BCE.

20 Aramaic Corpora in the Achaemenid Period[29]

20.1 *Elephantine*

Since the late–19th-century CE, a large number of Aramaic documents have been discovered in Elephantine, which had been the site of a Jewish garrison in Egypt. This Judean military colony yielded 43 contracts and several fragments. The oldest Aramaic contract, recorded on papyrus, was acquired in 1936 el-Hibeh, known today as the "Papyrus Bauer-Meissner," which contained a land lease. The contract is dated 515 BCE[30] while others are from the 5th-century BCE.

22 For documentary examples, see Pfeiffer and Speiser, 1936; Gadd, 1926.

23 For the structure of Old-Assyrian documents, see Hertel, 2013; and for marriage contracts, see Kienast, 2015.

24 The texts from Elkate were edited by Mayar, 2001.

25 Since 2004 Faist et al. publish a detailed bibliography for text from Emar in Ugaritforschungen, see Faist et al., 2004–.

26 For an overview of documents from Alalaḫ, see Lauinger, 2020. For documents from the Old Babylonian period see Lauinger, 2015; and for texts from the Middle Babylonian period, see Niedorf, 2008 and bibliography.

27 For the Akkadian documents, see Nougayrol, 1955.

28 For the legal documents in Ugaritic, see Vita, 2018; and for the texts, see KTU3 227–246.

29 For Aramaic Corpora in the Achaemenid Period, see Naveh & Greenfield, 1984 Dušek, 2013.

30 The text was edited initially by Bauer and Meissner in 1936.

The Elephantine legal corpus consists of two personal archives containing legal documents, one belonging to Mibtahiah and the other to Anani. The Mibtahiah (a wealthy woman) archive contains eleven documents and spans three generations (471–410 BCE) of a leading Jewish family on Elephantine Island. The contracts record the legal transactions of Mibtahiah's father, Mahseiah, son of Yedaniah, Mibtahiah herself, and two sons. The archive contains deeds of bequest, betrothal, grant, wifehood, withdrawal, and a deed concerning the apportionment of slaves.[31]

The archive of Anani, son of Azariah, an official at the Jewish temple in Elephantine, contains 13 documents covering two generations between 456–02 BCE. It documents the legal activities of his wife, daughter, and her husband, addressing deeds of bequest, loan, sale, wifehood, withdrawal, and concerning a dowry.[32] Further Aramaic legal texts, written during the Persian rule of Egypt, were discovered in Saqqara, although these are mostly fragmentary.[33] The legal formulae used in the Aramaic papyri from Elephantine are strikingly similar to those previously attested in Mesopotamia.[34]

20.2 *Wadi al-Daliyah*

In 1963, a trove of Aramaic papyri from Samira was found in Wadi al-Daliyeh, Palestine, ranging in date from 375–32 BCE.[35] The texts, written in the city of Samaria, were identified by some of the corresponding bullae naming the location. The papyri consist of at least 27 highly fragmentary documents and owing to their fragmentary condition, it's not possible to discern all of the content. However, at least ten are slave sales and one is the sale of a house.[36] Overall, the texts were influenced extensively by sale formularies common in Neo-Babylonian legal documents.[37]

---

31 Porten, 1969, 230ff; Porten, 1997, 214.

32 Ibid.

33 Porten & Yardeni, 1986–1999; and see the abbreviations.

34 These texts have been studied by Rabinowitz, 1956, Yaron, 1961; Verger, 1965; Muffs, 1969; (the latter source was reissued in 2003 with an introduction by B. Levine. I have used the new edition); Gross, 2008; and Botta, 2009.

35 Kottsieper, 2013; Dušek, 2013; and Dušek, 2020.

36 The papyri are edited by Gropp, 2001; Dušek, 2007; they have also been studied by Gropp, 2000; Gropp 2003; and Dušek, 2010.

37 Gropp, 2000, 834.

21 Aramaic, Hebrew, and Syriac Corpora from the Hellenistic and Roman Periods

21.1 *Documents from the Judean Desert*[38]

The bulk of the documentary materials from the Judean Desert stem from two sites along the west coast of the Dead Sea, Wadi Murabba'at[39] and Nahal Hever. The four caves excavated at Wadi Murabba'at yielded 173 inscribed items, including at least ten fragmentary deeds of sale, six written in Aramaic, and four in Hebrew. A. Yardeni dates all of these texts to the first Jewish Revolt against Rome (66–74 CE).[40] Additionally, in the caves at Nahal Hever, over 120 papyri were discovered, including deeds of conveyance during the second Jewish Revolt (132–6 CE).[41] Among these were documents written in Greek, Jewish Aramaic, and Nabataean Aramaic.[42] These contracts dealt with both immovable and movable items, e.g., gifts, sales, etc.[43]

22 Syriac Sources

22.1 *Syriac Documents*[44]

One of the oldest Syriac parchments was discovered in 1933 during the excavations of Dura-Europos, an important military outpost of the Parthian Empire and then the Roman Empire on the Euphrates. This document records the sale of a female slave, dated 243 CE.[45] In 1988, more documents were found that likely originated from Appadana (Neapolis), north of Dura-Europos on the Euphrates mostly in Greek. Two of them were Syriac parchments, the first,

---

38 Eshel, 2011 and for legal Papyri in the Near East see Cotton et al., 1995; for Hebrew documents, see Gross, 2012 (2014).

39 About documents from Murabbaat see Eshel, 2000, 583ff. All the epigraphic material from this site was published in 1961 by P. Benoit and J.T. Milik. A. Yardeni re-edited the Hebrew and Aramaic papyri from Wadi Murabba'at in 2000.

40 On this war, see Mason, 2016.

41 On the second Jewish Revolt, see Mor, 2016.

42 Yardeni and H.M. Cotton published the Jewish Aramaic and Greek papyri found by Bedouins in full in 1997. Additional papyri in Hebrew, Jewish Aramaic, and Nabataean Aramaic found by Yadin is published by Yadin, Greenfield, Levine and Yardeni in 2002. N. Lewis published the Greek material in full in 1989.

43 There are numerous studies on these documents, see for example Oudshoorn, 2007. Gross, 2008. Wise, 2015. Elser, 2017. Czajkowski, 2017.

44 See Butts, 2011, 314f.

45 See Healy, 2009, 264ff. The most accessible version of the texts is in Drijvers and Healey, 1999, 232ff.

Euphrates 19 is a transfer of debt dated 28 December 240 CE,[46] and the second, Euphrates 20, contains a lease for a piece of land.[47] On several of the Greek texts, there is additional writing in Syriac, for instance, P. Euphrates 6 (with its duplicate P. Euphrates 7) contains a deed for the sale of a slave in Greek, followed by seven lines of Syriac summarizing the sale and a list of witnesses and guarantors on the verso.[48] These documents reflect certain basic structural and individual elements observed elsewhere in Aramaic deeds of conveyance, but they are also influenced by Greco-Roman legal traditions.[49]

22.2 *Syriac Juridical Literature*

Alongside the legal papyri, another source for studying legal formulary in Syriac is the juridical literature concerning civil law.[50] Examples of legal terminology used in other Aramaic corpora can be found in these law books.[51]

23 Aramaic Inscriptions[52]

23.1 *Nabataean Tomb Inscriptions*[53]

A rich source of Aramaic legal terminology is tomb inscriptions from Mada'in Salih, an important Nabatean caravan city in the northwest of the Arabian Peninsula. The necropolis at Mada'in Salih includes more than 80 tombs with 38 bearing Nabatean Aramaic inscriptions—31 are dated between 1–75 CE.[54] The inscriptions record basic information about the tomb, such as who commissioned its construction and can be interred, but the most relevant part for Aramaic legal formulas, is a clause addressing ownership rights. Many of these tomb inscriptions contain a clause strikingly similar to the investiture clause in Aramaic deeds. Nonetheless, this clause served to restrict rather than confer ownership rights, which will be discussed below. A clue to the legal function of these inscriptions can be found in one example (inscription 37), stating that a copy of the tomb inscription had been deposited in a local temple. Therefore,

46 See Healy, 2008.
47 Drijvers and Healey, 1999, 237ff.
48 Feissel et al., 1997, 6ff and Doc 10.
49 Gross, 2008, 18.
50 For the Syrian legal literature, see Kaufhold, 2005; Selb, 1964.
51 Sachau, 1907–14 in 3 volumes; Selb and Kaufhold, 2002.
52 For more information on these texts, see Healy, 2005.
53 Healy, 1993; Hackl et al., 2003.
54 For sources on Nabataean law, see Healey, 1994; the latest and most comprehensive edition of these texts was published by J.F. Healey in 1993; see the German translation in Hackl et al., 2003; 302–53.

it seems likely that these inscriptions were copies of legal documents previously recorded in another medium, such as papyrus or parchment. Since these inscriptions lack some of the expected features common with a legal contract, e.g., the naming of witnesses, any other presiding officials, etc., it's possible they were mere summaries rather than verbatim copies.[55]

23.2 *Palmyrene Inscriptions*[56]

Some Palmyrene inscriptions containing clauses or simply references to sales of immovable property—portions of the tombs—are referenced in relevant literature as cession texts. Even though these are not legal documents, they contain legal clauses restating the right of the purchaser to the property already expressed in the sale contract.[57]

24 Greek Corpora

After Alexander the Great invaded Asia, Greek became the official language during the Hellenistic period. Regarding Near Eastern legal practices, this momentous event introduced new elements from Greek law, such as homologia, and the widespread use of local elements, namely double copies, in all regions. Greek documents from the Hellenistic Period in the Near East can be divided into two groups: the first, Greek documents from the territories of the Seleucid Empire, including documents from Western Iran (Avroman) to Palestine; and the second, consisting of Greek documents from Ptolemaic Egypt.

24.1 *Avroman*

In the early 20th-century, some documents were found in Avroman, Kurdistan. Two of the documents, Parchments I and II, dated to the Seleucid era in 225 (88–87 BCE) and 291 (22–1 BCE), respectively, are written in Greek,[58] and the third, Parchment III, presumably is from the Arsacid era (H)arwatāt of the year 300 (January–February, 53 CE).[59] Parchment I is a deed of sale for half a vineyard

55 Gross, 2008, 12f.

56 Hillers and Cussini, 1996; Yon, 2013, supplement.

57 Cussini, 2010; Cussini, 2016; for examples of legal texts, see Cussini, 1995; Kottsieper, 2004; 293–4.

58 Minns, 1915; Thommen translated the two documents into German with commentaries, see Thommen, 2010, 467–76.

59 Mackenzie, 1987, 111; for a new edition of this text, see Livshitz, 2010 (in English); Livshitz, 2011 (in Russian); Weber, 2010, 566f (in German).

inherited by two people totaling 40 silver drachmas, while Parchment II is a lease agreement and Parchment III is a short Aramaic-Parthian sale agreement.

24.2 *Dura-Europos and Euphrates*

24.2.1 Dura-Europos[60]

The Greek texts from Dura-Europos cover a wide range of genres, including legal documents. The majority of the texts date from the early–3rd-century CE, when the region was ruled by the Arsacids, before it was captured by the Roman Empire. Gift and sale contracts, along with divorce bills, are some examples of these legal documents.[61]

24.2.2 Euphrates[62]

In the 1980s, a total of 17 Greek documents were recovered in the middle Euphrates area, comprising legal matters such as sale deeds for slaves and letters. Their structure is similar to those from Dura-Europos. Nevertheless, due to the lack of Greek legal documents from Bactria, examples from Avroman, Mesopotamia, and Syria are excellent tools for studying Hellenistic changes, notably homologia or the validity clause, in the Near East, including Bactria.

24.3 *Egypt*

Numerous Greek documents have been discovered in Egypt dating to the Ptolemaic period, and some even after the Arab conquest in the 7th-century CE.[63] Owing to their number and chronological continuity, deeds recorded on reeds in Egypt provide valuable information on changing legal practices in the Near East, particularly after the Hellenistic period. Consequently, these documents are an invaluable body of evidence for a diachronic study of the changes in Greek deeds.

25 The Iranian World

25.1 *Pahlavi Deeds*

Pahlavi documents datable to the Sasanian period have not been forthcoming, despite a significant number from the early Islamic period in central and northern Iran having recently surfaced.[64] The majority of these are legal

60 For further information on these documents, see Czajkowski, 2020.

61 For an analysis of the documents from a legal point of view, see Welles's introduction to the texts; Welles et al., 1959, 11ff.

62 Feissel and Gascou, 1989. For the texts see Feissel and Gascou, 1995, Teixidor et al, 1997, Feissel and Gascou, 2000.

63 All these documents have recently been studied in Keenan et al., 2014; Lippert, 2012.

64 For the date of these documents see Weber, 2008(2012).

reports, letters, and receipts.[65] Another group of Pahlavi documents discovered in Tabaristan consist of mostly court reports, without any transfer documents.[66] As a result, I have cited them infrequently.

25.2 *Mādayān ī Hazār Dādestān*

Mādayān ī Hazār Dādestān (*Book of a Thousand Judgements*),[67] a law-book from the late Sasanian period (early–7th-century CE), is an important Pahlavi source for legal terminology.[68] The work was compiled by Farroxmard i Wahrāmān likely during the reign of Khosrow II (590–628 CE). It is the only extant legal work on pre-Islamic Iranian jurisprudence from the Sasanian era and one of the most important sources for social and institutional history.[69] The book includes numerous examples of Aramaic legal terminology, either as Aramogramm or terms translated into Pahlavi.[70]

25.3 *Sogdian Deeds*

During the 1930s, an important archive of Sogdian documents datable to the 7th–8th-centuries CE was recovered in the ruins of the Mug Mountains.[71] The collection is formed from legal documents, letters, and receipts; two texts detail marriage agreements,[72] one is a sales contract, and another is a leasing contract. Another Sogdian document from Turfan is a sales contract for a female slave in 639 CE.[73] The text shares more terminological and philological similarities with Bactrian deeds than documents from Mount Mug.

65 Weber and Gignoux have been working on them since the 1990s, and many of these documents have been published. See for example Weber, 2008 and Gignoux, 2009.

66 These documents have been edited and translated by Gignoux in 2012 and 2014. 2016 and reedited and translated by Weber, 2016, 2017, 2019, 2020, and 2022 with legal commentary by Macuch, 2016, 2017, 2019, 2020 and 2022, and published in series Res Orientales (Peeters Publishers).

67 We will use the abbreviations MHD and MHDA for this book. The book was edited and translated by Macuch (1981 and 1993, into German) and Perikhanian (1973, into Russian; and 1997, into English).

68 Perikhanian, 1983, 628.

69 For a detailed account of the contents of the book, see Macuch, 2009, online, and Macuch, 1993, 1–15; Perikhanian, 1997, 12–20.

70 See Sheikh, 2022.

71 See Livshitz, 2008, 11ff. He edited again the texts and published them in 2008 (English translation 2015). In 2006 Yakubovich edited and translated Doc No. 3 and 4 (Marriage contracts) with legal and philological notes. He reedited the same texts and published them in 2013 in Russian.

72 The Doc. No 4 is rather a prenuptial agreement, not a marriage contract.

73 This document is edited in Japanese by Yoshida in 1989, and in 2003 he issued an English translation of it with some commentaries.

25.4 *Khotanese Documents*[74]

Regarding the type of available documents, Khotanese texts are the second most common middle Iranian after Bactrian. These documents, dating from the 7th–8th-centuries CE, conclude contracts for adoptions, land purchases, loans, and sales of slave.[75] Following new discoveries, the quantity of documents is rapidly increasing, and these share some common terms with Bactrian texts. Despite their importance and larger number, the form and terminology in Khotanese texts have been often overlooked.

26 Arabic, Persian, and Old Uyghur Deeds

Certain documents written in Arabic, Persian, and Old Uyghur dating from the 11th-century CE have been discovered in Central Asia. Arabic and Old Uyghur deeds from Yarkand include transactions and legal processes,[76] but the oldest was a Persian marriage document discovered in Bamyan, written in 470/1078.[77] Another Persian document from Khotan, discovered with documents from Yarkand, is a land sale deed from 501/1107–8.[78] One can add two newly discovered sale contracts from Balkh to this collection, one dated to 545/1150 and the other from 607/1210.[79] In addition, a group of legal texts from the 12th and early–13th-centuries CE, including marriage and sale contracts, was recently discovered in central Afghanistan (Ghur).[80] Nevertheless, the structure of all these documents should be viewed through the lens of Islamic legal practices, despite some retaining elements of earlier legal formularies.

27 Rabbinical Works

Jewish literature from classical rabbinical Judaism (*c.*100–600 CE) is an important source for our research. Discussions about the wording of conveyance

74 See Zhan, 2018.

75 Published by Bailey, 1969; Emmerick and Vorob'eva-Desjatovskaja, 1995; Skjaervo, 2002; 2017; Daun, 2014; 2015; 2019.

76 Arabic documents are edited by Gronke, 1986; Huart, 1914; and Old Uyghur documents by Erdal, 1984.

77 Edited by Scarcia, 1963; Scarcia, 1966; and Roshan-Zamir, 2537(1357)/1978; it has recently discovered a considerable amount of early Persian texts (including documents) from northern Afghanistan. Some of these have been published by Ofir Haim, 2019a; 2019b.

78 Minorsky, 1942; Minovi, 1345/1966; although this Persian document is damaged, traces of affinities with Bactrian deeds can be read.

79 Sheikh Ol-Hokamai, 1388/2009.

80 Mirzā Khwājah Mohmmād and Sāqi, 1388/2009.

deeds can be found in rabbinical works such as the Mishnah, Talmud, and Tosefta. These rabbinical legal debates and decisions reflect common scribal practices at the time,[81] even though the development of Jewish laws were influenced by ancient Near Eastern and Greco-Roman practices. Consequently, there are significant legal parallels between rabbinical and Bactrian traditions because both share a common classical ancestry.

28 Magic Bowls[82]

Magic bowls are rich sources for legal formulae and terminology borrowed from rabbinical literature and other Aramaic legal corpora. The scribes used legal formulae during incantation blows for exorcising demons attached to a person or a household, especially in pronouncements of divorce.[83] These texts are composed of formulae such as the perpetuity and entitlement phrases or the validity clause.[84]

81 For the rabbinic tradition, see Stemberger, 2011; Fonrobert and Jaffee, 2007.

82 For an overview on magic bowls, see Müller-Kessler, 2017.

83 Bamberger, 2015a and 2015b; Shaked & Ford, 2013, 99ff.

84 Bamberger, to whom I owe my information, in her paper (2015a) examined some of the legal formulae in magic bowls.

CHAPTER 1

The Format and Opening Section

1 Form of the Documents

Before exploring the structure of Bactrian legal documents, let us first consider their format, which can be classified into simple, duplicate, and double copies.

1.1 *Simple Documents*[1]

A simple document comprises one copy, meaning it's only written once.[2] Normally, in the Aramaic tradition, these documents are signed within and at the end of the text. This practice is clearly exemplified in a deed from the Judean Desert:

כ[תב]א דנה פשיט וחתם בגוה

This d[e]ed is simple and signed inside.[3]

However, due to the length of the text, it does not always end in verso, so the signatures are on the reverse (recto).[4] More specifically, if the text is longer and extends onto the reverse of the document, the signatures and seals are placed there as well.

1.2 *Duplicate Copies*[5]

A duplicate copy is a simple document with more than one copy. In some Bactrian documents, it's noted that more than one copy is produced.[6] For example:

1 In Bactrian, docs. O, R, S, Ss, Tt, Uu, and Uv are examples of simple ones.

2 In Aramaic, its name is פשוט see Jastrow, 1901, 1244f, and in Qumran Aramaic פשיט Sokoloff, 2003, 74.

3 XHev/Se 8a in Yardeni, 1997, 36f and Eur, 14: εγραψα ιδια μου χιρι[α]πλουν αμαρτυρον "I wrote with my own hand, in a single copy, without [a] witness." Feissel et al., 2000, 185. Additionally, the rabbinical tradition mentions this practice even though it was abolished a long time ago; see below the section sealing and signature.

4 In Bactrian, see for example doc. S.

5 I borrowed the term from Roth, 1989, 19.

6 Doc. A, Nn, Tt, aa.

 | DOI:10.1163/9789004519985_003

> κιδο ι ωνδο λιβο ζαν̣ινδο ταδο αβο μασκο πιδοναμγο[7] νοβιχτιγινδο οδο κιδο ι ωνδο λιβο ναζανινδο ταδοιηνο αβο μο νιγο λιστοβαρο κιρδο
>
> Who witness the present document and (whose) signatures are written hereupon—and those who do not witness the present document have put (their signatures) on the other manuscript.[8]

Given that we do not have access to all of these individual documents, our knowledge of them is based on a single surviving copy of this document type. In Bactria, a document usually has one essential recipient; the recipient in sale deeds is the buyer, the recipient in peace agreements is the plaintiff, the recipient in loan contracts is the loaner, and the recipient in gift deeds is the donee.[9] If a document is produced with more than one copy, it means there are multiple recipients. Unfortunately, in Bactrian documents, there is no information provided about other recipients(s). Nonetheless, it's likely that one of the recipients was the city archive, as evidenced by the Syriac and Greek documents from Dura-Europos. For instance:

> ܘܐܬܟܬܒܘ ܠܙܒܢܬܐ ܗܕܐ ܫܛܪܐ ܬܪܝܢ ܚܕ ܦܣܩܗ ܐܚܝܕ ܠܐܪ̈ܟܝܘܢ
> ܢܥܠ ܒܐܪ̈ܟܝܘܢ ܕܐܢܛܘܢܝܢܐ ܐܘܪܗܝ ܢܨܝܚܬܐ
>
> And two documents of this sale have been written: one copy, kept as a record, will be entered into the archive of Antoniana Edessa the Glorious[10]

Since Bactrian documents are written in the presence of a ruler or a government official, and subsequently are composed and signed at a royal or administrative location,[11] it is reasonable to conclude that "the other copy" was intended for the city archive. Further evidence comes from a double document:

> οδο πισο μανδαρουανισο ζαβοργανο οιγαλφανο ακιδδηνο μοδδραγο χιρσοβωστιγο αβ μανιυο πιδοναμο οιγαλφο ναβιχτιγινδο οταβο μασκο ταβδοο
>
> And also, in the presence of the other freemen (and) witnesses who have written (their names as) witnesses (to this) sealed document, (this)

---

7 Based on a Mug document, Yoshida prefers the earlier translation of πιδοναμγο "copy" to the new version. (Yoshida, 2013, 157f.).

8 Doc. A.

9 In sale deeds the buyer holds the document. See chapter 2 section style.

10 Drijvers and Healey, 1999, 232f P1.

11 See this chapter below, sections Place and Authorities.

> purchase contract, on the other signed document and (who) have placed (their) seals hereupon[12]

The copy of the document appears to be a single one, which is most likely for deposit in the city archive. However, in the Neo-Babylonian period, one of the two copies could be passed to the seller or the opponent.[13] Moreover, document archiving occurred in the Parthian[14] and Sasanian[15] periods. As a result, the MHD recorded this function and a copy of the document must be kept in the temple treasury. According to one passage:

> ˀywkʾ ZNH ˀYK ˀthš y wrhrˀn hmbrkˀn NPŠH nˀmkʾ MNW ZNH ˀnd DYNˀ hc-š pytˀk pt nˀmkʾ ndˀn y ˀthš y hwrˀmˀrthštr y ˀrthštrʾ GDH nsng hbr hwrˀmˀr{thštr} MTˀ YTYBWNstʾ YHSNNd
>
> And the following: the document concerning the Varahran Fire-temple, which belongs jointly to the persons who drew it up and in which each one's share ("how much to whom") is set out, is preserved in the archives ("the depository of documents") of the Xurram-Ardax{šēr} Fire-temple which was founded in the province of Ardaxšēr-Xʷarreh in the village of Xurrarn-[Ardaxšēr] near the city of Xabr.[16]

Or

> dˀtwbr MN prwrtkʾ hmpcynʾ KN YHBWNtʾ rˀdynšnʾ y zrtwštʾ byšˀpwhr mgwptʾ pt y ṢBW y ˀthš krtʾ pytˀk
>
> A judge must prepare a copy of a document to be given out, as is evident from (the document) prepared by Zardušt, the magupat of Bišahpuhr, for the temple treasury.[17]

---

12 Doc. Nn.
13 See below.
14 Shaki, 1993, 222f.
15 See Choksy, 1988, 193.
16 MHD 78, 11–14; Perikhanian, 1997, 190f.
17 MHD, 93, 3–4; Perikhanian, 1997, 214f; MHDA 30, 7–9.

2 Historical Background of Duplicate Copies

The Neo-Babylonian period (the first millennium BCE) provides the first evidence for this type of document.[18] When duplicate documents for contracts began to be produced in the Neo-Babylonian period, a new type of recorded agreement emerged.[19] Some documents in the new format have two or more copies, which were given to each party. A document mentions this function:

> 1+en.TA.AM$_3$ gab-ri-ni-e TI-ú
>
> Each (party) took one copy.[20]

According to Roth, some duplicate documents have survived, and aside from minor differences, these correspond to each other.[21] In fact, a duplicate copy is a new type of double document that includes two identical but distinct versions of an agreement.

3 Double Copies (*Doppelurkunde*)

Remarkably, a large number of Bactrian documents are double copies,[22] which consist of at least two nearly identical[23] texts from the contract. One copy was written at the top (Scriptura interior) and sealed by the witnesses who attended the act as well as by the parties to the contract themselves and the other was written on the same sheet (Scriptura exterior) with a space in between them and lower text remains open.[24] They did so that if one of the parties had doubts about the authenticity of the open version and brought a charge against the opponent, the sealed version would be opened for consultation. Bactrians produced two types of *Doppelurkunde*:

---

18 San Nicolo, 1931, 164ff; Roth, 1989, 19f; Oelsner et al., 2003, 913.

19 In Akkadian, the word for duplicate copy is gabarû CAD, 5, 2, which is a Sumerian loan word GABA-RI, see Schramm, 2010, 48.

20 Roth, 1989, 127f, No. 42; MacGinnes, 1993, 149ff No.1.

21 Roth, 1989, 130f.

22 These are Docs. C, F, I, J, L, N, Nn, O, P, T, U, V, W, and X. in the receipts Aa, B, E, and H.

23 Even though the two texts should be identical, occasionally one of the two texts contains more detail, see below.

24 Turner, 1978, 26ff.

1. In the first type (Figure 1), the interior text was written and then rolled over and tied. The upper text was sealed[25]

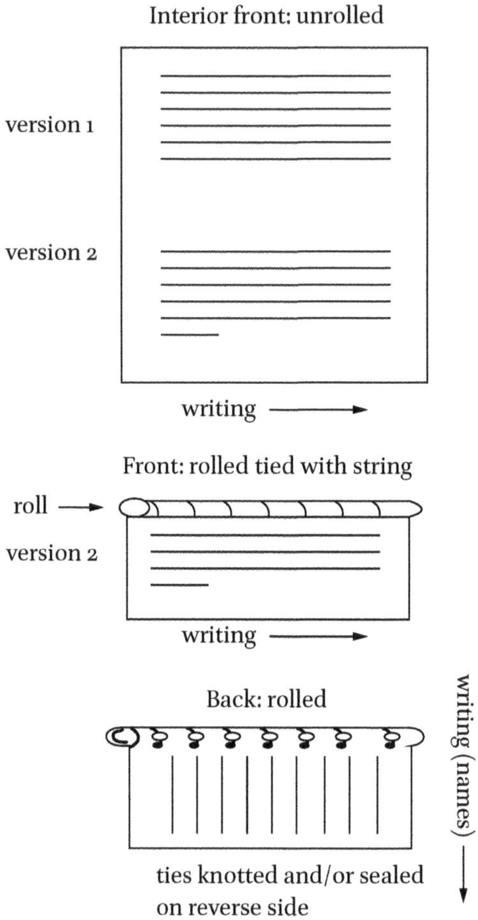

FIGURE 1 (Double copy type 1)
AFTER MEYER, 2004, 189

25 Docs. C, F, J, L, N, Nn, O, P, and V.

2. In the second type (Figure 2), the interior text was written first, and then a horizontal nick was cut across the document's center. It was rolled and folded, with the text and the upper part sealed within.[26]

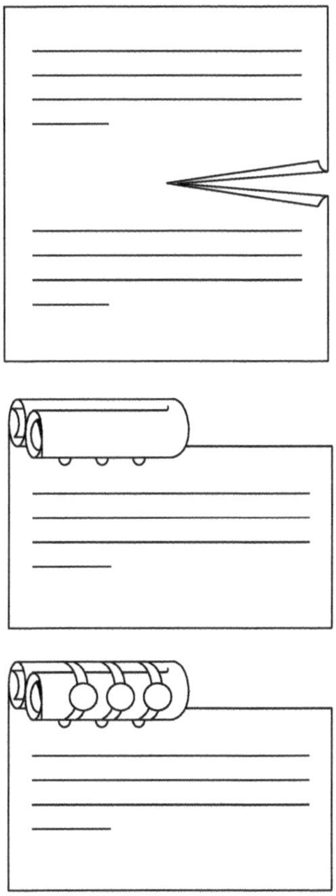

FIGURE 2
The second type
AFTER RUPPRECHT, 1994, 139

As noted previously, the open and tied versions are not identical copies of each other, and occasionally contain additions necessary for understanding the context and learning more about the agreement. These additions can be classified into various categories, ranging from linguistic features to legal elements. However, I will only address the legal issues here. For example, in doc. L, the Scriptura exterior on the last line explains the investiture clause:

26 Docs. T, U, W, and X; this practice was known in Greek documents from Elephantine and Dura-Europos. For more on this type of double copy, see Turner, 1978, 37f; Vandorpe, 1996, 232f.

τοι βαζανο̣κο αλο ι χ̣οβο καδγιγαν̣ο αβο ι μασ̣κο ναβιχτ̣ιγο αγγαργο παραλαδο οδο ναβαγ̣ο αβο ωσταδο οδο ι ο̣ιχρηγανο αβο κιρδο ο̣δ̣ο λαϸνο αβο αμβαγδο οδο χοαδο αβο δ̣δριγδο σαγονδο υαρσο χοαδο ριμαδο στακαλδο ιθαο ασταδο

(And) you, Bazanuk, together with the members of your household, have authority (over) it for the future, to sell the property described herein, and to pawn (it), and to put (it for) hire, and to give (it) away (as) a gift, and to hold (it) yourself, just as may suit yourselves.[27]

In doc. U, the validity clause is missing. Minor additions or omissions in other documents will be addressed below.

Throughout Central Asia, double wooden tablets found in Shan and Khotan are the closest examples to double copies. For these documents, the contract is written inside the tablet, while the cover contains an account (short or long) of the main points in the contract.[28]

4 Origin of the Double Document

The first attested double document from the Hellenistic period is a Greek marriage contract from Egypt, dated 311 BCE.[29] This format was used in various regions and traditions throughout the Near East.[30] Therefore, double copies in Aramaic, Bactrian, Latin, and Syriac have been discovered from Palestine to Bactria and can be dated from the Hellenistic period into late antiquity. These were used alongside other forms of deeds recorded in the eastern lands of the Seleucid and then Roman Empires.[31] Divergent views exist regarding the origins of this document type in the Hellenistic world; certain scholars believe they originated in Egypt,[32] others in Greece,[33] and some even contend the Hellenistic-era type began in Syria or Palestine during the 8th–7th-centuries BCE. The latter is based on the continuity of the case-tablet form in the Neo-Assyrian period.[34] which was used in ancient Mesopotamia from

27 Doc. L.
28 Felföldi, 2011, 107f; these documents in Khotanese are called pāḍā-, seeDuan, 2014, 349.
29 Hunt and Edgar, 1932, 2f Doc. 1.
30 Yiftach-Firanko, 2013, 2209f.
31 For a list of these documents in papyrus, see Cotton et al., 1995, 214–35; Taubenschlag, 1949, 49f.
32 Bilabel, 1925, 100f; Schönbauer, 1918, 234; Wilcken, 1920, 370.
33 Kunkel, 1936, 420.
34 Berges, 1993, 264ff; Kutscher, 1954, 246f n 129.

the Old Babylonian period onwards.[35] In Akkadian, such tablets were known as ṭuppum ḫarmum, translated as "case tablet"[36] or "valid tablet."[37] The steps for making a case-tablet were as follows: the agreement text was written on a clay tablet and then dried or burned. It was placed in a mud envelope, and the same text was recorded on the surface. Lastly, the envelope was closed and sealed.[38] This system protected the contract from forgery.[39] At the end of the Old Babylonian period, case-tablets became obsolete in southern Mesopotamia, and as previously stated, the duplicate form superseded this process during the first millennium BCE.[40] However, in the upper land, Assyria, the double form reappeared and continued to be produced for loans and debt-notes in silver until the 7th-century BCE.[41] This succeeding form is found in the Aramaic corpus from the Achaemenid era, but an anomaly was described in the Book of Jeremiah regarding a land purchase. It was recorded via ספר (letter) in two versions, one was sealed and closed, and the other was open:

ואקח את-ספר המקנה את-החתום המצוה והחקים ואת-הגלוי

> Then I took the sealed deed of purchase, containing the terms and conditions, and the open copy.[42]

Despite this description, documents from the region have not been forthcoming,[43] which also holds true in Bactria.[44] Given that the oldest attestation of double documents can be traced to Egypt, it is reasonable to assume this type of documentation was first introduced during the Hellenistic period, despite its Mesopotamian case-tablet origins.[45] In the rabbinical tradition, this

35 San Nicolo, 1931, 124f; Lipinski, 2010, 246f.
36 See CAD Ṭ/139 Ṭubbu CAD A part II/229ff arāmu.
37 Hertel, 2013, 138f.
38 Wenger, 1923, 2408f.
39 Schorr, 1913, XIX.
40 Neumann, 2003, 104.
41 Postgate, 1997, 161; for examples of double copies in Neo-Assyrian documents, see Jar, 1996.
42 Jeremiah 32.11; for a detailed discussion about this section, see Fischer, 1910 Lundbom, 2004, 498f; Jirko, 1923.
43 For the possibility of a double copy from Judea at the end of the 7th-century BCE, see Avigad, 1986, 125ff.
44 Lipinski suggests that "the use of dockets in Mesopotamia and Persia may have delayed the introduction of 'double documents' written entirely on Papyrus or parchment" Lipinski, 2010, 249.
45 For details on the *Doppelurkunde* in Bactria, see Bagnall, 2009, 108ff.

type of document was known as a גט מקושר (tied deed),[46] demonstrating that the format was well-known among Jews and Aramaic-speaking peoples in late antiquity. Before the discovery of Bactrian documents, scholars had deduced from other evidence that the use of the form for the composition of legal texts was gradually decreasing in the Fertile Crescent and Egypt during Roman rule in the 3rd-century CE.[47] This decline occurred in the following way: the inner text was compiled briefly with an abstract of the outer text's content—then the form eventually became extinct.[48] However, it's now clear, owing to the discovery of the Bactrian corpus, that the form survived in Bactria until the mid-8th-century CE, because unlike double documents from Egypt and Syria, Bactrians did not shorten the upper text.[49] On the contrary, the double documents from later periods are more detailed.[50] Nonetheless, following the Arab conquest of the region, the double copy was abolished, rendering these early documents (Persian), simplistic.[51]

Aside from Bactrian, no double document type in a Middle Iranian language has yet been discovered. The MHD, on the other hand, refers to an open (wišād) record of deposition (saxwan-nāmag) and the document (dib).[52] Does the word wišād in Pahlavi indicate an open copy (as the Hebrew word גלוי in Jeremiah) or outer text in double documents? We don't know because the text is obscure, and no double document has been discovered written in Pahlavi.

It should be noted, that there are various types of double documents in the Greek double tradition of Egypt.[53] The most well-known variation of this form is called the six-witness agreement or εξαμαρτυρος συγγραφη.[54] In some cases, one of the witnesses kept the duplicate document for future reference. This document type is called συγγραφοφυλαξ.[55]

46 Mishna, Baba Barṯa, 10.1; Tosefta, Baba Barṯa, 11.1.
47 Schiffman, 2003, 166.
48 Yiftach-Firanko, 2008, 205ff.
49 Doc. P is an exception among Bactrian deeds because the upper text in this contract is a shorter summary of the lower text. However, the use of complete double copies in later documents confirms that the shorter version of the upper text was limited and could not supersede the older custom.
50 For example, see docs. V and W.
51 For the marriage contract from Bamiyan Scarcia, see 1966; Sheikh Ol-Hokamayi, 1388/2009; Minovi, 1345/1966.
52 MHD 102. 15–16; 103. 2–4.
53 Lippert, 2012, 143f; Vandorpe, 1996, 232ff.
54 For further details on this type, see Wolff, 1974.
55 Mitteis, 1912, 53f; for this type of document, see this chapter section Witness. These double documents probably did not exist within the eastern frontiers of the Roman Empire.

5 Opening Clause

5.1 *Outer and Inner Elements*

The first line of Bactrian documents is entirely dedicated to the contract's outer elements, comprising the date, title, location, authorities and list of witnesses.[56] These outer characteristics are important for observing the legal system in Bactria and identifying differences and similarities among other Near Eastern traditions.

5.2 *Date (Year, Month, and Day)*

All Bactrian documents are dated and they are always opened with the date. In the complete version, the date formula follows the order—year, month, and day. The date formula begins with the word χþονο or αχþονο (year) and mostly ends with καλδο (when). The word χþονο or αχþονο was inserted for the year, which could be a Bactrian variant of the Greek χρονοσ (time).[57] The year is completely expressed by the use of letters. After providing the year, the month is next, with the Bactrian word for the month, μαυο.[58] The Bactrians had a month-naming system, a hybrid of Babylonian, Greek, and Iranian month names. The Bactrian word for the day is ρωσο.[59] Similarly to other calendars in the Middle Iranian languages, in Bactrian, every day has a name.[60] The day names are derived from the well-known Zoroastrian calendar.[61]

Based on this, one can categorize the date formulae into three groups:

1. The full version includes the year, month, and day.[62] For example:

   χþονο σ' μ' ζ' μαυο σπανδαρομιδο ρωσο

   (It was) the year 247, the month Spandarmid, the day Ormuzd[63]

---

56 This categorization was borrowed from Gropp, 2000, 831; in other words, they are called diplomatics, see Cotton, 2003, 50.

57 Humbach, 1966, 24; in Greek the word χρονος means "time" and not "year"; for more information, see Liddell & Scott, 1996, 2008; for an additional etymology of this word, see Scarborough, 2021.

58 Sims-Williams, 2007, 230f; Djelani Davary, 1982, 226.

59 Sims-Williams, 2007, 261.

60 Doc. R is an exception, with the letter κ (20) replacing the day's name.

61 Panaino, 1990, 658ff.; for a more detailed study on the name of days, see Raffaelli, 2014.

62 F, N, Nn, P, Q, S, Tt and Uu.

63 Doc. F.

In two documents,[64] the word σαχτο (passed)[65] is used to express dates in a more elaborate manner. For example:

χϸονο ρʹ ιʹ Αυρηζνο μαο σαχτο Αβαμοχοινο ρωσο καλδο

(It was) the year 110, the month Ahrezhn, the day Abamukhwin having elapsed, when[66]

2. The Middle version only includes the year and the month[67]

χϸονο ρʹ νʹ ζʹ δρηματιγανο μαο

(It was) the year 157, the month Drematigan[68]

3. The abbreviated version includes only the year.[69] For example:

αχϸονο υʹ ϙʹ

(It was) the year 490[70]

6 Historical Background

The date is consistently placed at the conclusion of documents in the ancient Near East.[71] However, the date appears for the first time in the Achaemenid period on the first line of contracts or legal records,[72] though writing the date or time at the beginning of documents is attested in the 2nd-century BCE in

64 Docs. A, R.

65 Sims-Williams, 2007, 293; for this word in Pahlavi and Sogdian, see Mackenzie, 1994, 125; Gharib, 1995, 353.

66 Doc. A.

67 Docs. C, I, Ii, L, O, T, V, W, X; the version of the date in doc. aa is uncertain.

68 Doc. C.

69 Docs. U and Y (in Doc Y the date is mentioned at the end of the text).

70 Doc. U.

71 For Ur-III, see Steinkeller, 1989, 10; for Old Babylonian, see Simonetti, 2013, 503f; Renger, 2008, 195f.; for Neo-Assyrian, see Faist, 2012, 211; for Neo-Babylonian, see Joannes, 2010, 271ff.; for the other regions in the ancient Near East, see Krecher et al., 1980, 490ff.

72 Rabinowitz believes this tradition was transmitted to the Jews via Aramaic texts; see Rabinowitz, 1961, 137ff.

northern and western Syria,[73] in documents from Alalaḫ,[74] Emar,[75] and Ugarit.[76] Akkadian documents begin with ištu ūmi annîm, meaning "from this day."[77] Additionally, the date appears in the first line of some Neo-Babylonian procedural documents,[78] while in Aramaic corpora, the date is normally placed at the beginning of the first line. More specifically, in the Aramaic papyri from Egypt,[79] the date is always placed at the beginning of the document, but in the Wadi al-Daliyah documents, the date is sometimes written either at the beginning or the end.[80] Later, the date appears in the opening formula of Greek documents from Avroman, Dura-Europos, and the Euphrates. As previously stated, the tradition with this form was introduced as an imperial regulation during the Achaemenid period and then spread throughout the Near East as a rule for dating documents in the Hellenistic period. Furthermore, this rule was supported by rabbinical and Talmudic traditions in late antiquity. Tosefta, for example, says:

גופו של שטר ביום פל בשבת בחדש פל בשנה פל ונמלכות פל

> The body of a writ [is as follows]: On such-and-such a day, in such-and-such a week, in such-and-such a year, in the reign of so-and-so.[81]

The same rule applies to Iranian documents: considering Parthian documents from Nisa, the date is penned mostly at the beginning, and only occasionally at the end.[82] Therefore, it seems that the legal corpora of the Sasanian period followed the Aramaic tradition. Based on a passage of the MHD, the date in documents is formulated at the beginning and by the regnal calendar.

> LWTH ZK y MDM pwrsšn' nˀmk'-1 y ŠNT 26 (y) hwsrwy y ˀwhrmzdˀn rˀdynˀyt' W BYN ˀrtxštr GDH … rˀd npšt'

---

73 Gross, 2013b, 135.
74 Niedorf, 2008, 139f.
75 1991, 296f, text no. 32.
76 For Akkadian documents in Ugarit, see Van Soldt, 2010, 92; for Ugaritic deeds, see Haase, 1967, 197.
77 For Ugaritic, **l. ym. hnd** (on this day), see Bordreuil and Pardee, 2009, 257ff, text no. 37.
78 Kessler, 1999, 254f; Holtz, 2009, 118f.
79 Yaron, 1961, 7f; for example, בו־3־3־2 לאלול הו יום 20־3־3־2 לפחנס שנת 10־3־2 חשיארש מלכא on the 18th Elul, that is the 28th day of Paḥons, year 15 of King Xerxes TAD B2.1.
80 Gropp, 2001, P 8 & 18.
81 Tosefta Baba Batra, 11.2; for more discussion on the date in the rabbinical and Talmudic traditions, see Fischer, 1912, 55ff; Gulak, 1935, 25; Friedman, 1980, 98ff; Schiffman, 2005, 188f.
82 Weber, 2010, 453 no.189; for more examples, see 501ff.

> In addition, (the following) is written concerning the record of a judicial investigation: in the twenty-sixth year of (the reign of) Xusrav son of Ohrmazd drawn up in Artaxsahr-Xvarreh.[83]

The judicial reports from northern Iran confirm this opinion; the date in these documents is at the beginning. For example:

> QDM ŠNT 90–3 Y ˀHL MN ˁLH bg yzdkrt' MLKˀn MLK'
>
> In the year 93 from the Lord Yazdgird the King of Kings[84]

Likewise, Sogdian documents begin with the date. For example:

> trxwn MLK' X srδ ''z m'xy msßwγγcy myδ 'sm'n rwc
>
> It was the tenth year [of the reign] of King Tarxun, month Masßogic, day Asmān[85]

In contrast to Bactrian and Sogdian, the day in other Middle Iranian and Khotanese languages does not have a name; only the number of the day is mentioned in documents:[86]

> Salī 20 māśtä cvātaja haḍa 10 3 ttye hvaṃnä rrāṃdä väśta 'vāhaṃ dädye ṣṣau vädyadattä
>
> Year 20, 13 days of the month of Cvātaja, of this king of Khotan, Viśa' Vāhaṃ. In the third (year) of the ṣṣau Vidyadatta.[87]

In the lands east of Bactria, the same rule was followed (the date at the top) in their formularies.[88] Although the placement of this formula in the Islamic legal formulary changed because the date was written at the end of the text in

83 MHD 100, 7–11; Peikhanian, 1997, 225f.
84 Gignoux, 2012, 68f. doc. 14.
85 Livshitz, 2008, 28f Nov. 3; Yakubovich, 2006, 310f.
86 Skjaervo, 2002, lxxv.
87 Ibid., 9 doc. or. 6397/1.
88 For the Kharoṣṭhi documents, see Burrow, 1940; for the Chinese documents from Turfan, see Scheil, 1995, 21; for the Tibetan, see Takeuchi, 1995, 34; for the Old Uyghur, see Yamada, 1964, 88f.

an agreement before the witnesses' signatures,[89] much like documents from ancient Mesopotamia.

Another intriguing and significant aspect of all these corpora is the manner calendars are utilized. Certain texts relied on a regnal or an era calendar,[90] and for Bactrian legal documents, the dates were calculated using the era calendar, which was first used in the Hellenistic period. The Aramaic texts from the Achaemenid period have been formulated in the regnal calendar, corresponding to earlier legal documents. Each calendar varies according to regional and time changes in the respective region.

A further note, the corpora from the eastern frontiers of the Roman Empire, e.g., Aramaic, Greek, Latin, and rabbinical traditions, not only record the date but also provide either brief or detailed information on the administrative and political conditions when the document was written. For example, the Syriac slave sale deed begins with the date as follows:

> ܒܫܢܬ ܫܬ ܕܐܘܛܩܪܛܘܪ ܩܣܪ ܡܪܩܘܣ ܐܢܛܘܢܝܘܣ ܓܘܪܕܝܢܘܣ ܐܘܣܒܣ
> ܐܘܛܘܟܣ ܣܒܣܛܘܣ ܒܗܦܛܝܐ ܕܐܢܝܘܣ ܐܪܝܢܘܣ ܘܕܩܪܒܘܢܝܘܣ
> ܦܦܘܣ ܒܝܪܚ ܐܝܪ ܫܢܬ ܚܡܫܡܐܐ ܘܚܡܫܝܢ ܘܐܪܒܥ ܒܡܢܝܢܐ
> ܩܕܡܝܐ ܘܒܫܢܬ ܬܠܬܝܢ ܘܚܕܐ ܕܚܐܪܘܬܗ ܕܐܢܛܘܢܝܢܐ ܐܕܣܐ ܝܩܝܪܬܐ
> ܩܘܠܘܢܝܐ ܡܛܪܦܘܠܝܣ ܐܘܪܠܝܐ ܐܠܟܣܢܕܪܝܐ ܒܟܘܡܪܘܬܐ ܕܡܪܩܘܣ
> ܐܘܪܠܝܘܣ ܐܢܛܝܟܘܣ ܗܦܩܘܣ ܪܗܡܘܣ ܒܪ ܒܠܫܘ ܘܒܐܣܛܪܛܓܘܬܐ
> ܕܡܪܩܘܣ ܐܘܪܠܝܘܣ ܐܒܓܪ ܗܦܩܘܣ ܪܗܡܘܣ ܪܗܡܘܣ ܒܪ ܒܠܫܘ
> ܘܒܐܣܛܪܛܓܘܬܐ ܕܡܪܩܘܣ ܐܘܪܠܝܘܣ ܐܒܓܪ ܗܦܩܘܣ ܪܗܡܘܣ ܒܪ
> ܡܥܢܘ ܒܪ ܐܒܓܪ ܘܕܐܒܓܪ ܒܪ ܚܦܣܝ ܒܪ ܒܪ [.]ܫ[..]

In the year six of Autokrator Caesar Marcus Antonius Gordianus Eusebes Eutuches Sebastos, in the consulship of Annius Arrianus and of Cervonius Papus, in the month of Iyyar, the year five hundred and fifty-four in the former reckoning, and in the year thirty-one of the liberation of Antoniana Edessa the Glorious, Colonia, Metropolis Aurelia Alexandria, in the priesthood of Marcus Aurelius Antiochus, eques Romanus, son of Belšu, and in the strategos-ship of Marcus Aurelius Abgar, eques Romanus, son

89 Khan 2019, 23; for the Persian, see Minovi, 1345/1966, 288; Minorski, 1942, 189ff; Sheikh Ol-Hokamayi, 1388/2009, 23ff.

90 After the fall of the Sasanian Empire, the calendar shifted from regnal to era, with the enthronement of Yazdgird III serving as the starting point. Therefore, Pahlavi documents from the early Islamic period bear a date based on the beginning of an era. The date in Sogdian and Khotanese is calculated using a local regnal calendar.

of Maʔnu son of Aggay and of Abgar son of Hapsay son of Baraqa for the second time, on the ninth day[91]

Despite the Bactrian documents having been written contemporaneously, there is no description or explanation of historical events, and instead, only the year, month, and day, were recorded as in Khwarazmian[92] texts and Parthian documents from Nisa.[93]

7 Title

In Bactrian conveyances, the title of the document is inserted after the time for recording the type of agreement. The word for "document" is π/βωστογο, which also means "letter, contract."[94] A component word is formed by combining a word characterizing the type of agreement and the word βωστογο that defines the type of contract (Table 3).

The second word in the title section is μολρογο, meaning "sealed"[95] and indicating that the document has been sealed and confirmed,[96] although in Documents F and X, the word μολρογο replaced the word βωστογο.

In Mesopotamian traditions, the title of the document, if recorded, was placed at the top of the document.[97] There is no title in Aramaic documents because it's written as an endorsement at the end of the agreement on the outside of the writ.[98] Some documents in the ancient Near East during the

91 Welles, 1959, Dura 28; Drijvers and Healey, 1999, 223f.

92 For example: BŠNT VII C VI YRḤʼ βwrtn BYWM βwrtn "in the year 706, on the month Frawardin, on the day Frawardin" Henning, 1964(1965), 179; for more examples, see Tolstov and Livshtz, 1964, 232–51; Livshitz, 1984, 258.

93 Weber, 2010, 494–561; for example, 550f; fortunately, there are some clues in the Parthian calendar allowing the identification of the era when it was compiled, see Avroman Minns, 1915; Weber, 2010, 552f.

94 Sims-Williams, 2007, 258f; and the Sogdian equivalent "**pwsty**" or "**pwst'k**" means "book writing"; for more details, see Gharib, 1995, 331 no. 8228; Sims-Williams and Durkin-Meisterernst, 2012, 352.

95 Sims-Williams, 2007, 235.

96 Sealing an agreement is one of the factors determining its validity; for more information, see chapter 3, under the section validity clause.

97 For example, n Nuzi tablet of adoption (ṭuppi māruti); for more details, see Maidman, 1994, passim.

98 Yaron, 1957, 54f; Yadin et al., 2002, 381f; for an endorsement in old Aramaic documents, see Lipinski, 2010, 251f; Fales, 2000, 117f.

TABLE 3

Subject	Title	Translation
Marriage	ολοβωστογο[a]	Marriage contract
Gift	λαϸνοβωστογο[b]	Gift deed
	παλọβωστιγο[c]	Familial contract
Manumission	αβησαχοανιγο[d]	Renunciation contract
Sale	μαχιρσοβωστιγο[e]	Purchasing contract
Peace	πιτανοβωστιγο[f]	Guarantee contract
	χοησαοοβωστιγο[g]	Contract of undertaking
Loan	παροβωστιγο[h]	Loan-contract
Farming	βονοοαρζοβωστιγο[i]	Farming contract

a Doc. A.
b Doc. C.
c Docs. Tt, Uv.
d Doc. F.
e Docs. J, L, Nn, P, V, W; in two of the last documents, without article μ (m); for this article, see Sims-Williams, 2007, 234.
f Doc. N.
g Docs. O, R, S, Uu.
h Docs. Q, Ss.
i Doc. U.

Hellenistic period include the title, but not as a rule. Consequently, it seems that writing the title in the first lines of the document was a local Bactrian custom.[99]

8 Location

Bactrian documents always include and precisely describe the location, which means the location where an agreement was drafted with witnesses. This section begins with the word **here** (**μαλο**):

> χϸονο υʹ ζʹ μαυο χανδιγο ρωσο αϸταδο καλδο ναβιχτο μολρạγο πιτανοβωστιγο
> **μαλαβο** σạμιγγανο ωδαγο αβο σανδαρανο αβο ρωβοχαραγγο αλβαρο

99 Except for Bactrians, Khotaneses are the only people in Central Asia occasionally following this rule; for an example, see Skjaervo, 2002, 9, or. 6397/1 and or. 6397/2; Duan, 2014, 350f.

> (It was) the year 407, the month Khandig, the day Ashtad, when (this) sealed document, (this) guarantee-contract, was written **here in** the district of Samingan, at Sandaran, the court of the Khars of Rob.[100]

The document specifies the city (þαυρο) or district (ωδαγο) followed by the location within the respective city or district where the agreement was drafted. The location can be public or a royal court with the local rulers. The precise location, found within the location clause, can be classified as follows:

1. in the borough of the city (ανδαγο)

   (αβιιο ανδαγο σιδο στηβο ριζδο) In the borough which is called Steb[101]

2. The Court (αλβαρο)

   αβο ρωβοχαραγγο αλβαρο In the Court of the Khars of Rob[102]

3. in the market (οασαρο)

   αβο ρωβοχαραγγο οασαρο At the market of the Khars of Rob[103]

4. Fortress (λιζο)

   αβο καυο αβο λιζο In the fortress Kah[104]

9 Historical Background

It was not customary to mention the location of the composition in Sumerian and Akkadian corpora. In fact, it is rarely mentioned in the text. However, the location is mentioned before the date at the end of Neo-Babylonian documents.[105] The Aramaic papyri from Elephantine, sometimes, but not always, include the location of composition, which could be mentioned at the beginning or the end of the corpus.[106] The place of composition consistently

100 Doc. N.
101 Docs. A, C, Ii, aa.
102 Docs. N, J, S, Tt, U, X.
103 Docs. P, Q.
104 Doc. V.
105 Joannes, 2010, 272; Oelsner et al., 2003, 913.
106 Yaron, 1961, 8f.; Yaron, 1957, 36.

accompanies the date in documents from the Judaean Desert, but this is not always the case. The place is mentioned after the date in Greek documents from Avroman, Dura-Europos, and the Euphrates.

10 Authorities and Witnesses

The presence of witnesses in a transaction is one of the factors determining the authenticity and validity of the conveyance. In Bactria, all conveyances are drafted in the presence of witnesses, who are classified as observing witnesses due to the nature of the documents (agreements and transactions).[107] The Bactrian word for "witness" is οιγαλφο[108] derived from the root, meaning *čai "to see, to observe, or to perceive."[109] The prepositions πις[110] (in front of, before, in the presence of) or **αζδηβδο**[111] (with the cognizance of) appear before the names of witnesses. Bactrians most likely used these two words interchangeably within the same text or context, implying they served the same purpose. For example, in doc. F in the Scriptura exterior, instead of αζδηβιδο, πισο is used:

αβο καδαγοβιδο αλβαρο **αζδηβιδο** ζαροοηρο οιβριιανο (interior or F)

In the court of the governor, **with the cognizance** of Zar-wer Wibriyan

αβο καδαγοβιδο αλβαρο **πισο** ζαροοηρο οιβριιανο (Exterior or F')

In the court of the governor, **in the presence** of Zar-wer Wibriyan

However, normally, the word **αζδηβδο** is devoted to officials and authorities.

11 Characteristics of Witnesses

The witnesses in the documents are free (ζαβοργο)[112] and based upon their names, are all males. For example:

107 For the types of witnesses in the ancient Near East, see Wells, 2004, 21ff.
108 For this word and its variants, see Sims-Williams, 2007, 246.
109 Cheung, 2007, 28.
110 Docs. C, J, N, O.
111 Docs. A, F, L, Nn.
112 Doc. C and for the meaning, variants, and more examples, see Sims-Williams, 2007, 188.

> Πισο εμουανο **ζαβοργανο** οιγαλφανο κιδο πιδο μιλανο αρομαστινδο πισο ωρομοζδο βορζαδορανο οδο πισο χοηο ικοσιρδαχμιγο οδο βαγολαδο μαϸοκανο οδο πισο φαροοαραζο μαλρογοσιγο οδο πισο μανδαρουανισο ϸαριγανο
>
> In the presence of these **freemen** (and) witnesses who were present amongst (them): (namely) in the presence of Ormuzd Burzaduran, and in the presence of the lord of Kusirdakhm, and (in the presence of) Bag-lad Mashukan, and in the presence of Far-warazan, [an] inhabitant of Malrug, and also in the presence of the other citizens.[113]

The other word for referring to situation witnesses is ϸαριγανο,[114] and equally, the term *mard ī šahr* in the Sasanian legal system, means freemen.[115]

There are no mentions of women or slaves as witnesses in the texts. The same exclusion applies to transactions from Mesopotamia in the Neo-Babylonian period onward.[116] Furthermore, in the Aramaic corpora, all documents feature only male witnesses, even when females are members of one or both parties.[117] As a result, only freemen could be witnesses in transactions.[118]

The witnesses whose names appear in the documents could be classified into two groups based on their social situation:

A. Freemen
B. Authorities

11.1 *Freemen*

Based on documents and our knowledge of the Sasanian period, the term "freemen" refers to ordinary people who were not slaves.[119] In Bactrian documents, the names of freemen serving as witnesses are usually listed in the following order: personal name, family name. Although in some cases, the place of origin[120] or a special appellation[121] is used in lieu of the family name. After

113 Doc. C.
114 Sims-Williams, 2007, 284.
115 Macuch, 2010, 209.
116 Sonnenschein, 1925 (1927), 214; Von Dassow, 1999, 16; Westbrook, 2003b, 39; women in the Neo-Babylonian period, on the other hand, could be called as witnesses in court; for more details, see Oelsner et al., 2003, 924.
117 Cussini, 2009, 186.
118 Naming freemen as witnesses is recorded in the Kharoṣṭhi documents as "azate jamna"; Burrow has noted the term Azate is an Iranian loanword, see Burrow, 1934, 509; Baums, 2018, 64.
119 Shaki, 1992, 656; De Blois, 1985, passim.
120 Doc. C, πισο φαροοαραζο **μαλρογοσιγο** in the presence of Far-waraz **inhabitant of Malrug**.
121 Doc. A, πισο βαγοβαο **ιαβιϸταδο** in the presence of Bag-bandag **the master craftsman.**

the introduction of the witnesses, the texts explain their actions and roles in two ways:

They either insert their seal on the documents:

> οδο πισο μανδαρουανισο αζαδοβοργανο οιγαλφανο κιδο οαλ[ο] π[ι]δο μιλανο αρμαστινδο οτηνο αβο μασκο μολρο ταβδο
>
> And also, in the presence of the other freemen (and) witnesses who were present there amongst (them) and (who) have placed (their) seals hereupon.[122]

or they were aware of the agreement before it was signed:

> οδο πισο μισο αζαδοκα{α}ρανο κιδο οαλο αβο μιλαγγο σταδδινδο οδασο εμο ερο ζανινδο
>
> And also, in the presence of the freemen who were present there amongst (them) and (who) bear witness concerning this matter.[123]

12 Number of Witnesses

In the Bactrian corpus, and similarly, in the Mesopotamian and Aramaic corpora, there probably was not a precise rule about the minimum or the maximum number of witnesses for any type of document. As mentioned above, in the Greek double tradition of Egypt, there is a well-known type of double document, the six-witness agreement (εξαμαρτυρος συγγραφη).[124] However, there is no evidence these documents were employed in Bactrian conveyances. In the rabbinical tradition, there is a rule regarding the number of witnesses. According to this rule, double copies have more witnesses than single copies, which is explained in the Mishnah as follows:

גט פשוט עדיו בשנים ומקושר בשלשה

> A simple document requires (at least) two witnesses, and a folded or tied document requires three (witnesses).[125]

---

122 See docs. A, C, J, Nn, O.

123 See docs. U, V, W, X.

124 For further information, see Rupprecht, 1995, passim; Wolff, 1978, 84ff.

125 Mishna, Baba Barṯa, 10.2; Tosefta, Baba Barṯa, 11.1.

Furthermore, Talmud Bavli explains why double copies require more witnesses:

סתור שנתר בה בקשריו נתרבה בעדיו

Since it has more folds, it [must also] have more witnesses.[126]

The Zoroastrian legal tradition requires a minimum of two witnesses for a deposition. Dinkard 8 states that the number of witnesses (gwkʾdʾnʾ) should be greater than one.[127]

12.1 *Mass Witnesses*

In some documents, we are confronted with a large number of witnesses who were present at the time the agreement was drafted. There are two ways to report their attendance:

1. οδο πισο υαμαχοανδο λιζαγοσιγανο χοιιαδαρο οδο κισαδαρανο

and in the presence of the assembled inhabitants of Lizag, greater and lesser[128]

2. οδο πισο μανδαρουανισο þαριγανο

and in the presence of other citizens[129]

A mass assembly of witnesses was noted in various Sumerian and Akkadian documents,[130] and in the Old Testament.[131] In summation, information gleaned from witnessed texts generally reveals at least two witnesses should have been present when a document was composed.[132]

126 TB, Baba Barṯa, 160a; Rabinowitz, 1956, 153f.

127 Dinkard 8, in Madan, 1911, 724 Shaki, 2011, 178 and Shaki, 1392/2013, 109.

128 Doc. Uu.

129 Doc. C, L.

130 Krecher et al., 1980, 493; Weinfeld, 1976, 392f.

131 Tucker, 1965, 42ff.

132 Doc. T is a gift deed—the queen gifted an estate and a slave girl to a temple in the presence of two officials: οδο πιδδι σαχοανο αβσιυο καδαγοστανο ποροβαργο πιδογαμοβαργο σταδο "And at this statement Absih, the spokesman (and) am[bassador] and treasurer of Kadagstan, was (present)."

12.2 *Authorities*

As previously stated, the Bactrian conveyances were drafted in an administrative office, a public place or a royal palace. Therefore, officials appeared before other witnesses in these transactions, and they can be classified into two categories:

12.3 *Administrative Staff*

According to Bactrian documents, administrative functionaries at all levels held judicial authority, and aside from functioning as the supreme judge, they also headed the bureaucracy. As a result, some deeds were composed in the presence of the local ruler, whose epithet was Khar. (χαρο):

> πισο φραμαριζμο þαβορα̣νο ιαβζοδοφαραυο χαγανο ταποαγλιγο υιλιτοβηρο ρωβοχαρο παροπαζο χοδ̣δηο
>
> In the presence of Frama-rizm Shaburan, the tapaghligh iltäbir of the qaghan prosperous in glory, khar of Rob, lord of Parpaz.[133]

Or agreements were made in his court:[134]

> μαλαβο μαδδρο ωδαγο ρωβοχαρανο αλοβαρο ... πισο βαιοριζμο μαδδρο φρομαλαρο
>
> Here in the district of Madr, (at) the court of the Khars of Rob ... in the presence of Bay-rizm, the steward of Madr.[135]

In the rest of the documents, local officials appear as witnesses and representatives of authority (Table 4).

Apparently, all of these officials hold two roles simultaneously—supervising transactions and witnessing transactions or agreements. Consequently, private documents were transformed into public documents, a decision endorsed by royal authorities. In other words, they serve as one of the marks or signatures both validating agreements and authenticating the documents.

133 Docs N, O, P, Q.

134 Docs. S, U, Tt, X.

135 Doc. U.

TABLE 4

Doc	Bactr	Trans
A	πισο οινδοωρομοζδο κολαγανο ιανδαγοβιδο	"In the presence of Wind-ormuzd Kulagan the chief of the borough."
C	πισο χοηο ικοσιρδαχμιγο	"In the presence of the lord of Kusirdakhm."
F	αζδηβιδο ζαροοηρο οιβριιανο οδο πισο ταλμοζηνο οα̣σ̣αροβιδο	"With the cognizance of Zar-wer Wibriyan[a] and in the presence of Talm- Zcn thc ovcrsccr of the market."
N	πισο χολχανο ιενηλο ταρχανο οιλαργανο χο̣δδηο οδο πισο σορηνο ρωβοχαρανο φραμαλα̣ρο	"In the presence of Khulkhan, the inal tarkhan, lord of (the estate) Wilargan and in the presence of Suren, the steward of the khars of Rob."
Nn	εζ⟨δδ⟩η{δ}βιδο κολζανο λιζγοσιγο καροοαλο	"With the cognizance of Kulzan, the leader of the people of Lizg."
P and Q	πισο ταρχανο χοσαροο ταρχανο πορο ο̣δο πισο δδηβοραζο ρωβοχαραγγο ο̣ασαροβιδο χαιιαχο	"In the presence of the tarkhan,[b] the son of Khusaru the tarkhan, and in the presence of Deb-raz, senior overseer of the market of the khars of Rob."
R	πισο σιτο γαζο υαμαρογαρο	"In the presence of Sit, the treasurer of Gaz."
S	πισο σηρο τορκο γαζο ταδονο οδαζδδηβιδο σιτο γαζο μαρογαρο	"In the presence of Ser the Turk, the tudun of Gaz, and with the cognizance of Sit, the treasurer of Gaz."
T	οδο πιδδι σαχοανο αβσ̣ιυ̣ο καδαγοστανο ποροβαργο πιδογαμοβαργο σταδο	"And at this statement Absih, the spokesman (and) am[bassador] and treasurer of Kadagstan, was (present)."
Tt	πισο υιλιτοβηρο λιζγο καροοαλο	"In the presence of Hilitber, the leader of the people of Lizg."
U	πισο βαιοριζμο μαδδρο φρομαλαρο	"In the presence of Bay-rizm, the steward of Madr."
Uu	πισο ραυολο λιζαγοσιγο καρ̣οοαλο οδο πισο οιιοσο οολαχο καροΔαρο οδο πισο ιακανο ταδανο	"In the presence of Rahul, the leader of the people of Lizag, and in the presence of Wiyus, the foreman of Wulakh."
Uv	Αβο μιροζινιιο υωρσανο οισβορο χηϸο χοαδδηι αλβαργο	"At the court of Mir-ziniy, lord of Khesh (Under?) the prince of Khorasan"
V	πισο σωρο σπανδαγανο χοδδηοο ριζμο ϸαραβο	"In the presence of Sor, the lord of (the estate) Spandagan, the satrap of Rizm."
W	πισο οισβοροζινιιο σαμοσιτανο ϸαβορανο φρομαλαρο	"In the presence of Wisbur-ziniy Samsitan, the steward of the Shaburan (family)."
X	πισο αζοδδ̣ηβιδο σαβολιυο οαργονανο χοδδηιο καδαγοστανο σπαλοβιδο	"In the presence (and) with the cognizance of Sävüglig, the lord of the Wargun (people), the commander of the army of Kadagstan."

a For more information on this person, see Sims-Williams, 2010, 62f no 148.

b For further details about him, see Sims-Williams, 2010, 152 no. 541.)

13 Historical Background

The practice of writing a document before an official or the king was common in the ancient Near East and can be found in a myriad of places and cultures. Documents from Ugarit[136] and Alalaḫ,[137] demonstrate this choice and begin with ina pāni X LUGAL (in front of the king X). Further documents began with other officials including the judges in Nuzi[138], Susa,[139] (ina pāni diāni) and Nippur in the Neo-Babylonian period.[140]

Regarding this action, Ishu-Bokht mentions in his law book the importance of composing a document before officials:

ܫܛܪܐ ܡܢ ܫܪܝܪܐ ܐܝܬܘܗܝ ܗܘ ܕܚܬܝܡܐ ܕܗܢܘܢ ܕܡܢ ܒܥܕܬܐ.
ܘܗܘ ܡܢ ܡܠܟܐ ܘ ܫܠܝܛܢܐ ܡܬܓܒܝܢ ܡܬܬܣܝܡܝܢ ܗܘ ܕܝܢ ܕܦܘܫܟܐ
ܐܝܬܘܗܝ. ܗܘ ܕܚܬܝܡܐ ܕܣܗܕܐ

A valid deed is a (document) which is sealed by whom he is selected and employed by Church, or King or Governor. A doubtful deed is a (deed) which (only) has seals of witnesses.[141]

13.1 *Temple Stuff: Divine Witness*

Gods are frequently called as witnesses from doc. L. The presence of Wakhsh increases in documents[142] and Ram-Set follows.[143] The texts introduce this type of witness (gods) in three ways:

1. simply giving his name

πιϲο βαγο ραμοϲητο

In the presence of the God Ram-Set[144]

136 Nougayrol, 1955, docs. 16.144, 16.160.
137 Niedorf, 2008, for example, see docs. 352.4, 353.1.
138 Pfeiffer and Speiser, 1936, doc. 15.
139 MDP. XXIII, doc. 315.
140 San Nicolo, 1929, 41; Bregstein, 1996, 57; Koschaker, 1931, 3f.
141 Sachau, 1914, 186f.
142 Docs. L, Nn, O, Tt, U, Uu, V, W.
143 Docs. P, Q, Ss.
144 Docs. P, Ss; notably, P' (Scriptio exterior of P) contains praise of the god Ram-Set.

2. introducing him and where he is worshipped

αζδδηβιδο βαγο ι οαχϸο κιδο μαλαβο οαρνο ασπισαμο

With the cognizance (or in the presence) of the god Wakhsh whom we worship here in Warnu.[145]

3. With epithets praising the god:

εζδδηβιδο βαγο οαχϸο οαρσοχοανδδιγο λαδοιανο λαδοαγαλγο ακιδδηιο ναμο αβ(ο) υαρογο ζαμιγο βοοαδογινδο

With the cognizance of the god Wakhsh, the wonderful, the granter of favors (and) granter of wishes, whose renown has reached the whole earth.[146]

The gods, like other witnesses, put their seals on the agreements.[147]

14 Historical Backgrounds

Divine witnesses were not recorded in Aramaic or Greek documents and only appear in certain examples from ancient Mesopotamia[148] and those recovered from ancient Chinese tombs.[149] Divine witnesses in ancient Mesopotamia emerge for the first time in some documents from the Old Babylonian period. In all of these examples, the name of the gods are written before all other witnesses, after the Sumerogram, IGI (Akkadian ina pāni or maḫar = before), and they, like other witnesses, place their seals on the agreements.[150] For many of these documents, Shamash, the god of justice, is frequently mentioned alongside a local god as a witness, again before the other witnesses, e.g., in Elam, Inshushinak, and Shamash,[151] in Girsu, Ammurum, and Shamash,[152] and in

145 Docs. L, U.

146 Docs. Nn, O, Tt, Uu, V, W.

147 Docs. L, P, Q, Uu; Lerner and Sims-Williams, 2011, 21, 37, 56.

148 Watanabe, 1985, 392 note 70.

149 Hansen, 1995, 152.

150 Opificius, 1957–71, 576ff.

151 Jalilvand Sadafi; 2014, 93f; Oppenheim 1936, 259f.

152 Goodeeris, 2009, 69; 70; for other cities, see Richter, 2004; Renger, 1967; Mercer, 1913; Mauer, 1979, 150f; Greengus, 1986, 212.

Nippur, Gula, and Shamash (UTU).[153] Although god witnesses have been read on only one document from the Middle Babylonian period,[154] there are numerous examples found in Middle Assyrian[155] and Neo-Assyrian documents.[156] Additionally, aside from private transactions, treaties between states and vassals include gods as witnesses—they witnessed and sealed treaties between kings.[157] In fact, they were guarantors of the oath sworn by kings, punishing those who broke the oath and rewarding those who kept it.[158] Another source for divine witnessing is the ancient Chinese tomb contracts.[159] The Chinese believed that gods ruled the underground and the layer beneath the land surface belonged to them. After purchasing a plot of land for his tomb, one made a contract with the gods to own not only the surface but also the layer underneath.[160] In these documents, Gods appear as the seller, witness, and guarantor all at the same time.[161] Further sources for divine witnessing are found on Old Uyghur documents datable to the 13th-century CE, and multiple gods appear as a witness.[162] However, unlike ancient Chinese tomb contracts there is no concrete explanation for "why does a god appear as a witness in Mesopotamian private transactions?"[163] Similarly, for Bactrian legal documents as well.

15 Differences

There are similarities and differences between Mesopotamian and Bactrian traditions regarding the appearance of divine witnesses in documents. Firstly, the number of gods in Mesopotamian texts is usually more than one, whereas, in Bactrian texts, only one god appears as a witness. Secondly, in Mesopotamia

153 Kraus, 1953, 60.

154 Donbaz, 1982.

155 Kochaker, 1928, 11; 21.1

156 Postgate, 1976, 9; Radner, 1999, 58f; Dally, 1986, 91.

157 Beckman, 1996, 2f; Beckman, 2017, 260; for an example of divine witnessing in diplomatic agreements, see Essarhaddon's succession treaty, Lauinger, 2012, 91; Weinfeld, 1976, 395ff.; Altman, 2012, 126.

158 Koch, 2008, 59; Westbrook, 2003, 84f; Parpola and Wilhelm, 2011–13, 47.

159 This was a contract between gods and humans for the purchase of grave plots; for more information on this type of document, see Hansen, 1995, 149ff.

160 Hansen, 1995, 152.

161 Hansen, 1995, 171f.

162 In these documents, first comes the name of gods and then other witnesses. For an example of divine witnessing in Old Uyghur documents, see Yamada, 1981, 373ff: tanug dört maxaranč tańgri-lär yiti äkä baldïz tärim-lär, witness: the four Maharaja gods and the seven sister-goddesses.

163 Veenhof, 1996(1993–94), 135f; Radner, 1999, 58f; Teissier, 1998, 115f.

Shamash whose name appears frequently in the documents as a witness from Mesopotamia is the god of justice[164] but in Bactria, Wakhshis the god of rivers.[165] Thirdly, unlike in Mesopotamia, praises and epithets for god(s) are mentioned in Bactrian transactional texts, while in Mesopotamian contracts, only their name appears before the names of other witnesses and after the preposition IGI (maḫar).

16 The Witnesses in the First Lines

As discussed above, witnesses were usually named in the first lines of documents following the location clause. Normally, the names of witnesses were recorded at the end of documents in the ancient Near East. However, there are a few exceptions where the names of witnesses are moved to the first line of documents. In Nuzi[166] and Elam,[167] these types of contracts are written in the presence of witnesses (ina pāni šibutī). This method was utilized for Greek documents from Avroman,[168] as well as some Greek documents from Dura-Europos,[169] Euphrates,[170] and Palestine.[171] In Bactria, naming witnesses without exception in the first lines of a document indicates this formula was the rule, rather than an option in other contemporary cultures.

17 The Sealing and Signature in Double and Single Documents

In these legal documents, there are three types of potential sealers: witnesses (freeman), the authorities (in whose presence the oral transactions were recorded by a scribe), and one of the principal parties (the issuer).[172] A legal document is typically a written instrument with the signatures of one or both parties, and these signatures acknowledge and create obligations to be fulfilled

164 Krebrenik, 2006–8, 354f; for the Hittite tradition, see Fauth, 1979, 227ff.

165 Biruni, 1380/2001, 297.

166 For example, Gadd, 1926, no. 3; Pfeiffer and Speiser, 1936, nos. 35 or 67; for example, nos. 29, 31, 54.

167 MDP, XXIII, no. 317.

168 Mines, 1915, Avr 1–2.

169 Welles, 1959, docs. 20, 23, 26, 31.

170 Teixidor et al., 1997, docs. 6–10, 12.

171 Lewis, 1989, 54ff doc. 14; docs. 15, 23–4.

172 Messina, 2009, 178, n 17; she categorized sealers into two types, "active parties to the contract (e.g., assignees, donors, exchangers, lessees, lessors, sellers) or they may be involved in the practice as professional (advisers, guarantors, officers, witnesses, writers)."

or rendered by such parties after the contract enters into force. In Bactria, the usual method for confirming the content of an agreement is sealing and signing, which differs in simple or double copies. Sealing is used only for authenticating the deed in simple documents, but in double copies, it's also used to close the inner text in the Mesopotamian tradition, thereby preventing forgery.[173] Although there is not a strict rule concerning the number of sealers, whether simple or double copies,[174] a Bactrian letter may reveal the minimum number of seals required for a document. In one example, an official reported to his lord via letter that he will not give any land to a certain Nawaz unless he brings a document with (at least) two seals from the lord:

> αλδομο ναοαζο ασο χοη̣οι πωστογο αβαραδο πιδο λοοι μολρο ταδοιηιο αζο οιζανδο ναβαρανο ασιδ̣οιηιο υαμοπαλο ζαμιγο λαυανο
>
> But if Nawaz brings me a document with two seals from the lord, then I will not do him any injury but will give him the land immediately.[175]

There are specific guidelines for how documents should be signed. Witnesses sign transversely on the verso of a double document in relation to writing on the recto. This practice was also used in Aramaic documents,[176] and was described clearly in the rabbinical tradition:

> גט פשוט עדיו מתוכו, ומקושר עדיו מאחוריו.
>
> A simple document has (the signatures of) the witnesses inside, and a tied (documents) has (the signatures of) the witnesses on the back.[177]

According to the Babylonian Talmud, signing on the reverse of double deeds prevented forgery.[178]

173 Schorr, 1913, XXXVII.
174 The number of witnesses and those signing a document are two different subjects.
175 Sims-Williams, 2007, 83f.
176 Hezser, 2001, 304f.
177 Mishnah, Baba Baṯra, 10, 1; TB, Baba Barta 160a.
178 BT, Baba Barṯa, 161a; Rabinowitz, 1956, 155f.

18 Authorities' Seals

The majority of seals on documents were issued by authorities, more specifically, rural administrative officials and priests. For example, doc. P is sealed by:

Yaskul (issuer) (A)
The god Ram-set (B)
The khar of Rob (D)
Deb-Raz (senior overseer of the market of the khars)[179] (E)

Considering the three seals in Doc. F, two bear the names of officials,[180] while a priest stands in for the respective god as the divine witness affixes the seal on the document.[181]

18.1 *Parties*

Only the issuer seals the agreement in Bactrian documents, which means that in sale deeds, sellers seal the document, in settlement contracts, the declarants, and so on, and usually one of these issuers completes the seal. However, in certain documents, more than one issuer might seal the document, and a collective seal is used. For example, in doc. I, a father and son each have a seal, while in doc. Q, a couple seals the contract together.

19 Historical Backgrounds

The practice of sealing in the ancient Near East was transformed over time.[182] Initially, sealing by parties was determined by the nature of the contract, following the Mesopotamian tradition. In sales, the seller usually sealed, and in short-term rentals and leases, the tenant and lessee usually sealed.[183] During the Neo-Babylonian period, sealing depended on the type of agreement;[184] in so-called dialogue documents, the contract was stamped by both parties,[185] while in some cases, three basic categories of potential seal users existed for

179 This explanation is my addition.
180 See docs. N, Q, Uu; in doc. J, five witnesses sealed the document, although none had been an official, while doc. L was sealed by a priest on behalf of the god Wakhsh.
181 Lerner and Sims-Williams, 2011, 21.
182 Renger, 1977; Oeslner, 1978.
183 Teissier, 1998, 111.
184 Oelsner, 1996, 101f.
185 Lewenton, 1970, 31.

these legal documents: judges, principal parties, and witnesses.[186] Documents from the Judaean Desert, unlike those from Elephantine, are signed by the two parties.[187]

19.1 *Witnesses*[188]

In Bactria, not all witnesses sealed the document, and have two types of seals: individual and collective. The first type, for the individual, is the private seal retained by each citizen. The second, the collective, was stamped for all of the document's witnesses or citizens.[189]

19.2 *Fingernail*

Making marks with fingernails is another way to confirm the content of an agreement. The impression of a fingernail was distinctive and when compared to a seal's symbolic potency, was just as strong. This tradition can be traced to the Old Babylonian period,[190] and three examples of this practice exist in Bactria.[191] In the outer text of doc. U, the issuer declares:

> μοδδρ̣ογο ταβδο μανο οαχþομαρηγο ορωλανο π̣ιδο χοβο þουο οδο πιδο μαναγγο πιδοοαυανο ταβ̣δ̣ο̣ [] μ̣οδδροδδηβανο
>
> (This) sealed document has been sealed by me, Wakhsh-mareg Urolan, with (my) own **fingernail**, and at my request, it was sealed by those who have impressed (their) seals (upon it).

The text indicates the importance of the fingernail press, which was equal to the importance of the seal, although the fingernail impression differs from the Chinese tradition of finger-seals. The latter has been found on documents from Bactria's neighboring lands with documents recorded in Tibetan and Tocharian. For this method, the name of the sealer(s) is written upside down, and the length of a finger and finger-joints for the respective person are drawn above the name.[192] Many examples of this practice exist in Khotanese

186 Bregstein, 1996, 57.

187 Schiffman, 2003, 178; for signatures in the Aramaic documents from Elephantine see Yaron, 1961, 31. Because of their fragmentary nature, the identity of the owners of signatures in the Aramaic papyri from Wadi al-Daliyah is uncertain. For more information see Dušek, 2007, 94.

188 Witnesses who are freemen, excluding authorities.

189 Doc. Uu, þαριγανο ταβαδο̣ (the citizen sealed).

190 Oelsner, 1978; Boyer, 1939; Postgate, 1976, 8; Wunsch, 2021, 159ff.

191 Docs. U, Uv, W.

192 Takeuchi, 1995, 110ff.

documents,[193] reflecting shared cultural practices. Nevertheless, the Bactrian method should be classified in the same tradition as Mesopotamian sealing,[194] but it's worth noting that pressing a fingernail on Bactrian documents differs from Mesopotamian examples due to the nature of the material. Bactrians favored documents written on leather or parchment, and therefore, the fingernail was pressed into a clay seal, while the Mesopotamian preference, clay tablets, necessitated the fingernail be pressed directly into the tablet or envelope.

20 Scribe

In the Ancient Near East, the scribe usually writes his name at the end of the document with the other witnesses, implying that he also served as a witness; we see this practice in Akkadian, Aramaic, and other corpora,[195] as well as in the Iranian legal traditions, i.e., Khotanese[196] and Sogdian[197] documents. However, the name of the scribe is not mentioned in the majority of Bactrian documents.[198] Bactrian legal formulary does seem to be inclined to avoid mentioning the name of the scribe.

193 Skjaervo, 2002, for example, 3f and 7f.

194 Sims-Williams, 2011(2015), 49.

195 For the presence of scribes in Mesopotamian documents, see Waetzoldt, 2009–11, 261; Cussini, 2013, passim; for examples from Elephantine, see Yaron, 1957, 38; for examples in Aramaic documents from the Judaean Desert and other Aramaic corpora, see Cussini, 2010, 352; Cussini, 2009, 195f.

196 For examples, see Duan, 2014, 351 and Duan, 2015, 136f.

197 For examples, see Livshits, 2015, 24ff No. 3 & 4. and Yoshida, 2003, 160.

198 There are docs aa and ab and Uv. (See also Sims-Williams, 2011(2015), 49). Docs aa and ab contain the scribe's signature, while Uv does not. Unfortunately, it is not clear why the name of the scribe is mentioned in these documents but not in others.

CHAPTER 2

Operative Section

1 Operative Section

The operative section in Bactrian deeds begins with an introduction setting out the facts of the transaction, thereby disclosing its purpose and nature. These documents are primarily concerned with facts, so stereotyped phrases in the introduction are very similar throughout most documents. The length and content of an operative section in a deed are determined by the nature of the deed, i.e., a sale deed contains the declaration, reason, description of the property, and quittance clauses, while in settlement agreements there is a warranty clause after the reason clause.[1] Other contracts, including gift, loan, and lease deeds containing some of the aforementioned clauses.

The term "operative section," first coined by Yaron, describes the section recording the transfer of rights. However, before discussing the clauses in this section, I should first explain the language or the style Bactrian deeds are written. In this case, style refers to the method of constructing and narrating a document. Bactrian deeds are distinguished by two characteristics:

1. It is usually framed in the first person through subjective declarations.
2. The deeds of conveyance are formulated from the perspective of the issuer.

Typically, only one party (in this case, the issuer, A son of B) speaks, who has accepted obligations under the contract. Usually, the obligation is bilateral because the other party has already fulfilled his part of the transaction, e.g., paying the price, providing service, etc.

2 Subjective Style

In the ancient Near East, there are two ways to write a document—objective and subjective:

1. Objective-style: the agreement is reported in the third person, as in "he bought X from him or sold X to him."

1 Sale deeds include more clauses and phrases than others, and I will focus on sale deeds in the following pages.

 | DOI:10.1163/9789004519985_004

2. Subjective-style: a transaction is declared in the first person to the second person (singular/plural). This style can be divided into two types: indirect and direct subjective. Indirect subjective is similar to reported speech in English and the objective mode from the perspective of witnesses. For example, "he said: I bought from you or sold X to you," while direct subjective is completely narrated in the first person (singular/plural). In this style, the issuer addresses directly the opponent party (addressee): "I said: I bought from you or sold X to you."

All Bactrian contracts are entirely formulated in the direct subjective mode:

> καλδο πιδοοιησαδο χογαμο χοσινδο **μανο̣** οιημο βορζομιυρο πορο οδο **μανο** βαγορημαρηγο βορο πορο μαλριγο þαυο μαρηγο **κιδομηνο** καδγο οιηþοοαραζανο ριζδο.
>
> When (this) declaration was freely (and) willingly made by **me**, Wyem son of Burz-mihr, and by **me**, Bag-re-mareg son of Bur, inhabitants of Malr, servants of the king, **we whose** estate is called Wyeshwarazan.[2]

Grammatically, the wording of Bactrian contracts is constantly switched between singular and plural forms, both in the first and second person, during the narration. This is a common feature of Bactrian contracts. For example:

> μισιδο ωσο α̣γ̣γ̣ιτο **μανο** δδηβο ι̣αλ̣ογανο πορο ταρμ̣ιδδιγο ζα̣δ̣αγο ασο λιζο ακιδομηνο χανο υωριγανο γιρλινδο.
>
> Now: there has now been received by **me**, Deb son of Yalgan, a native of Tarmid, from the fortress, **we** whose house they call Horigan.[3]

or

> οτο μισο **παδοαχþανηδ̣ο ασιδδηιο** υαρσο κιρδο αριμαδο χοαδο δδριγδο παραλαδο ναβαγο ωσταδο λαþνο αμβαγδο̣ αχρινο οιχρινο κιρδο πιδο γαοοανο πιδοκιþ̣το πιδο σπασο αζαδο υιρτο ταδδηιο.
>
> And also **you (pl.) have the right** (to do) **whatever** it may suit **you (sg.)** to do, to keep (him) yourself, to sell (him), to pawn (him), to give (him as) a

2 Doc. J.
3 Doc. Q.

gift, to put (him for) purchase (or for) hire, to detain (him) for a misdeed, (or) to let (him) free (in return) for service.[4]

3 Historical Background

The Mesopotamian legal documents are normally formulated objectively[5] and in the style of a protocol written from the perspective of the witnesses.[6] For example:

> 7 SAR qa-aq-qa-ru i-ṣú ù ma-du KI [d]Šu-bu-(lá)-a-bi [ù] dMÙŠ.EREN-a-bi (It)-ti-DIGIR-ba-li-iṭ i-šà-am
>
> 7 SAR estate, more or less, Itti-ilī baliṭ has bought from Šubula-abī and Šušinak-abī[7]

However, in some eras and lands, namely the Anatolian Old Assyrian Colony,[8] Emar,[9] Nuzi,[10] and Susa,[11] documents are written in an indirect subjective style.[12] For example, in a text from Emar we read:

> iš-tu UD-mi an-ni-im Imu-ZA-ZU DUMU ša-ma-nu i-na bu-ul-ṭì-šu ši-im-ti É-ti-šu i-ši-im ki-ia-am iq-bi a-nu-um-ma Ifḫ̮é-ba-te DAM-ti-ia a-bu ù AMA [ša] É-ia ši-it-ma
>
> From this day, Muzazu son of Šaman, in his good health, has decreed the disposition of his estate. He said as follows: Now then, my wife ḫ̮ebate is father and mother of my estate.[13]

4 Docs. N, P, R, S, T, Tt, Uu, V, W.

5 Krecher, 1980, 345.

6 San Nicolo, 1931, 133; Renger, 1977, 75.

7 Jalilvand Sadafi, 2014, 203. Doc 41; in the Old Babylonian period, sale deeds usually begin with a description of the sale object. For more details, see Skaist, 1990, 270ff.; Skaist, 2008, 221f.

8 Eisser, 1939, 119.

9 Heuhnergard, 1983, all documents.

10 Maidman, 1994, docs. JEN 682, 696, 699, 706, 740; Gadd, 1926, No. 3, 18, 54; especially documents beginning with the word Lišanšu, meaning "his tongue," which may imply a declaration. For more details about this type of document, see Koschaker, 1928, 21ff.

11 MDP, XXIII doc. 317.

12 Muffs, 2003, 175f.

13 Huehnergard, 1983, text. 3; Muffs labelled them fringe traditions, see Muffs, 2003, 15f note 5.

4 Style in the Aramaic Tradition

All the Aramaic deeds from Elephantine are formulated in the indirect subjective mode.[14] For example:

אמר קוניה בר צדק ... **אנה** אתית עליך ויהבת לי תרע ביתא זילך למבנה אגר

> Qwnyh son Ṣdq ... said: **I** came to you and you gave me the gateway of the house of yours to build wall there.[15]

However, the Samaria papyri used both styles; they began in an objective style but switched to subjective in the contingency clauses.[16] During the Hellenistic and Roman periods in the Judean Desert, Aramaic and Hebrew documents were also composed in the indirect subjective form,[17] whereas Syriac legal documents were written entirely in the direct subjective form,[18] and are homologous.[19] Although Aramaic documents from Palmyra and Nabataea, particularly Mada'in Salih, were formulated in an objective mode.[20]

In the rabbinical tradition, the operative section is also phrased in a subjective manner.[21] Furthermore, in the majority of Palestinian Ketubbot from the Middle Ages, the basic formulation of the document is written in the subjective mode.[22]

5 Style in the Iranian Languages

In the other Middle Iranian languages, both style forms are recorded. Seemingly, documents are composed in a subjective manner following the Zoroastrian tradition during the Sasanian period. This type of declaration appears in the MHD:

14 Yaron, 1961, 11.
15 TAD B2.1.
16 Gropp, 2000, 831.
17 Koffmahn, 1968, 62; Greek deeds from the Judean Desert are subjectively formulated and influenced by the Aramaic formula.
18 Cussini, 2010, 346f.
19 Goldstein, 1990, 45f; for further details on homology, see the section below on homologia.
20 Cussini, 1995, 24; Cussini, 2010, 253.
21 Gulak, 1935, 2.
22 Friedman, 1980, 18.

> ʾMT YMLLWNyt ʾYK-m ZNH dstkrtʾ ʿL LK YHBWNt ZK dstkrtʾ W KLʾ MH pt ZK dstkrtʾ dʾʾštʾ YKʿYMWNyt YHBWNt YHWWNyt.
>
> If he says: "I have given this dastkart[23] to you," (then), this dastkart and all the possessions in that dastkart will be given (to him).[24]

According to the MHD, it seems that contracts in the Sasanian period were mostly written in the subjective form, but the objective style was not abandoned because both styles are attested in Pahlavi receipts from the early Islamic period. More precisely, some receipts are written in the subjective mode, while others are composed in the objective mode.[25] For Sogdian documents, legal texts are mostly stylized in the objective form, with the exception of one document[26] and some receipts that use the subjective mode.[27] Those in Khotanese, much like Sogdian, have examples of both subjective and objective styles. Both forms are found in early Persian documents from Central Asia. Documents from Balkh and Gur are in the objective style,[28] while a Persian document from Yarkandi is written in the subjective mode and the legal Persian document from Bamiyan[29] is formulated as a dialogue document.[30]

In conclusion, Aramaic documents in Bactria probably were composed in the subjective mode during the Achaemenid period, similarly to Aramaic papyri in Elephantine, and this style did not change in Hellenistic Bactria. Later, during the Kushanid period, the subjective style was retained in the Bactrian language until the Islamic conquest (the first half of the 8th-century) over the region and the Islamic style replaced the local ones.

6 Homologia and Non-Homologia

Based on the declaration, one can divide the post-Hellenistic documents from the Near East into two categories: homologia and non-homologia.

---

23 For more information about this word, see Perikhanian, 1997, 349f.

24 MHD18. 6–7 Perikhanian, 1997, 62 and MHD 34. 3–15.

25 Weber, 2008, docs. 4, 5; Gignoux, 2009, doc. 33; the subjective form in receipts begins with the verb MKBLWNym (padīrēm) "I receive," see Weber, 2008, doc. 4.

26 Livshitz, 2008, doc. no. 4.

27 Livshtz, 2008, B.3, A.7.

28 Sheikh Al-Hokamayi, 1388/2009; Mirzā Khwājah Mohammad and Sāqi, 1388/2009 (except doc. 17).

29 Scarsia, 1963; 1966; for the Persian text in the Arabic alphabet, see Roushan-zamir, 2537/1978, 12ff.

30 For more information on dialogue documents or Zwiegeschprächsurkunde, see Petschow, 1965; Sand, 2002; Roth, 1989.

6.1 *Homologia*

Homologia was a common legal form in ancient Greek texts. The Greek word ομολογια means "promise,[31] say the same"[32] and "acknowledge"[33] in a legal context. Because the declaration begins with the verb ομολογειν,[34] this form is known as a homologia. A homologia form can be subjectively or objectively styled.[35]

This type of document in the Near East first appeared in Greek deeds from Ptolemaic Egypt.[36] Previously, in Greece, the verb was used as a legal term.[37] For sale and other contractual types, objective homology initially was the prevalent form, especially in double copies,[38] but subjective homology gradually prevailed.[39]

Homologia was accepted in Greek documents and even non-Greek deeds outside of Egypt and the western territories of the Seleucid Empire, e.g., the Fertile Crescent. Two Avroman Greek deeds are written in the objective homologia mode:

> εξωμολογησατο και συνεγπρααστοψατο Βαρακης και Σωβηνης οι του μαιφορρου υιοι
>
> Acknowledgment and agreement were made by Baraces and Sobanes, the sons of Maiphorres.[40]

Like documents from Avroman, Greek homologia contracts in Dura-Europos are written in the objective form.[41]

As mentioned earlier, certain Greek deeds from the Judean Desert were influenced by the Semitic tradition and are drafted in the subjective mode. I

31 Liddl, and Scott, 1996, 1226.
32 Gemoll, 2006, 577.
33 Wolff, 1957. 54ff; Muraoka, 2009, 496f.
34 For more details about the function of homologia, see Wolff, 1957, 53–65; Von Soden, 1973, 123ff.
35 Lippert, 2012, 141.
36 Von Soden, 1973, 8ff.
37 Mitteis, 1912, 72ff; Pringsham, 1950, 31f.
38 Seidl, 1962, 62.
39 Palme, 2009, 367f; Keenan et al., 2014, 31.
40 Minns, 1915, doc. 1.
41 See Welles, 1959, 100ff doc. 18 and 120ff doc. 23 for more examples of homologia in Greek documents from Dura-Europos see indices, section Greek and Latin words in Welles, 1959, 448 (the word εξομολογεω) and 450 (the verb ομολογεω). indices: the word εξομολογεω and the verb ομολογεω.

should also mention that many of these deeds are composed in the homologia type of subjective style.[42] The influence was not entirely one-sided, meaning some Aramaic and Hebrew deeds from the Judean Desert are written in homologia form.[43] The same holds true for Syriac deeds from Dura-Europos and the Euphrates.[44] The verb ידי in Aramaic[45] and ܝܕܐ in Syriac[46] in its causative (Afe'l) means "to acknowledge" and are a translation of the Greek verb ομολογειν.[47] For example:

> ܡܪܩܝܐ ܐܘܪܠܝܐ ܡܛܪܥܬܐ ܒܪܬ ܫܡܢܒܪܙ ܒܪ ܐܒܓܪ
> ܕܝܪܬܐ ܐܘܪܗܝܬܐ ܠܠܘܩܣ ܐܘܪܠܝܘܣ ܬܝܪܘ ܒܪ ܒܪ ܒܥܫܡܝܢ

> I, Marcia Aurelia Matarˁata daughter of Samenbaraz son of Abgar, Edessene resident, **declare** to Lucas Aurelius Tiro son of Barbaˁšamin.[48]

The verb πιδοοασ-[49] in Bactrian means "to declare" and "to reply" and it is equivalent to the Greek word ομολογια and serves the same function in Greek deeds.[50] A significant number of Bactrian deeds for conveyance are homologia.[51] In addition, homologia in Bactrian deeds, equally with Greek documents, do not prevent an exclusive type of deed.[52] Even though all early Bactrian documents are in the homologia form,[53] some of the later documents do not always use homologia.[54]

In the Bactria homologia form, the issuer normally expresses the declaration as follows:

---

42 Lewis, 1989, docs. 5, 11, 20, 21, 22; for an index of Greek words, see ομολογεω 159.
43 P. Yadin 42; Eshel and Yardeni, 2011.
44 Syriac deeds from Dura-Europos and Euphrates are drafted in the subjective homologia mode.
45 Sokoloff, 2003, 53.
46 Sokoloff, 2009, 563.
47 Gross, 2008, 86f, 199.
48 Drijvers and Healey, 1999, P I.
49 Sims-Williams, 2012, 255 and the variants.
50 Of course, the structure and roots of two words differ, but their meaning and function are similar. For more information see page 60. See also Sims-Williams, 2007, 255f.
51 Docs. A, C, F, I, Ii, J, L, m, Nn, R, S, V, W.
52 For Greek documents, see Wolff, 1978, 140f.
53 Docs. A, C, F, I, Ii, J, L.
54 Docs. Nn, R, S, V, W.

Καλδο πιδοοιησαδο ... μανο

When (this) **declaration made** ... by me

The presence of homologia in the Bactrian formulary indicates the influence of Greek on the Bactrian language, which may have happened during the Hellenistic period. Before this Greek influence, it is highly likely that Aramaic contracts in Achaemenid Bactria are narrated from the perspective of witnesses, as in the Aramaic papyri from Elephantine, where the declaration section begins in the third person.

If this hypothesis is correct, then the declaration in Aramaic deeds from Bactria would begin with the verb אמר (to say) similarly to those from Elephantine and changed during the Hellenistic period to homologia. This change can be reconstructed below:

אמר – ομολογια – πιδοοασ

The homologia form is found in Persian and Old Uyghur documents. In Persian, the verb (اقرار کردن),[55] and in Old Uyghur "Iqrar Bulmaq,"[56] mean "to acknowledge." These are an adoption from the Arabic verb ق رر which in a legal context means "to acknowledge or to confess,"[57] translated from the earlier Greek verb ομολογειν. As a result, Bactrian and Arabic/Islamic declaration formulae share a common ancestor, and declaration formulae in Persian and Old Uyghur documents from the region must undoubtedly be classified as belonging to the Islamic tradition.

6.2 *Non-Homologia*

Although the non-homologia form arrived in Bactria before the homologia form, it is only in later documents that this form appears.[58] In this type of document, the issuer expresses the subject of an agreement without the verb πιδοοασ, which can be classified into two types. In the first, the issuer expresses what has been agreed upon between the parties using a specific verb. The verb used in the text is determined by the type of document. For example, in a settlement deed, the declaration is made with the verb πιτιι- (to guarantee):

55 Steingass, 1963, 87.
56 Erdal, 1984, docs. I, II, III, IV, V.
57 Lane, 1863, 2499 قر.
58 Docs. N and onwards.

μισιδο πιτιιεμα̣ζο σαμοσιτο βιιανοβιδο πορο ... φαραφαγο τακο βητο πορο ...

Now, I, Sam-sit son of Samsit son of Biyan-bid ... **guarantee** to you Tak son of Bet ...[59]

The second begins with an explanation of the reason for conveyance. For example:

μισιδο ασταδο αχασο μανο ιωβιγο αστωφσιγο ακιδομο καδαγο ιωβιγανο ραζινδο πιδοοδδιγο χαρο μαρηγο οδο μαναγγο βραδο πορο πιδο δαγογγο ιαοοαρο ακιδο μανο ιωβιγο αβαφαγο βραμαρζο δαγογγο αχασαδδηιο ακιδο βραδο πιδο χαγγαρο ζιδδιμο ταδο ταοο βρα̣μαρζο αλμαγο ιωβιγο πιδολαδδιο πισαγαδαμο οτομο φαροφαγο βρ̣α̣μ̣[αρ]ζ[ο]

Now: I, Yobig, [an] inhabitant of Astof, whose house they call Yobigan, servant of the khar of Pidud, and my brothers (and) sons, had a quarrel, in the following circumstances, that I, Yobig, quarrelled with you, Bramarz, in such a way that I struck (your) brother with a sword. So, we-you, Bramarz, together with me, Yobig-" have agreed legally, and I have given you an undertaking, Yobig, and my brothers (and) sons-to you, Bramarz.[60]

In summation, the function of homologia and non-homologia documents is the same, with the only difference the rhetoric.

7 The λαδο οδο παραλαδο Pattern (Aramaic pattern זבן ויהב?)

In Bactrian sale deeds (homologia or non-homologia), the issuer usually expresses the sale-transaction with the verb **παραλαδο** (to sell).[61] For example:

μισιδο ωσο παραλαδο μανο

Henceforward: there has now been sold by me ...[62]

59 Docs. N, P, Q, Ss.
60 Docs. O, T, Tt.
61 Sims-Williams, 2007, 251.
62 Docs. J, L, Nn, P.

However, in two late sale documents (V, W), the issuer declares the transaction with two verbs, λαδο οδο, παραλαδο (to give, to sell) instead of just the verb **παραλαδο (to sell).** The issuer declares the transaction with two verbs, **λαδο οδο**, **παραλαδο** (to give, to sell). For example:

> καλδο πιδοοασαδο χογαμο οδο χοσινδο **λαδο οδο παραλαδο** μανο αβσιυο ...
>
> When a declaration was made by me, Absih, freely and willingly to give and to sell ...[63]

The phrase functions similarly to the Middle Assyrian iddinma ušabbi and Neo-Assyrian upišma ... iddin or utappiš ittidin, and the Aramaic זבן ויהב in Elephantine papyri. For Middle Assyrian sale deeds, specifically, those formulated from the perspective of the seller (*ex latere venditoris*), the transaction is written as follows:

> PN1(seller) ana PN2 (= buyer) iddin-ma ušabbi[64]
>
> PN1 gave and transferred to PN2[65]

In Neo-Assyrian deeds the formulation changes and statements are formulated below:

> Uppišma PN1... ana PN2 iddin[66] or išīm[67]
>
> PN1 contracted and gave or sold ... to PN2

Although in documents drafted from the perspective of the buyer (*ex latere emptoris*), this pattern changes.[68]

In all Aramaic sale deeds from Elephantine formulated from the perspective of the seller (*ex latere venditoris*), the sale declaration is expressed as follows:

---

63 Doc. V.
64 For the verb, see Postgate, 1997, 162.
65 Postgate, 1997, 168; Lafont, 2003, 546.
66 Postgate, 1976, 13f.
67 Donbaz and Parpola, 2001, docs. 234, 258.
68 Koschaker, 1928, 28f; Botta, 2008a, 103f.

אנחן זבן ויהבן לך ביתה

We sold and gave you (our) house.[69]

There are various explanations for use of the sale declaration in this form within Aramaic corpora. Muffs noted this phrase is a hendiadys construction,[70] while Yaron believes it's a "Fatty Degeneration of the Formula."[71] Botta recently rejected both previous viewpoints, claiming the two-term transfer formula is a formulaic addition intended to ensure the legal validity of the transaction in a new context (e.g., the Egyptian legal tradition).[72] However, the existence of this formula in Pahlavi (MHD) does not support his analysis. This two-term transfer formula as MZBNWNt W YHBWNt (frōxt ud dād) is mentioned several times in the MHD:

> ˀMT hwˀstk' Y nˀmcšt' rˀy YMLLNyt ˀYK ˁD KˁN ˀL L MZBNWNt W YHBWNt' ˀywyn' YHWWNt' mtryn' rˀy Lˀ ptkˀrm ywdtr YHWWNyt (W) cygwn ˀMT YMLLWNyt ˀYK ˁD KˁN ˁL L MZBNWNyt W YHBWNt' ŠLYTˀ YHWWNt' Y mtryn' rˀy Lˀ ptkˀrm ...
>
> If he says regarding a certain thing (Property): "I shall not bring [a] charge against Mihran (who) was obligated to sale and give me (the property) until now," (this) declaration differs if he says: "I shall not bring [a] charge against Mehran who has authority (on the property) to sale and give me until now."[73]

It not only indicates that Aramaic-speaking people in Egypt used this Aramaic two-term transfer formula but also contemporaneously in Iran during the Achaemenid period. Aramaic scribes used the term in legal documents, and after the Achaemenids, the term entered into Pahlavi legal terminology as an Aramogram. Therefore, 1it is unlikely that Egyptians influenced this Aramaic legal practice.[74]

Nevertheless, the Bactrian two-term transfer formula cannot be a direct translation of the Aramaic because it begins with the verb λαδο (to give) and

69 TAD, B. 3.4 and B.12.
70 Muffs, 2003, 34 n1.
71 Yaron, 1958, 18.
72 Botta, 2008a, 106.
73 MHDA, 22. 8–10; Machuch, 1981, 169; Perikhanian, 1997, 286f.
74 For more detail on this subject, see Sheikh, 2022, 279f; Pardee thinks it can be "a bit of evidence for a Northwest Semitic law," see Pardee, 2008, 312.

then follows with the verb παραλαδο (to sell), unlike the Aramaic. The Bactrian version seems to be a regional formula.

8 Perspective

Bactrian documents are written from the perspective of the issuer. The identity of the issuer can be determined based on the nature of the document. In a sale contract, the issuer is the seller (*ex latere venditoris*); in settlements—the defendant, in gift contracts—the donor, in manumission deeds—the lord, etc. Given the majority of Bactrian documents are sale deeds, more details on their perspective have been addressed below.

8.1 *Ex latere venditoris*

In the ancient Near East, sale deeds were drafted from one of two perspectives: the purchaser (*ex latere emptoris*) or the seller (*ex latere venditoris*). Sale deeds in Bactria are narrated by the seller (*ex latere venditoris*), similarly to Aramaic deeds from Elephantine, which are compiled from the seller's viewpoint.[75] However, in earlier cuneiform deeds, the pervasive formulation is from the viewpoint of the buyer.[76]

9 Linguistic and Grammatical notes

9.1 *Timeline*

From the operative section to the final clauses, Bactrian deeds are narrated from the past through the present and into the future.[77] In other words, these documents are reports on a process of agreements beginning in the past (the operative section), then property transfers to the new owner in the present (the investiture clause), and finally, promises and obligations to avoid future problems (the non-contest and warranty clauses).

9.2 *Ergativity*

The verb in the declaration section is in the third person, but this does not imply the style of Bactrian deeds is objective, since the Bactrian language,

75 Yaron, 1961, 124f.

76 Yaron, 1961, 125; *ex latere emptoris* prevails in the Old Babylonian period, but *ex latere venditoris* predominates in the Hellenistic period, see Oelsner et al., 2003, 944f; San Nicolo, 1974, 31f; Petschow, 1939, 43.

77 Our explanation is based on Porten's paper on time in the Aramaic papyri from Elephantine. For more information, see Porten, 1981, 169f.

along with some other Iranian languages, is an ergative language.[78] In some Iranian languages, the subject-agent (A) in the ergative split is expressed by an oblique case, or by a personal enclitic, while the direct object-patient (P) is expressed by the direct case and person agreement in the verb.[79] Bactrian ergative constructions indicate the subject-agent in the oblique and the object-patient in the direct case.[80] For example, as we have seen above in the sentence καλδο πιδοοιησαδο ... μανο, the verb πιδοοιησαδο (to declare) is third person singular but the subject-agent μανο (I or me) is first person singular and oblique.[81] Consequently, this grammatical rule does not impact the declaration and operative sections of Bactrian deeds in the subjective mode.

9.3 Figurae per adiectionem

Characteristic pairs of homonymous or complementary words and expressions in volition, satisfaction, and investiture clauses are common features of Bactrian documents.[82] These features are not found in any of the Aramaic corpora. On the contrary, the clauses in those texts are declared in a one-term style, similar to other legal deeds in cuneiform corpora. Since the 3rd-century CE, the above features have been documented in Greek legal documents originating in the Byzantine Empire, and their popularity increased steadily.[83] The objective was to ensure that any relevant point of a legal event was certain and explicit. At the same time, the style may have been intended to impress and please. This fashionable Greek chancery style, therefore, has been labeled "the theorization of the style."[84]

10 Parties

The issuer introduces himself, his family or partners, and then the addressee(s) in the declaration section. The parties are introduced in a variety of ways,

78 In an ergative language "the property ascribed to grammatical systems in which the subject of an intransitive verb and the direct object of a transitive verb are similar in grammar, while the subject of a transitive verb is different," see Brown & Miller, 2013, 156.

79 Windfuhr, 2009, 31f; Payne, 1998, 555f; Haig, 2015.

80 Sims-Williams, 2011, 29f.

81 For more examples, see Golami, 2009, passim.

82 I will deal with this feature in detail wherever it appears.

83 Zilliacus, 1956, 158; Zilliacus, 1967, 48ff; the Byzantine style did not influence Bactrian documents, instead, these features developed independently within the two legal traditions.

84 Keenan et al., 2014, 85f; interestingly, this isn't the only element they have in common. Other affinities exist, including the subjective mode mentioned above. Even though studying these affinities is beyond the scope of our project, it's important to note they shared a common ancestor, the Greek style of the Hellenistic period.

which vary depending on the document. Four factors appear more frequently than others in documents when introducing the parties: location, master, patronymic, and personal name—their frequency has been recorded (Table 5).

In its most basic form, the issuer introduces himself or the addressee as X son of Y or X from the Y family. For example:

> Καλδο πιδοοασ̣αδο χοακ̣α̣μο οδο χοα̣σ̣ινδο ασβιδο̣ νονοκανο
>
> When this acknowledgement [is] made by me, Asbid Nonokan freely and willingly.[85]

Whereas in its most detailed form, the issuer describes the personal name, patronymic, place, his/their master, and family name or clan. For example:

> πιδοοασαδδιδο χογαμο χοσινδο μανο βαι̣ο οδαζο χαιο οδαζο ιωζο οδαζο οανακο χοασο πορανο λιζγοσιγο καναγο γωζογανο μα̣ρηγο καδαγο νανανο ραζινδο
>
> (Then this) declaration was made freely (and) willingly by me, Bay, and (by) me, Khay, and (by) me, Yoz, and (by) me, Wanak, the sons of Khwas, inhabitants of Lizg, servants of Kanag Gozgan, we whose house they call Nanan.[86]

In the case of authorities having an interest in an agreement or transaction, the relevant consideration in the introduction of a person is his/her rank or post in the government. For example, in doc. T a queen granted an estate and a slave girl to a temple. She introduces herself in the following manner:

> βαγοαζιιασο στορογο τοροσανζο οισλογδο χοτ̣ολογο ταπα̣γλιιο βιλγαυο σαβοουο χινζωιο χαλασαν̣ο οισλογδο καδαγοστανο
>
> Bag- aziyas, the great Turkish princess, the queen of Qutlugh Tapaghlĭgh Bilgä Sävüg, the princess of Khalach (people), the lady of Kadagstan.[87]

85 Doc. F.
86 Doc. Nn.
87 Docs. T (scripter exterior), Tt.

TABLE 5

Doc	Personal name	Patronymic	Location	Master	Family name	Origin	Rank	
A	+	+			+			Father and two brothers
C	+	+	+					One person
F	+			+				One Person
I	+	+		+				A family
Ii	+	+	+	+				A family second version of I
J	+	+	+	+	+			A family may be brothers
L	+	+	+	+	+			A family father and son
N	+	+	+	+	+			Individual one person
Nn	+	+	+	+	+			Family brothers
O	+	+		+	+			One person at the behest of family
P	+	+	+					Two brothers
Q	+	+	+	+		+		Father and son
R	+	+	+					Family brothers
S[a]	+	+	+		+	+		Family brothers
Ss	+	+						Partners
T	+						+	Queen
Tt	+		+	+			+	Lord
U	+			+				Family
Uu	+	+	+		+	+		Family
Uv	+	+						Family
V	+	+		+	+			Family brothers
W	+	+		+	+		+	Family
X	+	+						Family
aa	+	+						
ab[b]								

a Issuers in this document are not native and live in the city Gaz and might serve masters, thus they named their master in the introduction: μισιδο πιδοοασαδο χογαμο χοσινδο μανο πωτανο οδο μανο μιιαρο φαρνοα- γαδο πορανο ασο βονοσογολιγο κιδο ωσο πιδο αγαδαγο ιανο αβο γαζο αρμαυαμο οδαβο σηρο τορκο γαζο ταδονο σπισαμο αχþαγγο μαρηγανο αβοφαγο βαζο οδαβοφαγο γογναγο οδαβοφαγο γωρδο λιζγιγανο χοδδηοο μαγατορο βοκολαυο μαρηγανο:

"Now: (this) declaration was freely (and) willingly made by me, Potan, and by me, 'Miyar, the sons of Farn-agad from Bonchuqligh, who now on account of a summons are present in Gaz and (who) serve Ser the Turk, the tudun of Gaz, the servants of Akhsh to you, Baz, and to you, Gugnag, and to you, Gord, khabitants of Lizg, the servants of Lord Magatur Buklah"

b The declaration section in this document is lost.

Parties are typically men; however, women may participate in a sale process with their husbands. As a result, their seals bear the name of the husband.[88] This action is common in Zoroastrian laws, where a woman can engage in conveyance with the permission and consent of her husband.[89] The rule is mentioned in the MHD.[90]

11 Historical Background

The basic factor for introducing a party in ancient Near Eastern legal practice is providing the personal name and patronymic in the form "A son of B," while other factors vary by region. There are two ways for introducing parties in Elephantine Aramaic papyri: the first is as simple as A son of B, and the second is to provide more information about the parties, e.g., their career, ethnic background, and origins.[91] For example:

> אמר דרגמן בר חרשין חרזמי זי אתרה ביב בירתא עביד לדגל ארתבנו למחסיה בר ידניה יהודי זי בבירת יב לדגל וריזת
>
> Said Dargamana son of Khvarshaina, a Khwarezmian whose place is made in Elephantine the fortress of the detachment of Artabanu to Mahseiah son of Jedaniah, a Jew who is in the fortress of Elephantine of the detachment of Varyazata.[92]

This rule applies to other Hellenistic documents in Aramaic and Greek corpora.[93] Thus, there is no significant difference when introducing parties in Bactrian and other ancient Near Eastern deeds, particularly Aramaic examples. It appears likely that the Bactrians continued to use the Aramaic pattern with limited change during the Hellenistic and Sasanian periods.

12 Volition Clause

The issuer declares in many documents that he does the acknowledgement freely and willingly. Moreover, the issuer completes the deed without pressure

88 Doc. Q.
89 Elman, 2014, 255ff.
90 MHD, 64, 2–9; Perikhanian, 1997. 161f.
91 Yaron, 1961, 9; Porten, 1996, 81.
92 TAD B.2.2.
93 For Aramaic deeds from the Judaean Desert, see Schiffman, 2005, 190.

from the addressee or another party. This clause is known as a volition clause in legal terminology. In Bactrian texts, the keywords for this clause are χογαμο (freely) and χοσινδο (willingly).[94] Nonetheless, the clause is not found in all Bactrian deeds, and it's not limited to a specific type of agreement, meaning the rule was optional (Table 6).

TABLE 6

Doc	Freely	Willingly	At our own wish
A	χοακαμο	χοασινδο	
C	χοακαμο	χοασινδο	
F	χοακαμο (οδο)	χοασινδο	
Ii			πιδο μο χọβο σιν[δο
J	χογαμο[a]	χοσινδο	
L	χογαμο	χοσινδο	
Nn	χογαμο	χοσινδο	
N			
P			
Q			
R			
S	χογαμο	χοσινδο	
T			
Tt			
U	χογαμο (οδο)	χοσινδο	
Uu			
Uv			
V	χογαμο (οδο)	Χοσινδο	
W	χογαμο	Χοσινδο	
aa	-	-	
ab	-	-	

a In documents from the later periods, the cluster χοα simply becomes χο (from doc. J onwards) as in the transmission of this cluster from Pahlavi to Persian. For more details, see Weber, 1997, 619f.

94 An exception was found in doc. Ii, instead of freely and willingly, the phrase πιδο μο χọβο σιν[δο] (at our own wish) is inserted (Table 6). The document is heavily damaged, making it difficult to comment on its provenance. If originating from another region, there was an alternative form(s) to the prevalent terms χογαμο (freely) and χοσινδο (willingly).

13 Historical Background

The volition clause has a very long history in ancient Near Eastern legal practice.[95] The earliest examples with expressions of joy indicating volition can be found in Akkadian deeds from Susa during the Old Babylonian period as ina ṭūbatišu ina nar'amātišu (in his joy, in his love).[96] For example:

> is-qa-tu-šu šà KI aḫ-ḫi-šu ina ṭù-ba-ti-šu ina na-ar-a-ma-ti-šu i-zu-zu
>
> He divided in his joy, in his love his portion, which shared with his brother.[97]

In the same era, the volition term also appears in documents from the city of Mari:

> x É.DÙ.A PN PN_2 inḫil ina ṭú-ub libbim x KÙ. BABBAR PN_2 PN inḫil
>
> PN handed over x house plot to PN_2, PN_2 handed over willingly x silver to PN[98]

This clause is expressed in some Akkadian documents from Ugarit. For example:

> Anāku ina DÙG. GA-ma (ṭâbima) E.ḪI (bīta) A.ŠÀ (eqla) attadnaššu
>
> I have willingly granted him the houses and fields[99]

This term appears in Emar slave sale deeds as ištu or ana SAG.Du-šu /-ši /-šunu (voluntarily or of his/her/their own free will).[100] After a long absence, the clause reappears in many Neo-Babylonian deeds of movable property and in the majority of so-called "dialogue documents" in Mesopotamia.[101] The

95 Muffs, 2003, 129ff; Muffs in his book explored the term extensively through history in the ancient Near East and later in an article (1992) discussed the term and its metaphoric rule and legal function.

96 Cuq, 1931, 61; Klima, 1960, 25; Salonen, 1967, 97; Jalilvand Sadafi, 2014, 84; CAD, N1, 345.

97 Jalilvand Sadafi, 2014, 182ff No. 33.

98 CAD, Ṭ, 117f; the volition terms appear in Old Babylonian letters, see CAD, Ṭ, 118.

99 Nougayrol, 1955, 83 doc. 16.143.

100 Demare-Lafont, 2010, 51; Tsukimoto, 1991, 277.

101 Muffs, 1992, 144.

volition clause in Neo-Babylonian texts differs from earlier versions because it's expressed in the form ina ḫud libbišu "of his own free will" (literally "with joy in his heart"),[102] and is only recorded in deeds of movable property, including sales of slaves and gift deeds.[103] For example:

> [^{md}Nergal-ina-eši-êṭir] apil-šú šá ^{md}Nabû-iddina^{na} [apil ^{m}Dannu]-^{d}Adad ina ḫud libbišu ^{md}Nabû-[rîm]-šu-kun ^{m}Man-nu-ki-i- ^{d}Bel u mâri-šu a-na 3 manû 10 šiqlu kaspi a-na šêmi gam-ru-ú a-na ^{m}Mu-še-zib-^{d}Markuk apil-šú šá ^{md}Marduk-ušallim apil ^{m}Ši-gu-ú-a id-din
>
> [Nergal-ina-eshi-etir], son of Nabu-iddina, [descendant of Dannu]-Adad, of his own free will, Nabu-[rimu]-Shukun, Mannu-ki-Bel, and his son for 3 minas 10 shekels of silver, for the full price to Mushezib-Marduk, son of Marduk-Ushallim, descendant of Shigua, has sold.[104]

The use of the volition clause was extended to all types of transactions during the Seleucid and Arsacid periods,[105] and thereby in all types of documents.[106]

The volition clause is stated with ברחמן (in affection) in Aramaic conveyances from Elephantine.[107] For example:

אנה ענניה יהבת לכי[תמת] ברחמן

> I, ʿAnaniah, gave it to you (Tamet) in affection[108]

or

אנה מפטחיה יהבת לכי[אסורי] ברחמן

> I, Miptahiah, gave it to you **(Isweri)** in Affection ...[109]

---

102 Muffs, 1992, 144f; CAD Ḫ, 25ff; regarding the verb ḫadû, it is necessary to say the term ina ḫud libbišu is recorded before the Neo-Babylonian period in an Akkadian letter from Ugarit, see Nougayrol, 1955, 8; Muffs, 2003, 202.

103 San Nicolo, 1928, 577; Joannes, 2010, 263f; Petschow, 1939, 45; Oelsner, 2009, 45.

104 Moore, 1975, 113 doc. 116.

105 Lewenton, 1970, 5; Muffs, 1992, 144.

106 Petschow, 1939, 69; Krückmann, 1931, 28.

107 See Muffs, 2003, 36ff.

108 TAD, B3.5.

109 TAD, B5.5; Porten, 1996, 168 no 52.

According to Szubin and Porten, "in the entire corpus of Aramaic legal texts, this term appears exclusively in documents drawn up within the family circle."[110] Additionally, Muffs indicated that the word רחם is found within three contexts of the Aramaic papyri from Elephantine, one is the volition clause.[111] The documents from Wadi al-Daliyah begin with the object of sale, and there is no mention of the volition clause.[112]

Notably, as Muffs discovered, law language in the Akkadian and Aramaic traditions is symbolic, figurative, and metaphorical,[113] whereas Bactrian is literal. Not only in this clause, but also in other clauses, Aramaic formulae are translated into a non-metaphoric style in Bactrian. We see this function again in the satisfaction term and warranty clause, which have been discussed in Chapter 3.

The term appears again in documents from the Judean Desert, but in different forms.[114] In Hebrew deeds, the term is expressed as מן רצונם (of their own free will). For example:

רצו וחלקו בינותים בינותום **מן ריצונם**

They have consensually divided between them, of their **own free will.**[115]

While in Aramaic deeds the volition clause is expressed as מן רעותי (of my own free will):[116]

יהב ומקים במלה קימה מתנת עלם די לא תעדיה **מן רעונתי**

I (hereby) bestow with validity, by a valid statement, a perpetual gift that shall not pass away, of my **own free will** ...[117]

110 Szubin and Porten, 1983, 35f; Yaron, 1961, 80f.
111 Muffs, 2003, 41f.
112 Gropp, 2001, 21.
113 Muffs, 1992, 121ff.
114 Koffmahn, 1968, 66f.
115 Yadin et al., 2002, 45ff; Yadin 44.
116 Sokoloff, 2003, 80; Sokoloff, 2002a, 1089f.
117 Yadin et al., 2002, 92; Yadin 7.

The term appears in rabbinical and Talmudic literature for other contexts,[118] although during the Middle Ages, the volition clause was still recorded in legal documents of Jewish communities.[119]

This clause was preserved in Islamic legal practice and was usually recorded in the following manner:

> بعد أن قرئ عليه وعرفه وأقرّ بفهمه في صحّة عقله وبدنه وجواز أمره طائع غير مكره ولا مجبر ولا مضطهد طالب راغب...
>
> After (it) had been read to him and he is cognizant of it and has acknowledged that he has understood, he being in the state of sound mind and body and capable of transacting his business, voluntarily, without compulsion and not against his will and not under constraint, (but) demanding (and) desiring (it) ...[120]

As part of the Islamic tradition, Persian documents from the 12th–13th-centuries CE record the volition clause either in Arabic:

> اقرار کرد خواجه هندو بن محمدبن احمد الريكان /(؟) عونى، فى حال [صحته و جواز]/ اقراره و نفاذ كل اموره، طائعاً راغباً غير مكره و لا مجبر عليه ...
>
> Khwājah Hindu bin Muhammad bin Ahmad Al-Rikān(?) ʔOwni, in his soundness and with regard his acknowledgement, and effectiveness of all his affairs, voluntarily and demanding, without compulsion and not against his will ...[121]

or in Persian, the translation:

> معترف شده بعد از ثبوت معرفت او بطريق مشروع بی هيچ اكراهی و اجباری بل بطوع و رغبت ...

118 TB Yoma, 86b–87a בצבו נפשיה in Hebrew: רבא כי הוה נפיק לדינא אמר הכי בצבו נפשה לקטלא נפיק
"When Rava went to judge (and) said as following: he, from his own free will, goes to die ..."
the same text in Aramaic in TB Sanhedrin 7b ברעות נפשיה ; see also TB Yevim 54a and TB Nedarim 91a; however, a Hebrew document from the 5th-century CE preserved this term as a volition clause in the phrase מן דעתי מן צביוני נפשי (of my own decision and free will), see Sirat & Cauderlier, 1985, 355f lines 6–7.

119 Friedman, 1980, 1.121f.

120 Grohmann, 1936, 157ff no. 119.

121 Sheikh-Ol-Hokamai, 1388/2009, 1388/2009, 25 doc. 2.

> He is recognizant after his reorganization has been proved by the legal way without compulsion and not against his will, but (he has done) of his own free will and desiring it …[122]

In Greek documents from Egypt, the volition clause is placed at the end of the document when submitting it to a third person for preservation.[123] The keyword in the Greek version of the volition clause is εκων (willing).[124] Nonetheless, the volition clause in the Greek documents from the Judean Desert is apparently translated from Aramaic and Hebrew into Greek by the two terms θελησιζ (to be willing)[125] and συνευδόκησις (to consent to).[126]

As Lewis has indicated, these words are probably translations of the Aramaic term מן רעות into the two Greek terms Επη τες θεληεως και συευδοκησεως (**of his own free will and consent**) because the word רעו means both "will" and "desire."[127] Oudshoorn thinks "perhaps the scribe sought to express these different meanings of the word by translating them into two separate Greek words."[128] This clause is absent from the Greek deeds of Avroman and Dura-Europos.

Regarding the presence of the volition clause in Mesopotamian and Jewish traditions, it seems more probable that it was first used in Bactrian Aramaic documents of the Achaemenid period, then migrated into Bactrian Greek documents during the Hellenistic period, and finally, entered the Bactrian language through Greek.

In summation, the declaration section in Bactrian documents is a hybrid of Aramaic and Greek traditions, which means that its style (subjective mode) and the volition term are based on the Aramaic tradition, whereas the homologia form is based on the Greek.

14 The Cause Clause

In all Bactrian conveyance deeds, the issuer gives a reason for committing to the agreement. Such action provides us with information about the agreement's background, which is useful not only for our understanding of legal

---

122 Gronke, 1982, 174f doc. VI (dated 602/1205). Urkunde VI (dated 602/1205).

123 Seidl, 1962, 163f.

124 Taubenschlag, 1955, 312f; Taubenschlag, 1934, 138; for further examples, see P. Elephantine 2 in Hengstl, 1978, 197f; Schulz, 1922, 213 note 2; and for the volition clause in the Byzantine Empire, see Keenan, 2014, 94.

125 Muraoka, 2009, 326.

126 Muraoka, 2009, 656.

127 Lewis, 1989, 74, 132.

128 Oudshoorn, 2007, 128f.

practice in Bactria but also for economic and socio-political conditions.[129] The reason varies from each document depending on the nature of the deed, with the majority of sale deeds stipulated because of a debt.[130] For example:

> μισιδαζο οαραζ̣οοιηþο οδαζο μοζδο παρο πορδδιγο α̣σταδαμο ταδομηνο αβο καδγο ανδαρο σ̇αγισο τα̣οι ν̣ιστο ασταδο ασιδομηνο αβο ι παρο α̣ματηιο
>
> Now: I, Waraz-wyesh, and I, Muzd, were owing a debt, and we had no other assets (left) in the house "which might have been disposed of by us towards (our) debt."[131]

In gift deeds, the donor expresses that he has received fulfilled service by his servant(s) or a god and that in exchange, he has rewarded him. For example:

> ασιδο τοο βαβαιο οδο τοο α̣β̣γ[α]σο οδο τοο ζολ[α]δο γωζογανο καναγο πορανο λιζγιγο χοβομο̣ μα̣ρ̣ηγανο αβομαγο ασπριγγο κανδορα̣ν̣ο ορβιι̣αν̣ο λιζγο χοηοο χοζο γαβδδιγο
>
> It so happens that you, Babay, and you, Abgas, and you, Zhulad Gozgan, the sons of Kanag, inhabitants of Lizg, my own servants, serve me, Aspring Kanduran Urbiyan lord of Lizg, exerting yourselves well and willingly.[132]

In contrast, agreements in peace contracts are the result of a lawsuit (λαδο) or a quarrel (αχασο). Example:

> μισιδο ασταδο αχασο μανο ιωβιγο αστωφσιγο ακιδομο καδαγο ιωβιγανο ραζινδο πιδοοδδιγο χαρο μαρηγο οδο μαναγγο βραδο πορο πιδο δαγογγο ιαοοαρο ακιδο μανο ιωβιγο αβαφαγο βραμαρζο δαγογγο αχασαδδηιο ακιδο βραδο πιδο χαγγαρο ζιδδιμο
>
> Now: I, Yobig, [an] inhabitant of Astof, whose house they call Yobigan, servant of the khar of Pidud, and my brothers (and) sons, had a quarrel, in the following circumstances, that I, Yobig, quarrelled with you, Bramarz, in such a way that I struck (your) brother with a sword.[133]

---

129 For an example, see Rezakhani, 2010.

130 Debt has been a major issue throughout the history of the ancient Near East and has been the subject of numerous legal documents. For an overview of debt history in the ancient Near East, see Van der Mieroop, 2002; Westbrook and Jasnow, 2001.

131 Docs. L, J, Nn, P, W, aa.

132 Doc. Tt.

133 Docs. O, R, S, Uu, X.

In Bactria, identifying the reason for an agreement was a rule, although the cause clause was less frequent in other documents.[134] For peace contracts, the final clauses follow the cause clause, whereas, in transaction conveyances, the description of property, payment, and investiture clauses are inserted between the cause clause and the final clauses. Therefore, transaction deeds have been discussed further below.

15 Description of the Property

In gift, lease, and sale contracts, the issuer describes the property, whether mobile or immobile, about to be transferred to the addressee after providing the reason. In the case of mobile property, the description of the object, slaves (male or female), is very brief and restricted to the slave's gender and name:

> ειο βαλακο ασιδο **χαλασο** ναμδο
>
> This boy who is called **Khalas**[135]

or in doc. T where a princess donates a slave girl to a temple:

> οδομο λαδδηιο μισο μασκονδο ιωγο ζινο κιδο **οαραγο** ναμο σιδομο ασο βρηδαγ̣ο οδασο οηβορογο ασο οονο πιδ̣ο στορογο γαοανο πιδο σανο σηρο βινζο.
>
> And also, there was given to you by me a certain person, a woman whose name (is) **Warag**, who was received by me from the bredag and from the prince…, as (a mark of) great obligation, (as) a slave girl for (your) pleasure (and) use[136]

In other slave sale deeds during late antiquity, identification of the slave is usually more detailed, including his/her name, age, place of residence, and a description of physical features. For example, in the Syriac sale deed of the slave girl, she is introduced in the following manner:

---

134 A cause clause is included in some Khonanese documents, although it's based on the reason for writing the contract rather than selling; the latter was more common in Bactrian documents.

135 Doc. P.

136 Doc. T.

> ܘܙܒܢܬ ܠܗ ܐܡܬܨܝܢ ܐܡܬܐ ܕܝܠܝ ܙܒܝܢܐ ܬܗܘܐ ܒܪܬ ܫܢܝܢ ܥܣܪܝܢ
> ܘܬܡܢܝܐ ܝܬܝܪ ܐܘ ܒܨܝܪ ܡܢ ܫܒܝܐ
>
> And I have sold to him Amatsin my female purchased—she is aged twenty-eight years, more or less—from captivity.[137]

Contrary to mobile contracts, the issuer provides more information about the property in the transaction of immovable property. He describes the property's boundaries, location, neighbors, and water rights. Most properties have names,[138] and the size of the estate is sometimes recorded as well. All of these factors work together, creating the most complete description of an estate.

Not all documents include these elements. The only common denominator among documents is the location name. Except for three documents, the others omitted one or more factors (Table 7).

TABLE 7

Doc	Location	Name	Boundaries	Neighbors	Water right	Size
C	+	+	+	+	+	–
J	+	+	+	+	+	+
L	+	+	+	+	+	+
Nn	+	–	+	+	–	–
T	+	+	–	–	+	–
Tt[a]	+		–	–	–	–
U	+	+	+	+	–	–
V	+	+	+	+	+	–
W	+	+	+	+	+	+
aa[b]	+	+	+	+	+	–

a Doc. Tt is damaged and the estate name is unknown.
b In doc. Aa, the boundary description is unclear because the text is fragmentary.

137 Drijvers & Healey, 1999, 232, 1; for other examples see Hunt and Edgar, 1932, 96ff, docs 31–32 (two slave sale contracts from Egypt).

138 Interestingly, in Bactrian land sales, the property has a name, which was a tradition recorded in Greek documents from Avroman. It's unclear if this was an Iranian tradition.

Regarding information from the documents, the most complete description of an estate contains the boundaries, location, name, neighbors, water rights, and size. For example, in doc. L:

> ασιδομηνο αστο μαληλο αβο οαρνο αγγαργο παροιαβιγο ειο αγγαργο ασιδο σαγαδαγο ριζδο αστο πιδο ιαοι παραγανο μιδο β′ αλο κασοκο φροιαχοδαρο οδαλο κασοκο καμβαταρο ασο κοαδα̣βο ι μασκο ναβιχτιγο αγγαργο εμο παδουαμονδδινδο ασο μιυροασανο οαχϸοιαμϸο αγγαργο παδουαμονδο οδασο νιμορωσο τωοιηλο βαζανοκο χοβο αγγαργο παδουαμονδο οδο πιδοβιλδο αβχαραγανο αγγαργο οδασο μιυροναφρανο βορζομιρανο αγγαργο πα̣δουαμονδο ο̣δασ̣ο αβαχρανο οαχϸοιαμϸο αγγαργο παδουαμονδο ταδομηνο ωσο παραλαδο α̇βο̇ ι μασκο ναβιχτιγο αγγαργο σαγονδο πιδο παδουαμονδδιγανο αβανδαρο ναβισιδο ιαββο οδο ι πα̣νδαγο ασιδο οαρο ναυαγγινδο φαροφαγο βαζανοκο οδο φαροφαγο ζονολαδο οδο φαροφαγο σαγο οδο φαροφαγο τοτο οδο φαρο τωμαχο βραδο οδο φαρο τωμαχο πορο φροζανδανο αβο ζαροζιδαγο δδιναρο κ′
>
> But we have a disposable property here in Warnu, this (same) property which is called Sagada. (This property) is (of a size requiring)— two measures–either a little more or a little less for-sowing with grain, in respect of which these are the boundaries of the property described herein: to the east the property of Wakhsh-yamsh (is) the boundary; and to the south the property belonging to you, Bazanuk, (is) the boundary, and beyond (it) the property of the Abkharagan (family); and to the west the property of the Burzmiran (family is) the boundary; and to the north the property of Wakhshyamsh (is) the boundary Thus the property described herein has now been sold by us, just as is stated within with reference to the boundaries, (and) the water and the path which are adjacent thereto, to you, Bazanuk, and to you, Zhun-lad, and to you, Sag, and to you, Tut, and to your brothers and to your sons (and) descendants, for twenty dinars of struck gold.[139]

Among these factors, I will focus on the property's boundaries and size in the following pages. A property in Bactrian documents is defined by its four boundaries. This rule is explicitly stated in two documents:

139 Docs. J, L, W.

ταδομο ωσο λαδδηιο σαγονδο πιδο δ' παδουαμονδο βανδαρο ναβισιδο

Thus (the property) has now been given to you by me, just as it is described with **reference to the four boundaries.**[140]

Only two documents, gift deeds, lack a description of boundaries.[141] The boundaries are ordered from east to west, but there is no set pattern. The issuers describe the boundaries in a clockwise direction in docs. C, L, as ESWN, whereas in three documents EWNS,[142] and in further documents EWSN[143] (Table 8).

Along with the description of borders, the text also includes the names of neighbors. Sometimes a neighbor is a buyer, or the neighbor's properties are owned by the buyer.[144]

TABLE 8

Doc	East	West	South	North	City
C	1	3	2	4	Rob
J	1	2	4	3	Malr
L	1	3	2	4	Warnu
Nn	1	2	4	3	Lizg
U	1	2	4	3	Madr
V	1	2	3	4	Rizm
w	1	2	3	4	Gandar
aa	1	3	2	4	–

140 Docs. V, W.
141 Docs. T, Tt.
142 Docs. J, Nn, U.
143 Docs. J, U; due to the long time elapsed between the composition of the two documents, the standard sequence in the city of Malr was most likely EWNS.
144 Docs. J, L, Nn; in the lease contract, doc. U, the leaser.

16 Historical Background

16.1 *Description of the Boundary and the Estate*

The four-part description of boundaries is a Mesopotamian element that developed through Aramaic and then Greek legal practices to Bactrian conveyances. The dimensions of the fields in ancient Mesopotamia, usually four sides conventionally oriented to cardinal points,[145] are based on the four quadrants of heaven in Mesopotamian cosmology.[146]

The delineation of the property according to its four boundaries is first attested in Mesopotamia and dates back to the pre-Sargonic period.[147] In the Neo-Sumerian period, the cardinal points mir (north), kur (east), u_5 (south), and MAR.TU (west) were used to indicate the four sides of a field,[148] though there is no fixed rule for the arrangement of the four sides.

The majority of documents from this period begin delineation with the north direction.[149] In subsequent land sale deeds during the Old Babylonian period, there were two methods for describing the dimensions of a field; the fields in the south were delimited by the four quadrants of heaven, upper and lower borders, and two sides, while the fields in the northern part of lower Mesopotamia were delimited by cardinal points.[150] Only a few cities in the Old-Babylonian period recorded transaction deeds with a description and definition of all four boundaries.[151] These cities are Dilbat,[152] Larsa,[153] Nuzi,[154] and Sippar.[155] Beyond Mesopotamia, contemporary to the period, the two cities Ekalte[156] and Terqa[157] follow the same rule. During the late Bronze Age,

145 Liverani, 1990, 148.
146 Kraus, 1955, 51f; Horowitz, 1998, 259f.
147 Deimel, 1924, 37f.
148 Kraus, 1955, 52; Liverani, 1990, 158.
149 Kraus, 1955, 52; Levine assumes that "derivative of the river orientation with its topographical implications is the convention of upper = north, lower = south in boundary descriptions of real estate, buildings, etc., going back to Sumerian, where cartographers indicated north as "above", and south as "below"," see Levine, 1975, 51.
150 Liverani, 1997, 219.
151 Podany, 1997, 430; Liverani, 1996, 20ff.
152 Gautier, 1908, 60f doc. XXV; Koshurnikov and Yoffee, 1986.
153 Harris, 1983. passim.
154 Zaccagnini 1979: 82ff.
155 Harris, 1978, 213f; docs. 220–2.
156 Mayer, 2001; Beckman, 1997, 116.
157 Rouault, 1984, TFR 1 1–3; Podany, 1997, 430.

in ancient Syria, descriptions of land borders are frequently attested from Emar[158] and Hana.[159]

The boundary stones, Kudurru or Naru,[160] are another source of evidence from the Middle and Neo-Babylonian periods, where a significant portion of the text is devoted to the description of boundaries. These boundary descriptions combine the northern and southern parts of lower Mesopotamian measurements, e.g., wind direction, and the four quadrants of heaven.[161] For example:

> eqla im-šú-ḫu-ma a-na ^{md}en-lil-ia mār ^{m}kar-zi-ia-ab-<ku> ú-kin-nu itû(ÚS-SA-DU) elû(AN-TA) ^{uru}ter-qa-an bīt-^{md}sin-ma-gir iltānu(IM-SI-SÁ) itû(ÚS-SA-DU) šaplû(KI-TA) ^{uru}ka-za-la bīt-^{md}sin-ma-gir šûtu(IM-U$_{18}$?-LU) pūtu(SAG) elû(AN-TA) šadû(IM-KURRA) kišād ^{íd}bi-na-ni-ti pūtu(SAG) šaplû(KI-TA) amurru(IM-MARDÚ) kišād ^{íd}ḫi-ba-ri-ti
>
> They measured the land and confirmed (it) for Enlilya, son of Karzi-yabku. Upper border: (city) Terqan, Bīt-Sîn-magir, north. Lower border: (city) Kazala, Bīt-Sîn-magir, south. Upper front: east, bank of the binanītu canal, Lower front: west, bank of the Ḫibarītu canal.[162]

The description of land dimensions in most ancient Mesopotamian and Syrian documents begins with the northern or upper border.[163] Documents delimited with quadrants of heaven have the directions arranged as a lower border, upper front, and lower front, while documents delimited with wind directions are arranged as south, east, and west.

In the Neo-Assyrian period, land transaction deeds from northern Mesopotamia do not follow the above-mentioned traditions. Instead, the description of borders is not arranged according to wind directions or quadrants of

---

158 Beckman, 1997, 116; for more documents from Emar, see Beckman, 1996; Tsukimoto, 1990.

159 Podany, 2002, for sides in Hana: see Podany 2002, 224f: the sides are mentioned as follows: Side 1: US$_2$.SA.DU AN.TA (upper border) Side 2: US$_2$.SA.DU KI.TA (lower border) Side 3: SAG.KI 1 KAM or SAG.KI AN.TA (upper side) Side 4: SAG.KI 2 KAM or SAG.KI AN.TA (lower side) Podany, 1997, 424; Podany, 2016, 83ff; even after Assyrians seized Hana, the definition of four borders is still mentioned in contracts. For an example, see Kümmel, 1989, and Tsukimoto, 2011.

160 For an overview of Kudurrus, see Brinkman, 1980–3, 267–74; for studies in detail, see Slanski, 2003; Paulus, 2014.

161 Paulus, 2014, 84.

162 Lambert, 2011, 19.

163 Levine, 1975, 51.

heaven, but neighboring properties, roads, and waterways, are used.[164] Nonetheless, throughout the Neo-Babylonian period, land sale deeds from southern Mesopotamia, namely Kudurrus, mark the borders by two measurements simultaneously, namely wind direction and the four quadrants of heaven.[165]

In the Aramaic papyri from Elephantine, two ways of delineating an estate are recorded: the first begins with the upper side, which is common in Egypt and adopts Egyptian terminology for the description of borders—upper side (עלי), lower side (תחת), west (מערבא) and east (מועא).[166]

> והא תחומי ביתא זי אנה ענני יהבת ליהוישמע ברתי **מועה שמש** לה אגרא זי הנפנא זי בנהו מצריא הו תמואנתי **עליא** לה בית קנחנתי דבק לה אגר באגר **תחתיא** מנה אגר דרגא ובית חור בר פטאסי גנן זי חנום אלהא דבק לדרגא דך **מערב שמש** לה אגר תרי רבתא
>
> And now these are the boundaries of the house which I, Anani, gave Jehoishma my daughter: **east** of it is the protecting wall which the Egyptians built, that is the way of the god **above** it the house of the shrine of the god adjoins it wall to wall **below** it is the wall of the stairway and the house of Hor son of Peteese, a gardener of Khnum the god, adjoins that stairway; **west** of it is the wall of the large room.[167]

However, there is no regular sequence for the description of borders[168] and setting the order for describing borders:

The second is most likely of northwest Semitic origin. Evidence from the Judean Desert supports this theory.[169] In Aramaic deeds recorded during the Hellenistic period, the measure is completely changed to compass points, and the description of the borders begins with the eastern side:

> ת]חומי אתרה דך מד[נח]ה ארחה וח[רנין מערבה יהוד]ה זבנה ו[ח]רנין[דרומה]
> ארחֹ י[ר]תי צפן וחרנין צפונה ירת[י]צפן וח[רנין]

164 Fales, 1990, 84; for land sale contracts in Neo-Assyrian see Kwasman and Parpola, 1991 and Matila, 2002.

165 Liverani, 1996, 33ff; Sonnenschein, 1925 (1927): 186ff; Joannes, 2010, 271; San Nicolo and Ungnad, 1929–1937, 51f; for texts on land sale see Brinkman, 1989; Weisberg, 2003, 16f doc. 3; Baker 2004, doc. 80, 92; Wallenfels, 1998, 15ff doc. 3.

166 Porten, 2000, 854ff; Porten 1996, 160, n. 28; Levine, 1975, 48ff; interestingly, the terms for east and west in Aramaic are מועה שמש (rising of the sun) and מערב שמש (sunset), and in Bactrian, the word for east is μιυροασανο, which also means rising of the sun, and the word μιυροναφρανο means sunset.

167 TAD B 3.10; B. 2.1 B. 3. 11–12.

168 Porten, 2000, 855f.

169 Yadin et al., 2002, 8.

> [The boundaries of that place: Ea[s]t—the road and o[thers; west—Yehuda]h the buyer and [o]thers; [south the road(s) of the h[ei]rs of Ṣpn and others; north—the hei[rs] of Spn and o[thers].[170]

The same rule applies to Greek deeds in the Judean Desert, more specifically, Greek deeds, much like Aramaic deeds, begin the description of boundaries with the east.[171] In Mesopotamia and western Iran, the situation is different; a Greek deed from Dura uses compass points to describe the four dimensions of the estate,[172] whereas Greek deeds from Avroman lack the boundary description. Documents in other Middle Iranian languages, including Khotanese, contain descriptions of neighbors, but not in four quarters, in fact, some do not contain descriptions of boundaries at all.[173]

Early Arabic and Persian documents from Central Asia provided the four boundaries according to the older tradition, but without defining the directions according to compass points or quarters of heaven. The neighborhood estates were mentioned in these documents with the word حد (border), e.g., first border, second border, etc.

17 Size of the Property

There are two units for measuring surfaces, one similar to the metric system, for example, λοχσο ζ'[174] (seven Lukhs), and another using grain, ιαοο δ' γωρο[175] (four bushels of grain). These two measurement systems are well known in the ancient Mesopotamian[176] and Aramaic corpora.[177]

18 *Clausula Salvatoria*

In four Bactrian land transactions,[178] the issuer does not provide an exact statement of the field size. Instead, the agreement contains a clause waiving future

170 Yardeni, 1997, 38ff XḤev 9.
171 Lewis, 1989, 45.
172 Welles, 1959, 134ff. doc. 26; the dimensions in P. Dura 26 are provided in the order east-west-south-north.
173 For an example of description of boundaries in Khotanese documents, see Duan, 2014, 350f.
174 Doc. J.
175 Docs. V, W.
176 Powell, 1984; 1987–1990.
177 Powell, 1992, 901f.
178 Docs. Ii, J, L, V, W.

claims on the size by both the issuer and the addressee. It is called *Clausula Salvatoria*.[179] For Bactrian deeds, this disclaimer is expressed as κασοκο φριαχοδαρο οδαλο κασοκο καμβοδαρο (little more or little less). For example:

> μασκο ναβιχτιγο αγγαργο πιδο ιαοι παραγανο λοχσο ζ′ αλο **κασοκο φριαχοδαρο οδαλο κασοκο καμβοδαρο**
>
> (This) is the property described herein, (of a size requiring) seven lukhs-either **a little more or a little less**-for sowing with grain.[180]

18.1 *Historical background*

Clausula Salvatoria appears in various forms in the Old Babylonian land sale documents for the first time.[181] The function of this phrase is explicitly described in a land sale deed from Nuzi:

> šum-ma eqlu ma'adu la i-na-ak-ki-is ù šum-ma mi-iṣ la u-ra-at-ta.
>
> If the land is great(er) he will not shorten it and if small(er) he will not add (to it).[182]

One of the most common variations of this phrase is līṭir limṭi (more or less).[183] The other form is found in house or land sale deeds from Elam[184] and Nuzi[185] as iṣi[186] u mādu:[187]

> É.DÙ.A i-ṣú ù ma-du ù ^{ĝeš}KIRI$_6$ i-ṣú ù ma-du
>
> A roofed space, (its size) greater or smaller, a Garden, (its size) greater or smaller.[188]

---

179 Lewenton, 1970, 101f; Yaron, 1960c, 167f; Petschow, 1939, 37f.

180 Docs. Ii, J, L, V, W.

181 Mauer, 1979, 23; San Nicolo named it "salvatorische Klausel," see San Nicolo, 1974, 208f; Matuš, 1950, 30.

182 Gadd, 1926, 86 doc. 2.

183 CAD, 10, M part I, 431–32 maṭû.

184 Jalilvand Sadafi, 2014, 47; she translated the term "so wie er ist"; Mauer, 1979, 21.

185 Gadd, 1926, for example docs. 3, 15; Pfeiffer and Speiser, 1936, docs. 58, 65.

186 CAD, 7, 219ff iṣu specifically 222 eqlum i-ṣú-um u mādum.

187 CAD, 10, M part I, 24f; mādu to be or become much.

188 Jalilvand Sadafi, 2014, 143 Doc. 13.

In subsequent periods, the term iṣi u mādu appears more frequently than other variants in Akkadian conveyances,[189] particularly in Neo-Babylonian field sale contracts from the Achaemenid[190] and Seleucid periods.[191]

There is no mention of this clause in Aramaic sale and gift deeds from Elephantine, but it appears later in some immobile deeds from the Judean Desert in Aramaic and Hebrew[192] with the form חסר הו יתיר (less or more):

> אנה מרעותי יומה דנה זבנ[ת] לך לאתרא דלי די מתקרה ח[ק]ל פרדסה[בית זרע חנטי]ן סאין תלת הן חסיר או יתר לזבנה
>
> I, of my own free will, this day, have sol[d] to you the place of mine, which is called the F[iel]d of the Orchard/Garden, [the area of sowing of three se'ahs of [wheat. If it is less or more—(it belongs) to the buyer.[193]

This term, in the same form, was preserved in the rabbinical tradition during late antiquity and the Middle Ages:[194]

> בית כור עפר אני מוכר לך הן חסר הן יתיר
>
> I am selling you a bet kor of dust, whether less or more.[195]

The same clause appears in Islamic deeds as کثیر و قلیل (more or less), for example, in a Persian land sale:

> [و آنچه بدو مضاف] و منسوب است از قلیل و کثیر و مراعی و مرافق و مزارع، جملگی حق این مشتری گشت.
>
> [And everything is added] and related to (it), less or more and pastures, appurtenances, and sown fields, all have become the buyer's property.[196]

---

189 Jalilvand Sadafi, 2014, 66f.
190 Oelsner, 2009, 34f; Jursa, 2005, 26f; Doty, 1978, 72f.
191 Wallenfels, 1998, 9ff doc. 2.
192 Yardeni, 2000, Mur 22, 30 (Hebrew). XḤev/Ṣe 50 + Mur. 26 (Aramaic).
193 Yardeni, 1997, 38ff XḤev 9.
194 Rabinowitz, 1958, 486.
195 Tosefta, Baba Barṯa, 6.25; Mishnah Baba Barṯa, 7.1–4 and TY, Baba Barṯa, 15c.
196 Sheikh Ol-Hokamai, 1388/2009, 24 doc. 1; Gronke, 1986, docs. III, IV; Huart, 1914, all three documents.

In fact, the Islamic formula (از کثیر و قلیل) and the Bactrian κασοκο φριιαχοδαρο οδαλο κασοκο καμβοδαρο share a common ancestor.

19 Payment Clause

For land transaction deeds, after describing the estate, the issuer states that the price was received and acknowledges the agreement. The Bactrian receipt declaration is divided into two parts. The issuer declares in the first part that the full price of the good was received, and in the second part, he expresses satisfaction with the payment. This declaration is manifested approximately as follows:

> μασκο ναβιχτιγο αγγαργο σαγονδο πιδο παδουαμονδδιγανο αβανδαρο ναβισιδο ιαββο οδο ι πανδαγο ασιδο οαρο ναυαγγινδο φαροφαγο βαζανοκο οδο φαροφαγο ζονολαδο οδο φαροφαγο σαγο οδο φαροφαγο τοτο οδο φαρο τωμαχο βραδο οδο φαρο τωμαχο πορο φροζανδανο αβο ζαροζιδαγο δδιναρο κ′ οτομηνο αγγιτινδο ι οαυαγο οισπο ασπο\ριγο οτο κιρδδαμο þαδο οδο υονοσινδο
>
> Thus, the property described herein has now been sold by us, (just as is stated within with reference to the boundaries, (and) the water and the path which are adjacent thereto,) to you, Bazanuk, and to you, Zhun-lad, and to you, Sag, and to you, Tut, and to your brothers and to your sons (and) descendants, for twenty dinars of struck gold; and the price has been received by us all complete, and we have become satisfied and content.[197]

Before discussing the full price element, it's important to review currency units in Bactrian deeds. Bactrian currency units are dinar[198] and drachma,[199] and their amounts are written in letters.[200] The price is paid with dinars in the first four documents and drachmas for the rest (Table 9).

Aside from the payment, fines must also be paid in coins, and the currency units for penalty and payment clauses are remarkably similar. Moreover, if the payment was made in dinars, the fine would be paid in dinars as well.[201]

---

197 Doc. L.
198 Docs. J, L, m, Nn.
199 Docs. P, Q, Ss, V, W.
200 Except doc. V which has at once letter and digits as the amount of price.
201 See chapter three for penal provision.

TABLE 9

Doc	Type	Quantity	Metal	Minted	Quality	Condition
J	δδιναρο	Η (8)	ζαροζιδαγο			
L	Δδιναρο	Κ (20)	ζαροζιδαγο			
Mm	Δδιναρο	Ιζ 17	Ζαρο			
Nn	Δδιναρο	Κ οδο ε (25)	Ζαρο	þαυοζιδαγο		
P	δδραχμο	Γ (3)		παρσαγγο		
Q loan	Δδραχμο	Μ (40)	σιμινο	καοοαδο παρσαγ[γο	þιζγο	οιζινδδιγο ωδαγο
Ss loan	Δδρ̣αχμο	Σ (100)	–	–	–	–
V	Δδραχμο	σαδο ρ′ οδο πανζασο ν′ (150)	σιμιγγο	ταζαυο	þιζγο	ωδαγο οιζινδδιγο
W	Δδραχμο	χοατο ξ′ (60)	σιμιγγο	ταζαγο	þιζγο	ωδαγο οιζινδδιγο

Normally, not only is the quantity of coins mentioned, but also the metal type. Additionally, one may find more information about the type of coinage in some documents, including the location of minting, quality, and condition. The most complete description of a coin is its denomination, metal type, quality, quantity, and condition.[202] The next sections examine two key terms in Bactrian sale deeds: full price and satisfaction.

20 Full Price

According to Bactrian documents, the price was paid in cash and in full. For Bactrian conveyance deeds, this phrase is expressed in various forms (Table 10).

All these forms have been organized into three types:

1. The noun οαυαγο (price) with the preposition πιδο (for) and the adjective σποριγο (complete);
2. The noun οαυαγο with two adjectives σποριγο (complete) and οισπο (full).
3. The third type deviated from the preceding two, with only a couple documents containing the full price element. In documents **aa** and **ab**, the issuer declares that he has received the full value (αργο σπορ̣ο̣).

202 Docs. Q, V, W.

TABLE 10

Doc	Full price in Bactrian	Translation
F	Πιδο σποριγο οαυαγο	For the full price
J	Οαυαγο σποριγο οισπο	The price, full and complete
L	Οαυαγο σποριγο οισπο	The price, full and complete
U	πιδο σποριγο οαυαγο	For the full price
V	σποριγο οισπο οαυαγο	The full and complete price
W	πιδο σποριγο οαυαγο	For the full price
aa	αργο σπορο	The full value
ab	ιαγρο σπορο	The full value

All three variants address the full price element in Bactrian legal documents, and the variation does not affect the term's function. The documents with the full price element are transaction deeds, whether direct or indirect. For example, doc. F. iterates an "indirect" transaction because the issuer explains that he bought a slave and paid full price. After the slave repaid the cost, he was freed:

> κοοαδομο αβο ζηρο βαγοβανδαγο πορο ασο ιαμβολαδο οδασο σαδαιωλο οδασο ταιαγο πιδοοδιγο ζαδγο χιρδο πιδο σποριγο οαυαγο ταδομο ωσο ασαφαγο ζηρο πιδο χοβο σαρο οαυαγο σποριγο αγγιτο
>
> That I had (formerly) bought (you), Zer son of Bag-bandag, from Yamsh-lad and from Sadayol and from Tayag, natives of Pidud, (in return) for full payment (or price), and (that) now the full price has been received by me from you, Zer.[203]

21 Historical Background

There are extensive research works on the history of the full price element in ancient Near Eastern legal practice.[204] The full price element is a fairly pervasive feature of cuneiform sale formularies. Going back to deeds of sale from the Ur III period (*c.*2112–2002 BC.), this element is attested in sale documents

203 Doc. F.

204 Two pioneers are Muffs, 2003, and Skaist, 1995. Our analysis here is based on their observations, with some modifications.

throughout the ancient Near East.[205] In the Old Babylonian period, this phrase is recorded as sumerograme ŠÁM.TIL.LA.BI/NI.ŠÈ (its full price)[206] in many of sale deeds from lower Mesopotamia:[207]

> KI DUMU-ša-ba-ia ^{Id}IŠKUR-MA.AN.SUM DUMU ^{d}IŠKUR.i-din.nam IN.ŠI. IN.ŠÁM ŠÁM.TIL.LA.BI.ŠÈ 6 GÍN KÙ.BABBAR IN.NA.AL.LÁ (išqul)
>
> Adad-iddinam, son of Adad-iddinam has bought from Mār-ša-Baja. He paid its full price, 6 shekels of silver[208]

In addition to Lower Mesopotamia, in other neighboring lands like Susa and Syria the full price element was inserted in legal transactions. In Susa many sale documents contain the phrase as ana šīmī(šu) (NÍĞŠÁM) gamrūti (for its full price):[209]

> ^{ǧeš}KIRI$_{6}$ ... KI ip-qù-ša ku-bu-ra-bu a-na da-ra-tim i-ša-am a-na ší-mi-šu ga-am-ru-ti 1/3 MA.NA KÙ.BABBAR iš-qú-ul
>
> A garden ... from Ipqūša, Kūbu-rabû has bought forever. He paid 1/3 Mina silver as its full price[210]

The phrase is also employed in documents from Ekalte,[211] and Tell Hadidi[212] in Northern Syria:

> KI ^{d}Ba-a̯ha-la-ka ù LÚ.MEŠ.ši.bu-ut URU.KI Be-lu-ú A.ŠA m.Ḫu-ra-ru DUMU ^{d}IŠKUR.EN ana ½ GI.[N]A KÙ.BABBAR ṣur-pu a-na ŠÁM.TIL.LA A.ŠA i-ša-am
>
> From Baˁalka and the elders of the city Belu, the owner of the land, Ḫuraru son of Addu-Baˁla, has bought the land for ½ refined silver as its full price[213]

---

205 Steinkeller, 1989, 13–14 also Doc. 65, 82 and 84.
206 Landsberger, 1937, 27, No. 40–45.
207 Skaist, 1990, 260f.
208 Dekiere, 1995, 96 Doc. 424.
209 Jalilvand Sadafi, 2014, 78ff.
210 Jalilvand Sadafi, 2014, 135f Doc. 9.
211 Mayer, 2001.
212 Whitting, online http://www.helsinki.fi/~whiting/hadidcat.html.
213 Mayer, 2001, 80 Doc.7.

Even though these documents were written in different locations, the function of the phrase is the same in all of them. The purpose is to protect the buyer from accusations of shortchanging the seller.[214]

In Old Assyrian sale deeds from Anatolia, instead of ŠÁM.TIL.LA.BI/NI.ŠÈ, the verb šabā'um/šabbu'um (to be full) was used to express that the price has been fully paid:

> Na-ab-Sú-en$_6$ aṣ-ba-at-ma um-ma a-na-ku-ma URUDU SIG$_5$ ša a-hi-ib-lá-ku-ni ša-bu-a-tí ṭup-pí dí-nam
>
> I seized Nabi-Suen, and I said, "You are fully paid for the copper of good quality that I owe you. Give me my tablet."[215]

During the Late Bronze Age, (1595–1155 BCE), the full price element, šīm gamer, as in the Old Babylonian period, was inserted into many sale deeds from cities, including Alalaḫ,[216] Emar,[217] Ugarit,[218] and Ur[219] in Syria and lower Mesopotamia. In tandem, throughout upper Mesopotamia, the Old Assyrian term for the full price was omitted in documents from the Middle Assyrian period and instead the term ana šīmī gamrūti (for its full price) was inserted, documents from the Middle Babylonian period are an example.[220] This action means the Old Babylonian formulation for full price replaced the Old Assyrian payment clause in upper Mesopotamia, ensuring people used šīm gamer in their legal tablets instead of šabā'um/šabbu'um.[221] Eventually, this term was replaced by kaspu gammur tadin (the money is paid completely) in Neo-Assyrian sale deeds,[222] while in lower Mesopotamia, the full price element is recorded using two terms, ana šīmī gamrūti or ana šīmi ḫariṣ (for its stipulated price) in contracts:[223]

> (S) ina ḫūd libbišu (O) ana x kaspi ana šīmī gamrūti/ana šīmi ḫariṣ ana (B) iddin

214 Skaist, 1995, 619.

215 Hertel, 2013, 155f; the verb šabā'um/šabbu'um was used in quittance/settlement records Hertel, 2013, 137.

216 Niedorf, 2008, 187.

217 Démare-Lafont, 2010, 46f; Fijalkowska, 2014, 116.

218 Van Soldt, 2010, 94 note 52.

219 Gurney, 1983, 5.

220 Krecher et al, 1980, 516.

221 The verb šabā'um/šabbu'um was used in quittance-settlement records; Hertel, 2013, 137.

222 Postgate, 1997, 162; for details about kaspu gammur tadin, see Radner, 1997, 349f.

223 Petschow, 1939, 45ff; Oelsner, 2002, 309; Oelsner, 2009, 34.

> Seller has sold (given) Buyer, from his own free will, the object of sale for its full price/its stipulated price.[224]

It is obvious that the full price element was widely used in the ancient Near East, and that Aramaeans were aware of this term as a Near Eastern people. One reason is use of the term כסף השלם יהב (the money has been paid in full) in Old Aramaic in lieu of the Neo-Assyrian term **kaspu gammur tadin** (the money has been paid in its entirety).[225] Although the phrase כסף השלם יהב is an Aramaic version of the Akkadian PN X MA.NA KUBABBAR ušallam (PN has paid x mina silver in full), borrowed from the Neo-Assyrian judicial procedures formula for the fine clause.[226] Nevertheless, the Aramaic papyri from Egypt do not contain the full price element, instead, the issuer states he received the price of the good:

> ויהבת לן דמי ביתן כסף כרש חד הו 1 שקלן תלתה הו 3 כסף יון סתתרי 3־3 שקל חד
> וטיב לבבן בגו זי לא אשתאר לן עליך מן דמיא

> And you gave us the price of our house (in) silver, one, that is 1 karsh three, that is 3 shekels, (in) Ionion silver 6 staters, one shekel and our heart was satisfied herein that there did not remain to us (incumbent) upon you (any) of the price.[227]

Its absence does not imply that people in Elephantine, particularly the Jewish community, were unfamiliar with the term because it's reported in some Old Testament passages on land sales when the buyer paid the price completely (בכסף מלא).[228] Furthermore, Egyptians were aware of the term and used it in some of their legal documents.[229] The term was used in Palestine during the 4th-century BCE when the full price element occurred several times in slave sale deeds from Wadi al-Daliyah as שחרין דמין גמירן (the stipulated price, the full price):[230]

---

224 Oelsner, 2002, 309.

225 Fales 2010, 192 and note 12.

226 For an example of a full-price term from Neo-Assyrian judicial procedures, see Jas, 1996, 60 doc. 38.

227 TAD 3.12; Schwiderski, 2009, 212f.

228 Genesis 23:9; Skaist, 2015, 173f.

229 Ritner, 2002, 353; Porten's comment on the verb מלי in TAD 3.1 is not correct. Lipinski has indicated it's not the full-price element, see Lipinski, 2000, 592 n. 226.

230 Dušek, 2007, 107.

ליהוחנן שמה בר שאלה דנה עבד זילה תמים [חנניה בר בידאל זבן ליהונור בר לנרי בכסף ש 2-3-10-20] שחרץ דמין גמירן כספא [זנ]ה ש 2-3-10-20 חנניה [מקבל מן יהונור]

[Hananiah son of Beyadʾel sold] a certain Yehohanan son of Seʾilah, this slave of his, without defect [to Yehonur son of Laneri for 35 silver sheliels,] the stipulated price, the full price. [Th]is sum of 35 shekels Nananiah [has received from Yehonur].[231]

Gropp has suggested that the term used in these documents was borrowed from the Babylonian legal formulary and is a combination of two Neo-Babylonian legal terms, šīm ḫariṣ and šīmī gamrūti, created by Aramaic scribes.[232] Later, in Nabataean sale deeds from the Judean Desert, a similar combination (שי חרץ דמין גמרין) is preserved.[233] In fact, the second part of the term דמין גמירין (full price) was produced as a full price element in Aramaic deeds from the Judean Desert:

וכס[פ]ה אנה מקבל דמין גמרין

And the money I have received, (the) full price.[234]

In the Syriac slave sale deed, the issuer mentioned only the price of the purchased item (a female slave) twice in the text, the first in the declaration section:

ܩܒܠܬ ܡܢܗ ܕܝܢܪܐ ܫܒܥܡܐܐ ܘܙܒܢܬ ܠܗ ܐܡܬܨܝܢ ܐܡܬܐ ܕܝܠܝ

I have received from him seven hundred denarii and I have sold to him Amatsin my female slave

And the second is at the end of the document without the full price element:

ܕܙܒܢܬ ܐܡܬܐ ܗܕܐ ܕܝܠܗ ܘܩܒܠܬ ܕܡܝܗ ܐܝܟ ܕܟܬܝܒ ܡܢ ܠܥܠ

231 Gropp, 2001, 34ff P 1.

232 Gropp, 2001, 37f; Gropp, 2003, 31.

233 Yadin et al, 2002, P Yadin 2 and 3; for more about the payment clause in Aramaic documents from the Judaean Desert, see Gross, 2008, 46ff.

234 Yardeni, 2000, XḤev/Ṣe 9.

She has sold this female slave of hers and received her price as written above[235]

Further evidence for the payment clause, in the same way, can be found in an inscription for the transfer of property from Palmyra, where the issuer declares:

מקבלא מנה כסף דנרין מאה ועשרין

He has received from him money (price), 120 denarii.[236]

Unlike the Syriac and Palmyrene texts, a Nabataean inscription from Mada'in Salih uses the full price element in the fine clause as לדמי מגמר (for its full price):

ומן יעבד כעיר מה די עלא כתיב פאיתי עמה לדושרא אלהא בחרמא די עלא **לדמי מגמר** סלעין אלף חרתי ולמראנא חרתת מלכא כות

And whoever does other than what is written above shall be liable to the god Dushara regarding the inviolability referred to above, **for the full price** of a thousand Haretite sela's, and to our lord King Haretat for the same amount.[237]

Certain Greek deeds in Egypt, influenced by the Egyptian formulary tradition, bear the full price element,[238] although Greek sale deeds from Avroman, Mesopotamia, and Palestine do not.

This element was recorded in conveyances for Khotanese texts as well, with the payment clause usually written after the description of the property. It can be recorded in two ways:

235 Drijver and Healey, 1999, P. 1.

236 Cussini, 1995, 239 PAT 1791.

237 Healey, 1993, 68 n.1; however, the full price element was dropped in other inscriptions. Based on available evidence and whether it contains the full price element or not, Aramaic deeds can be divided into two groups: those with it and without. The first group includes deeds from Wadi al-Daliyah, Aramaic and Nabataean papyri from the Judean Desert and a Nabataean inscription from Mada'in Salih. The second group consists of the Aramaic papyri from Elephantine, a Syriac sale deed, and Palmyrene and Nabataean tomb inscriptions. The Aramaic conveyances from Bactria would almost certainly be classified in the first group.

238 Blau, 1912, 210.

1. The new owner declares he has paid the full price:

   uspurrä prahänaji hoḍi u-ṃ dī mārāpyara pajistāṃdä mūri 500 u drai chā śaṃcī 200 mūri

   He paid the prahänaja in full, exactly as much as the parents requested: 500 mūrās and 3 chās of white silk (worth) 200 mūrās.[239]

2. It's declared that the new owner has paid the price and the former owner has received the full price:

   hauḍämī ṣi' yagurä tti mūri 2000 500 nāṃdūṃmūṃ mihi braṃgalä u saṃgaśūrai u puñadarmä tti mūri uspurri 2000 500

   So, Yagura paid those 2,500 mūrās. We Braṃgala and Saṃgaśūrai and Puñadarma received those 2,500 mūrās in full.[240]

Regarding Sogdian transactions, the payment clause is simple, meaning it's declared in the contract that the buyer pays the price of the good, but there is no indication of the full price element. The payment clause in a contract for the sale of a slave girl from Turkestan reads:

> xr'yn šmny y'nsy'(n) 'xw 'wt' BRY c'n-kwtr MN … δ'yh … pr 120 δrxm šyrw kr'nw p'rsxwstw
>
> A monk [by the name of] Yansyan, the son of Uta, who is from the family of Chan, bought a female slave … for 120 Drachms very pure and minted in Persia.[241]

However, in one of the transactions, namely a lease contract from Mount Mugh, there is evidence indicating that Sogdians were very familiar with the full price element. The lessor declares that the lessee must pay the full price each year in flour:

239 Skjaervo, 2002, 67f Or. 9268.2.

240 Skjaervo, 2002, 66f Or. 9268.1; for more examples of the full price element in Khotanese documents, see Duan, 2015; Duan et al., 2016.

241 Yoshida, 2003. 159f.

> ZY ms cw ZK MLK' δyw'št(y)-c ZKn xwβ 'wrnyk'm δ'ty δstβ'r kwn't 'PZY šn 'm'y-δ 'rtkw 'spwrnw prwyδ't
>
> And also, if King Dhēwāshtīch, by the law, instructs an official to recover this flour in full for the king, then Mākhyān, his sons and kin shall be answerable and pay for all of it.[242]

Concerning the declaration of receiving the price, all three languages use the same word for the adjective "full"—in other words, the Bactrian word ασποpo[243] is cognate with the word *uspurra-*[244] in Khotanese, and the word *'spwrn*[245] in Sogdian. These three words share the same etymology, meaning, and function.[246] The question to be asked now is whether one of these languages used this word before the others and then it was borrowed or all three borrowed it from an older Iranian language (maybe Old Persian). Unfortunately, due to the fragmentary nature of the evidence, it's not easy to discern the origin.

In Islamic deeds, after stating the price of the property, it is mentioned immediately its half to prevent falsification of the amount in the future.[247] However, in some Persian deeds from Central Asia the seller declares that he has received the price in full:

> [زمین] یحیی بن ایوب را فروختم بهای تمام یافتم.
>
> I have sold Yahyā ibn Ayyūb (the land) and received the price completely.[248]

Furthermore, a combination of these two formulae appears in Persian documents from Ghur:

> مر حاجب حسن مودود را فروختن به دو دینار ملکی فیروزکوهی که نیمه بود یک دینار ... فروشندگان بها تمام و کمال قبض کردند

242 Livshits, 2008, doc. B-4.

243 Sims-Williams, 2007, 197.

244 Bailey, 1979, 43.

245 Gharib, 1995, 65; Durkin-Meisterernst and Sims-Williams, 2012, 46; ᶜspwrn-. the same word appears both in Parthian ᶜspwryft (Durkin-Meisterernst, 2004, 87) as well as Pahlavi uspurrīg or spurrīg (MacKenzie, 1971, 76), but not in the legal context.

246 For the etymology of this word, see Bailey, 1979, 43.

247 Gronke, 1986, 467f; Gronke, 1984, 167.

248 Minovi, 1345/1966, 288.

> [they] sold [it] to Hājib Hasan Mawdūd for 2 dinars of gold struck by the king in the city Firūzkūh that its half is 1 dinar … the sellers received the price completely and entirely.[249]

The full price element in these documents demonstrates the continued use of pre-Islamic payment clauses in legal documents, as well as their coexistence with the Islamic form. The same practice was exercised among the Turks who knew this term well and inserted it into sale contracts written during the 10th–14th-centuries CE: for most, the full price element used the word tükäl:

> bu X qanpuγ bitig qilmiš kuntä **tükäl** birdim
>
> This X qanpu (the price) I have received **completely** on the day the contract [has] been elaborated.[250]

Interestingly, the term for the full price element is mentioned in two sale contracts (one in Uyghur script and the other in Arabic) in a Turco-Persian term, bähasi tükäl or بهاسی تگال:

> Bahanı tükäl buldum
>
> I have received the price completely.[251]

and

> بو تورت حد ایچنداکی یيرنی ساتتم بهاسی تگال بولدوم
>
> I have sold the land within these four boundaries. I have received its price completely.[252]

The term is most likely borrowed from Persian, but could also be derived from legal terminology in one of the eastern Middle Iranian languages.

249 Mirza Khwaja and Saqi, 1388/2009, docs. 6, 7, 9, 13, 14.
250 Yamada, 1993 passim and Yamada, 1964, 98f Tugushevoi, 2013, 204 index.
251 Erdal, 1984, 281ff doc. IV.
252 Minorsky, 1942, 191ff; Erdal, 1984, 291ff doc. VI.

22 Satisfaction Term

After or before the description of the property, the issuer states that he is satisfied and content with what he has received from the addressee, either the price or service. One can categorize the satisfaction term into two groups based on the type of document:

1. Documents containing a payment clause: this group includes lease,[253] manumission,[254] and sale contracts.[255] In these texts, after the payment has been fully paid, the issuer declares satisfaction with the price received.

   οτομηνο αγγιτινδο οαυαγο οισπο ασπορο οτο κιρδαμο þαδο οδο υονοσινδο

   And the price has been received by us [in] full and complete and we have become satisfied and content.[256]

2. The gift deeds:[257] in Bactrian gift deeds, the donner expresses his satisfaction for the service performed by the done.

   ταδομο λαδο μασκο ναβιχτογο ζαμιγο οδο ιαβο σιδο οαρο ναυαγγο λαþνο φαραφαγο ιαμþο(σπαλο) πιδο κιρδο ασπαχτο οτομο αγγιτο ασαφαγο ιαμþο-σπαλο παλαþνο πισιδο þαδο υονασινδημο

   Thus, the vineyard described herein and the water which (is) adjacent thereto has been given (as) a gift by me to you, Yamsh-spal, for service rendered, and (this) counterpart of (my) gift has been received by me from you, Yamsh-spal. Thereupon I am satisfied and content.[258]

The keyword for the satisfaction term in Bactrian is þαδο (satisfied or happy) (Table 11). After the word þαδο, the word υονοσινδο (content or glad) has more frequency in documents. However, in the last two documents (aa and ab), instead of the word υονοσινδο, the word ναμιυγαρημο (I am not suffering loss) was inserted.

253 Doc. U.
254 Doc. F.
255 Docs. J, L, V, W, aa, ab.
256 Docs. J, L.
257 Docs. C, Tt.
258 Docs. C.

TABLE 11

Doc	Satisfied	Content	
C	ϸαδο	υονασινδημο	
F	ϸαδο {ϸαδο} οδο	υονοσινδο	
J	ϸαδο οδο	υονοσινδο	
L	ϸαδο οδο	υονοσινδο	
Tt	ϸαδο		
U	ϸαδο οδο	υονοσινδο	
V	ϸαδο	υονοσινδο	
W	ϸαδο	υονοσινδο	
aa	ϸαδημο οτι		ναμιυγαρημο
ab	ϸαδημο οτο		ναμιυγαρημο

Furthermore, some sales contracts include more complementary words and phrases in the satisfaction term.

> οτο κιρδαμο ϸαδο οδο υονοσινδο οταλο φρογαοαμο ασιδο ναλο μιυγαρο
>
> And we have become satisfied and content and are profited and not subject to loss.[259]

or

> ϸαδο υονοσινδο κιρδαμο πιδοσαχτο οαυαγο φρογαοο ζαναμο ναγο μηγαρο
>
> (And) I have become satisfied (and) content, (and) the price agreed I acknowledge (to be) profitable and not damaging.[260]

As mentioned earlier, these complementary words and phrases are appropriate for ensuring that all relevant aspects of a legal event are certain and explicit. The satisfaction term in Bactrian contracts is very important because these deeds preserve a very old term from ancient Mesopotamian legal practice, which had disappeared following the Middle Babylonian period.

259 Doc. J.
260 Docs. W, V.

Nevertheless, the clause was used in Egyptian transaction documents from the 8th-century BCE through the Islamic period.[261]

23 Historical Background and Function of the Satisfaction Term

The satisfaction term is first attested in Old Babylonian documents from Mesopotamia and ancient Syria as the summerogram ŠÀ.GA.NI AL.DU$_{10}$ or Akkadian libbašu ṭāb "his heart is satisfied."[262]

The term occurs in two types of texts: legal texts, including sales, settlements of litigation, receipts for the bride-price,[263] within the law code of Hammurabi,[264] and non-legal texts, namely letters.[265] I will only address the transaction texts. Muffs noted that the satisfaction term in Old Babylonian deeds originated from the archaic law on sales written in Mesopotamia during the third millennium BCE.[266]

The formula appears in deeds from lower Mesopotamia and ancient Syria, particularly in sale deeds, when the seller declares satisfaction with the price after the buyer has paid or the seller has received full payment. This phrase is typically stated in sale deeds as follows:

> IN.ŠI.IN.ŠÁM ŠÁM.TIL.LA.BI.ŠÈ 2 1/3 GÍN KU.BABBAR IN.NA.AN.LÁ ŠÀ.GA.A.NI AL.DÙG (or DU$_{10}$)
>
> He (the buyer) paid 2 1/3-shekel silver as its full price. His (the seller's) heart is satisfied.[267]

Following the Old Babylonian period in Mesopotamia, scribes removed the satisfaction term from documents, but in the late Bronze Age, scribes in the city of Emar continued to use the formula in their transactions.[268] After a long absence, the formula reappears in Aramaic papyri from Elephantine through

261 Frantz-Murphy, 1988, 106f.

262 See CAD, 19, 36 Ṭ ṭâbu.

263 Muffs, 2003, 46f; Westbrook, 1991, 219; Dušek, 2009, 87.

264 L. 264; Westbrook in his article (Westbrook, 1991) analyzed the satisfaction term in the code of Hammurabi, but instead, I will concentrate on legal transactions.

265 For an example of the satisfaction term, see Van Soldt, 1994, no. 58; Veenhof, 2005, no. 101.

266 Muffs, 2003, 105ff.

267 Dekiere, 1995, 88f No. 418.

268 Skaist, 1995 passim; Gross, 2013a, 333f; for additional documents, see Beckmann, 1996; Westenholz, 2000; Tsumiko, 1991; the phrase is almost written as ŠÀ-bu.šu DÙG.GA, see Beckman, 1988, 65.

deeds of sale, marriage contracts, withdrawal documents, a document of obligation to deliver grain, and a mutual quitclaim, particularly in the context of payment, oath, or marriage.[269] The clause in the Aramaic deeds from Elephantine is attested as לבבי טיב (my heart is satisfied).[270] For example, in a sale deed:

> אנחן זבנהי לך ויהבת לן דמוהי כסף כרש 1 שקלן 3–1 באבני מלכא כסף זוז לכרש 1 וטיב לבבן בדמיא זי יהבת לן
>
> We sold it to you and you gave us its price (in) silver, 1 karsh, 4 shekels by the stone(-weight)s of the king, silver zuz to 1 karsh, and our heart was satisfied with the price which you gave us.[271]

As we have said above, there is a 700-year chronological gap between Emar and Elephantine,[272] and no evidence for filling this gap has been discovered. New excavations will hopefully shed more light on this dark corner.[273]

Returning to the function, in Akkadian and Aramaic traditions, there are two views on the satisfaction term. Muffs in his book assumes it was a quittance term,[274] which was criticized by Westbrook. The latter emphasized the satisfaction term is "purely empirical, relating to what has been observed, as befits a clause dealing with the performance stage of the contract rather than the stage of its conclusion." Therefore, he concludes the legal function of satisfaction is a conclusive evidence clause, "which bars the seller from claiming later that he in fact received short measure, even if subsequent verification should prove that this was truly the case."[275] Furthermore, the satisfaction term is found not only in Akkadian legal texts but also in Demotic deeds from Egypt dating to the 8th-century BCE.[276] This additional evidence raises questions about the

269 Dušek, 2009, 87f.
270 Schwiderski, 2009, 479f.
271 TAD B. 3.4; B. 3.12.
272 Other similarities between the documents from Emar and Elephantine should be noted but are beyond the scope of this study. For further information, see the term BA.UG7 TIL. La (in death and in life) in Emar; and for the term בחיי ובמותי (in my life and my death) in Elephantine, see TAD B2.3.
273 When Muffs was writing his book, the documents from Emar were not yet discovered. These documents have subsequently helped to bridge the chronological gap between Akkadian and Aramaic deeds.
274 Muffs, 2003, 43ff; Levine, 2003, XVI.
275 Westbrook, 1991, 222; for another critique of Muffs' approach, see Malul, 1988, 332f; Yaron, 1971, 407ff.
276 For the earliest demotic deed datable to 707 BCE, see Vleeming, 1981.

origins of the satisfaction term in Aramaic papyri, with some scholars believing it has an Egyptian ancestor.[277]

Muffs concludes that the clause in Aramaic deeds was not borrowed from the Egyptian tradition, but rather it was adopted by the Aramaeans from the Assyrian legal formulary.[278] Bactrian is the only Middle Iranian language incorporating the full price element as well as the satisfaction term within the payments clause. However, an Egyptian origin does not seem suitable in Bactrian legal documents,[279] because in the payment clause of Demotic and Aramaic sale deeds from Achaemenid Egypt, only the price is mentioned, without indication of full payment. In other words, these Egyptian deeds do not contain the full price element within the payment clause, whereas Bactrian sale deeds include both, much like those in Akkadian documents. Furthermore, there are lands between Egypt and Bactria that continued practicing their legal formulary, namely Babylonia. Finally, even though the satisfaction term in papyri from Wadi al-Daliyah differs from the Akkadian and Egyptian deeds, it expresses the satisfaction of both sides:

> ליהוחנן שמה בר שאלה דנה עבד זילה תמים [חנניה בר בידאל זבן ליהונור בר לנרי
> בכסף ש 20־10־3־2] שחרץ דמין גמירן כספא [זנ]ה ש 20־10־3־2 חנניה [מקבל מן
> יהונור ויהונור ליהוחנן זך החסן עבד יהוה] לה ולבנוהי מן אחרוהי לעלמא שליט
> יהונור ליה[וחנן זך לעלמא **ורעיו חד מן חד אסרא ביניהם**]
>
> [Hananiah son of Beyadel sold] a certain Yehohanan son of Se>ilah, this slave of his, without defect, [to Yehonur son of Laneri for 35 silver shekels,] the stipulated price, the full price. [Thlis sum of 35 shekels Nananiah [has received from Yehonur. And Yehonur took possession of the said Yehohanan. He will be a slave] of his and of his sons after him in perpetuity. Yehonur has authority over the [said] Yeh[ohanan in perpetuity. **And they were mutually satisfied with the bond between them.**[280]

As Gropp and Dušek suggested, it's the Aramaic equivalent of Neo-Babylonian in a ḫud/migir libbišu (from my own free will or voluntarily).[281]

---

277 Ritner, 2002, 347f; Porten, 1992, 260 no. 4.

278 Muffs, 2003, 179; Geller, 2011; in his review of Botta's book, (Botta, 2009).

279 See Geller's review of Botta's Book, Geller, 2011, 150f; I am inclined to accept his critique because as he said: "it is usually a safe bet, when dealing with legal matters, to rely upon conservatism and resistance to change", and for other reasons see also Pardee, 2008, 311f.

280 Gropp, 2001, 34 P. 1.

281 Ibid., 49; Dušek, 2007, 77f; Dušek, 2009, 93.

During the Hellenistic period, Greek deeds from Egypt include the full price element and satisfaction phrase following the Demotic formulary but with a combination of the Aramaic formula.[282] The satisfaction term is one of the sections where this type of formulation was used. It is worth noting in some Greek settlements from the 6th–7th-centuries CE that the satisfaction term is formulated with two or three complementary words or verbs, and the issuer expresses his satisfaction as follows:

> τουτων τοινυν ουτω γενομων και στερχθεντων και αρεσθεντων
>
> Because these things, then, have taken place in this way and we are content and pleased with them,[283]

This is similar to the process in the Bactrian legal formulary.[284]

The gaps between legal corpora concerning the satisfaction phrase in the ancient Near East are enormous. Therefore, it's difficult to explain how the satisfaction term was inserted into Aramaic deeds and then in Bactrian conveyances. Nevertheless, Skaist's theory about the satisfaction phrase in Aramaic papyri from Elephantine sounds plausible.[285] He first proposes the following hypothesis to explain the geographical and chronological distribution of the Akkadian formula libbašu ṭāb. He reminds us that it's a type of formula in the conveyances from the Ur III period named type A by Steinkeller.[286] He also claims that in texts from Alalaḫ, Ekalte, Emar, and level VII, type A of the Ur III period conveyances formulary was used, particularly the first part of its operative section.[287] This adoption he suggests: "such a loan could only have taken place during the Ur III period when Type A was standard and when West Semitic peoples particularly the Amorites came into extensive contact with

282 Blau, 1912, 210, 212f; Keenan et al., 2014, 55.

283 Gagon & van Minnen, 1994, 54ff; 96.

284 See this chapter section Figurae per adiectionem.

285 Skaist, 1995, 625; Skaist, 2008, 224f.

286 Steinkeller, 1989, 11f.

287 Steinkeller designed the operative section of the Ur III period conveyances as follows:

(1) Object of Sale	(1) Object x,
(2) Term for Price	for its price,
(3) Amount(-šè)	amount y,
(4) Seller(-šè-ra/-a) / ki Seller(-ta)	from the seller
(5) Buyer (-e)	the buyer
(6) Term for "to buy"	bought

See Skeinkeller, 1989, 11ff.

lower Mesopotamia."[288] In another paper, he explains how the term libbašu ṭāb made its way from Akkadian texts to Aramaic ones from Elephantine. He hypothesizes that it may have taken place when "an Aramean who purchased land from a native would have had the sale deed drawn up in the manner current in that area-very likely in Akkadian, as were all the available sale deeds. With the passage of time, it was felt necessary to draw up the deeds in Aramaic. The simplest way of doing this would have been to translate the Akkadian directly into Aramaic. Thus it would have been possible for libbašu ṭāb to become לבבי טיב either as the accepted Aramaic equivalent or as a loan translation."[289] As mentioned above the satisfaction term after the Old Babylonian period disappears from legal deeds in Mesopotamia while it continued to be used in Emar, Northern Syria—part of the homeland of the Aramaean-speaking people—until the 12th-century BCE.[290] Accordingly, it appears plausible that the Aramaean scribes in Bactria continued to use their pattern, learned in their homeland (Syria), and brought with them to Bactria. In other words, it appears in Aramaic documents from the Achaemenid period, meaning insertion of the full price element or satisfaction term in the payment clause was optional, so it is likely that Aramaic scribes in Bactria inserted both in the payment clause because they were familiar with the practice from their homeland.

Another alternative explanation for the existence of the satisfaction term in Bactrian sale deeds, it was introduced into Bactrian legal terminology during the Hellenistic period. This theory seems to be weak and implausible because Greek sale deeds from Mesopotamia and the Levant do not include the satisfaction term,[291] and it's also absent in Aramaic and Hebrew deeds from the Judean Desert. In other words, the satisfaction term is completely eliminated from Levantine legal formularies during the Hellenistic period, and previously in Mesopotamia.

Remarkably, the satisfaction term appears in Pahlavi litigations as well, and the word for satisfaction is hwnsnd (content, satisfied), which serves the same goal, much like the Bactrian word υονοσινδο (content).

> ˀMT ktkxwdˀy ŠNT ˀywk' xwˀstk' ZY-š NPŠH cnd 100 wˀhk ˀrcyt' pt xwyšyh ˁL mtr ˀtwr'prnbg y BRH YHBWNt W ŠNT 2 hndrc' pt' hndrc' krt' ˀYK-m xwˀstk' y ˁL L mt' ˀbxt' PLG ˁL ˀtwr'prnbg ˀpryk' ˁL mtrˀtwrprnbg

288 Skaist, 2008, 224.

289 Skaist, 1995, 625f.

290 Arnold, 2011, 184; for more details on the homeland of the Aramaeans, see Lipinski, 2013; Younger, 2014.

291 Dušek, 2009, 95f; just one document (Welles, 1959, P 26) contains the term. However, the term refers to more than just price satisfaction and encompasses the entire agreement.

y BRH YHBWNt mtrˀtwrprnbg krtˈ ˀYK pt ZK y ktkxwtˀy hndrcˈ krtˈ hwnsnd W hmDYNˀ HWHwm gwmˀynkyh ˀYK mtrˀtwrprnbg YHBWNt y pyš ŠBKWNt YHWWNyt

If a head of household in one year conveyed a thing valued at 100 personal as a possession property to his son Mihr-Ādurfarrbay, and in the second year he gave the following Testament in his will: "I have conveyed a property received by me, in an undivided fashion: half to Ādur-franbay and the other (half) to my son Mihr-Ādurfarrbay." (And if) Mihr-Ādurfarrbay declares: "I am satisfied and agree with the testament given by the head of household in his will," then the doubt created by the original transfer of the thing to Mihr-Āturfarrbay is thereby cleared up.[292]

Similarly, this term serves the same purpose in Pahlavi as it does in Akkadian and Aramaic, and it's reasonable to conclude that **hwnsnd** in Pahlavi legal practice is an Aramaic element equivalent to לבבי טיב in Aramaic litigation documents.[293] Additionally, in the Islamic legal formulary, the satisfaction term is recorded in a few Islamic sale deeds from Egypt[294] while in the eastern borders of Islamic lands, e.g., Northern Afghanistan and Turkistan, the term had been dropped from contracts written in Arabic, Old Uyghur, and Persian.

Lastly, it seems that the satisfaction term in Bactrian deeds has an Akkadian origin, which was transferred to Bactria through the Aramaic tradition in the Achaemenid period. Later in the Hellenistic period, even though scribes did not omit it from Greek legal deeds, the metaphoric role was lost.[295]

292 MHD, 94.14–95.2; Macuch, 1993, 595ff; Perikhanian, 1997, 216–17.

293 For more examples of the satisfaction term in the MHD, see Perikhanian, 1997, 400 in the Glossary, see the word xonsand/xunsand būtan.)

294 For example, the phrase رضاهم بثمنه (their satisfaction with the price) in some sale contracts, for more discussion, see Frantz-Murphy, 1988, 105ff.

295 The same occurred with Greek deeds in Egypt when the term lost its metaphoric role.

CHAPTER 3

The Investiture and Final Clauses

1 Investiture Clause in Sale Deeds

In this chapter, I have examined the investiture clause in deeds of conveyances, e.g., gifts, leases, and sales, and then explored the contingency or final clauses in all of these documents. In the conveyances, the issuer acknowledges the addressee's rights and declares the transfer of property to him after the addressee has fulfilled his obligations, for example, paying the price of the property in cash or through services. To accomplish this, the former owner declares that the new owner, as well as the children and descendants, will have full power over the property in perpetuity. This clause usually consists of four parts: 1) the opening declaration, 2) the perpetuity phase, 3) the rights of alienation phrase, and 4) the heritability phrase.

For sale deeds, the issuer declares that upon receiving the price, he has recognized the addressee's (buyer's) rights to the property and transferred the estate:

> ταδο ωσο ασο μανδορονιγο ρωσο παρσο μαβαρο ζαμα{α}νο ι μασκο ναβιχτιγο αγγαργο σαγονδο πιδο παδουαμονδδιγανο ναβιχτιγινδο ιαββο οδο πανδαγο ασιδο οαρο ναυαγγο ταδο ταοι ριϸτακο οδο ταοι οαραζοϸαβορο οδο τωμαχο βραδο οδο τωμαχο πορο οδο τωμαχο φροζανδανο χοβο οδο χοζο αβοδδηιο ασο μωσο αβο ιαοιηδανο ζοριγο αβηιουαργο αβηιοτωγο αβηιουαγγο αβηιοαβφαγγο κοαδδηνο υαρσο κισο οιζανδογαρο μαβοδδηιο

> So now, from tomorrow (and) for (all) future time, (as for) the property described herein, just as has been stated with reference to the boundaries, (and) the water and path which (are) adjacent thereto, to the property-then may it belong properly and well to you, Rishtak, and to you, Waraz-shabur, and to your brothers and your sons and your descendants, from now to eternity, without dues, without tax, without exaction, without deduction, so that no-one may be able to cause injury to you.[1]

In gift deeds, this declaration is made after the addressee has completed services for the issuer (master):

1 Docs. J, L, V, W.

 DOI:10.1163/9789004519985_005

> ιϑαο ατανο μαπορσο ζοριγο μασκο ναβιχτογο ζαμιγο οδο ιαβο σιδο οαρο ναυαγγο ταοι ιαμþοσπαλο χοβηιο χοζηιο χοαρηιο ληρηιο αλο ποραναvo αλο φορζινδαvανο αβσαχοανο αβοισαρο ασο μωσο αβο ιαοηδανο ζοριγο
>
> So that in the future the land described herein and the water which (is) adjacent thereto may belong properly and belong well to you, Yamsh-spal; you may have (and) hold (it), with (your) sons (and) with (your) descendants, without claim (and) without argument, from now to eternity.[2]

The vocabulary arrangement in the transfer declaration varies from each document. The differences are due to two factors: the location of the document's composition and the nature of the document. However, the differences have no bearing on the role of the clauses and terms. In the majority of transfer deeds, the issuer uses the verb "to be" (βο-) as the first step in declaring the transfer of property.[3] The verb "to be" (βο-) is usually followed by the adverbs χοβο οδο χοζ (properly and well).[4] Although in two late sale deeds, the transfer declaration is expressed by two verbs, λαυ (to give) and παραλαδο (to sell),[5] and the investiture clause is entirely dropped in one text.[6]

For some deeds, the issuer declares that the addressee can do whatever he wants with his new property, which means that he reaffirms the new owner's full authority over the property[7] (Table 12).

TABLE 12

Doc	Perpetuity	The verb to be βο-	Obligations	Properly and well χοβο οδο χοζ	The verb to have ληρ-	The verb to hold χοαρ-
C	+	+	+		+	+
J	+	+	+	+		
L	+	+	+	+	+	+
Nn	+		+			

2 Docs. C, T, Tt.

3 Docs. C, J, L, P, Tt, U, aa, ab; for additional information, see Sims-Williams, 2007, 203f; in a number of documents, the verb χοαρ- was used to demonstrate the new owner's affirmation of authority over the property; for further examples, see docs. C, L, U, V, W, aa.

4 Docs. J, L, P, U, aa, ab.

5 Docs. V, W.

6 Doc. Nn; for this document, the issuer expresses that the property belongs to the addressee in perpetuity without using the investiture clause.

7 Docs. P, T, V, W.

TABLE 12 (*cont.*)

Doc	Perpetuity	The verb to be βο-	Obligations	Properly and well χοβο οδο χοζ	The verb to have ληρ-	The verb to hold χοαρ-
P	+	+		+		
T	+		+		+	+
Tt	+	+				
U	+	+		+	+	+
V	+		+		+	+
W	+		+		+	+
aa	+	+		+	+	+
ab	+	+		+		

2 Perpetuity Language/Phrase

When the issuer cedes property to the addressee in a Bactrian deed, he declares the property is his forever. This phrase can be stated in two ways:

1. ασο μανδορονιγο ρωσο παρσο μαβαρο ζαμανο (From tomorrow for future time.)
2. ασο μωσο αβο ιαοιηδανο ζοριγο (From now to eternity.)

These two phrases can be used separately or together, but their functions are similar.[8] The pair also can be found in settlement documents as part of the peace clause.[9] The purpose of the phrases was not to convey the length of time, but rather the continuation of time.[10] It denotes the property belongs to the new owner(s) until transferred to another party.

3 Historical Background of Perpetuity Language/Phrase

The perpetuity language in Bactrian deeds, ασο μωσο αβο ιαοιηδανο ζοριγο (from now to eternity) is a literal translation of the Aramaic term מן יומא זנה ועד עלם (from this day and forever). When compared to the Aramaic papyri from

8 Even in doc. S, the perpetuity phrase is a combination of both preceding phrases, ασο μανδορονιγο ρωσο οιταβο ιαοοηδανο ζοριγο (From tomorrow until eternity).

9 Docs. S, Uu.

10 Botta, 2008b, 161f; Yaron, 1958, 39f.

Elephantine, we find similarities in the function and location of the perpetuity language used in Aramaic and Bactrian deeds. The perpetuity language is included in both investiture clauses. To understand why perpetuity language in Bactrian deeds has an Aramaic origin, a brief historical review of perpetuity language, particularly in Aramaic papyri, and in ancient Near Eastern legal practices is required.

Before looking deeper into the origins of perpetuity language, it's important to distinguish between its usage and etymology. The first part of the perpetuity phrase is attested in many Akkadian legal documents from Bronze Age Syria (Alalaḫ, Ekalte, Emar, and Ugarit) as ištu ūmi annîm (from this day).[11] This form evolves, eventually becoming longer, but begins with ištu ūmi annîm (from this day) and ends adi dārīti (and forever),[12] among the first Akkadian documents from Ugarit:

> iš-tu U$_4$.KAM an-ni-i-im a-miš-tam-ri DUMU níq-me-pa LUGAL ^{uru}ú-ga-ri-it it-ta-ši É.ḪI.A A.ŠÀ.ME[Š] ša ^{p}aš-tar-a-bi DUMU a-ri-iš-bi ù A.ŠÀ.ḪI.A ša ^{p}ḫa-ṣí-qá-ta-na DUMU ba-dì-da-na ù it-ta-din-šu a-na ^{p}EN-ki-li ù píl-ku-šu-nu mim-ma ia-nu É-tu$_4$ A.ŠÀ.MEŠ ša ^{p}aš-tar-a-bi ù A.ŠA.MEŠ ša ^{p}ḫ-ṣí-mi-id a-na ^{p}EN-ki-lil a-di da-ri-ti
>
> From this day, ˁAmmiṯtamru, son of Niqmêpaˁ, king of Ugarit, has "lifted" the house(s) (and) field(s) of ˁAṯtarˀabu son of Arišbi and the field(s) of Ḫaṣiqatānu son of Badidānu and he has given it to Ewrikili the house(s) (and) field(s) of ˁAṯtarˀabu and the field(s) of Ḫaṣiqatānu are "bound" to Ewrikili forever[13]

This phrase appears in Ugaritic documents as well, and it is written as ym hnd....ˁd ˁlm.[14] For Example:

> l ym hnd ˁmṯtmr bn nqmpˁ ml[k] ugrt ytn šd kḏǧdl d št[n] d b šd [–mt] [y]d gth [-d] z[t]h yd [–]rmh yd [–]lklh [w] ytn nn l bˁln bn kltn w l bnh ˁ[d] ˁlm

11 For documents from Elkate, see Meyer, 2001; for documents from Qatna, see Richter and Lange, 2012, 78f; the most recent document beginning with this formula was written in Hama during the 8th-century BCE, for more details, see Arnaud, 2013, 8f.

12 Van Soldt, 2010, 92.

13 Ibid., 102; only one document from Alalaḫ has a perpetuity phrase, for further detail, see Niedorf, 2008, 406ff, doc 36.1; Loewemann, 1956, 222.

14 For the word ˁlm in Ugaritic, see Del Olmo Lete and Sanmartin, 2015, 155.

On this day, ˁAmmiṯtamru, son of Niqmêpaˁ, kin[g] of Ugarit, has given the land of Kudugadal, which was (previously) transferred (to him), which is situated in the fields of -MT, with its buildings, [wi]th its olive orchard, with its [vine]yard, with [every]thing pertaining to it—(all) this he has given to Baˁlanu, son of Kilitenu, and to his sons forever.[15]

This archaic form persisted, but certain changes occurred over time. The words "from now" and "forever," which had been separated in ancient documents, were combined into a single continuous phrase reminiscent of the poetic formula "from now and forever." The formula appears in another form within Ugaritic literary texts:[16]

ˁwrt yštk bˁl l ht w ˁlmh l ˁnt p dr dr

'Baal shall make you blind from now and for all generations i.e., forever[17]

Loewestamm believes that Aramaic perpetuity language evolved from perpetuity language found in Alalaḫ, and more specifically, Ugaritic texts.[18] As discussed below, Aramaic scribes eventually shifted this phrase to the investiture clause, combining it with the existing perpetuity phrase of the transfer clause. However, Syria was not the only place in the ancient Near East where the phrase "perpetuity" was used in legal documents.

Already in the Old Babylonian period, this phrase occurs in transfer deeds from Elam with a shorter form, ana dārīti (forever), which also appears frequently in sale deeds from Susa:

kīma abu ana māri išāmu B ina kiden Šušinak ana dārīti išām

Like a father has sold (his) son, (the Buyer) has sold (object) with kiden[19] of Šušinak forever.[20]

15 Bordreuil and Pardee, 2009, 257f; for more examples, see KTU3 T. 3.13, 3.33; Kienast, 1979, 434; Marquez Rowe, 2006, 251ff.

16 Loewestamm, 1980, 168.

17 KTU3, 1.19 IV, 5–6; the formula appears in the Old Testament as מעתה ועד עולם (from this time and forever) with some texts on legal transactions, for example, see Ps 113:2 115:18 121:8 131:3; Is, 9:6 59:21 Mi, 4:7; Loewestamm, 1980, 166; Spieckermann, 2014,74f; for the word עולם in the Old Testament, see Preuss, 1999; Jenni 1997; Levine, 2013.

18 Loewestamm, 1980, 167.

19 For divine protection, see CAD, 8, 342f.

20 Jalilvand Safadi, 2014, 85f; for ana dārītī in other texts, see CAD, 3, 107f.

Later, the shorter form of the perpetuity phrase was inserted into several transaction deeds with Mesopotamian legal formularies; for Neo-Assyrian deeds, the term was expressed with ana kal šatti or ina kal ūmī (forever) in the warranty clause of slave sale deeds:

> ṣib-ti be-en a-na 1-me UD-me sa-ár-tu a-na kal UD.MEŠ
>
> (Guaranteed against) seizures of epilepsy for 100 days (and against) fraud forever.[21]

In the operative section of Neo-Babylonian legal documents, the perpetuity phrase was stated as ana miâti or adi mâtu (forever): ana ūmi ṣâti or adi ūm ṣâtu (forever):[22]

> ^{md}A-ŠEŠ-it-tan-nu DUMU šá ^{m}Ni-[din-tum-^{d}A-nu] ina ḫu-ud lì-bi-šú ^{fd}Na-na-a-bul-liṭ-in-ni GÉME-su šá ŠU$_{11}$ 15-šú a-na ^{f}GAŠAN-s[u-nu šaṭ-ra-tum] a-na re-mu-ú-tu a-na ^{f}GAŠAN-s[u-nu] DUMU.SAL šá ^{m}Ni-din-tum- ^{d}A-nu NIN-šú DAM ^{md}UTU-DIN-su-E DUMU ša ^{md}EN-SU a-di U$_{4}$-mu ṣa-a-ta id-din
>
> Anu-ah-ittannu, son of Nidintu-Anu, from his own free will, has sold his slave woman, Nanâ-bulliṭinni, whose right hand [is inscribed] with (the name of) Bēlessunu, to Bēlessunu, daughter of Nidintu-Anu, his sister, wife of Šamaš-balāssu-iqbi, son of Bēl-erība, in perpetuity.[23]

This clause was also included in the warranty and fine clauses of cuneiform legal texts from the Seleucid period.[24] For example:

> U$_{4}$- mu pa-qa-ri a-na UGU-ḫi É ŠUII MU.MEŠ [it]-tab-šu-ú ^{m}ú-bar A šá ^{md}60-TIN-iṭ A šá ^{m}ú-bar A ^{m}MU.MEŠ ú-mar-raq-ma a-di 12-TA.ÀM a-na na-^{md}na-a-MU A šá ^{md}60-AD-GUR a-na U$_{4}$-mu ṣa-a-tú i-nam-din pu-ú-ut a-ḫa-a-meš a-na mu-ur-ru-qu šá É ŠUII MU.MEŠ ^{m}NÍG.SUM.MU-LUGAL A šá ^{m}ri-ḫat-^{d}60 u ^{m}ú-bar A šá ^{md}60-TIN-iṭ a-na ^{md}na-na-a-MU A šá ^{md}60-AD-GUR a-na U$_{4}$-mu ṣa-a-tú na-šu-ú

---

21 Krescher et al., 1980, 521; for further documents, see Kwasman and Parpola, 1991, docs. 6, 48, 61, 85; Mittila, 2002, docs, 8, 48, 50, 64; Donbaz and Parpola, 2001, docs. 123, 125, 146, 178.

22 CAD 16, 116f ṣâti.

23 Stolper, 1990, 563f.

24 Petschow, 1939, 69f n.1; Van der Spek, 1995, 188f.

> When a claim is brought concerning that storehouse, Ubar, son of Anu-uballiṭ, son of Ubār, [the] descendant of Šumāt will clear (it) and pay the 12-fold (penalty) to Nanâ-iddin, son of Anu-ab-utēr, in perpetuity. Nidintu-šarri, son of Riḫat-Anu, and Ubār, son of Anu-uballiṭ, mutually assume guaranty for the clearing of that storehouse for Nanâ-iddin, son of Anu-ab-utēr, in perpetuity.[25]

The abbreviated version of the perpetuity language was used in various forms of all cuneiform documents, but the situation differs with Aramaic corpora. There are two versions of perpetuity language in these documents:
1. short לעלם (forever)
2. long מן יומא זנה ועד עלם (from this day and forever)

The long version predominates in the Aramaic papyri from Elephantine,[26] and it places in the investiture clause.[27] For example:

אנתי שליטה בה מן יומא זנה ועד עלם ובניכי אחריכי למן זי רחמתי תנתנן

> You are empowered in it from this day and forever and your children after you. To whomever, you want you may give (it).[28]

Only one of the papyri incorporates the perpetuity language in the warranty clause:

אנה בגזשת ואובל כל אנחן זבן ויהבן לך ורחקן מנה מן יומא זנה ועד עלמן

> I, Bagazushta and ʾwbl, all (told), we sold and gave (it) to you and withdrew from it from this day and forever.[29]

In Palestine, on the other hand, papyri from Wadi al-Daliyah use the abbreviated version of the perpetuity phrase as לעלמא (forever) in the transfer clause, as in cuneiform deeds:

[עבד יהוה] לה ולבנוהי מן אחרוה לעלמא

25 Wallenfels, 1998, doc. 4.

26 An abbreviated form of perpetuity language appears in two documents as עד עלם (forever), see TAD, B2.7, B2.10.

27 Gross, 2008, 110; perpetuity language occurred in the investiture, reaffirmation of the investiture, and second investiture clauses exactly as he demonstrated.

28 TAD B2.3; Yaron, 1960a, 257f; for more examples, see Schwiderski, 2009, 655f.

29 TAD B3.4; Gross, 2008, 110 n. 53.

> [He will be a slave] of his and of his sons after him in perpetuity[30]

The perpetuity phrase appeared in two versions of Aramaic legal corpora from the Hellenistic period, as it had previously. In light of this, these documents can be divided into two groups: Group A) scribes in this group writes the long version within the document. This group includes Aramaic, Hebrew, and Nabataean from the Judean Desert, as well as a Syriac deed from Dura-Europos and a Nabataean tomb inscription from Mada'in Salih. For conveyances in the Judean Desert, the investiture clause begins and ends with the perpetuity phrase, as it does in Bactrian documents. For example:

> לעלם רשאין זבניא די מן עלא באתרא דך וירתהן למקנה ולמזבנה ולמעבד בה כל די יצבון וירתהן מן יומא דנה ולעלם
>
> Forever are the purchasers who are (mentioned) above empowered with regard to that place and their heirs to acquire, sell, and to do with it all that they desire and their heirs from this day and forever.[31]

There are two possible explanations why the perpetuity phrase in Palestine and Bactria is identical: the Seleucid administration created this form of perpetuity phrase for all its territories, even though it was optional, or the perpetuity phrase independently changed into a common form within these two lands, Palestine and Bactria.

However, the formulation of perpetuity language in other documents differed. For example, a Syriac sale deed from Dura-Europos starts with perpetuity language, but does not end there:

> ܕܡܢ ܝܘܡܢܐ ܘܠܥܠܡܐ ܬܗܘܐ ܐܢܬ ܛܝܪܘ ܙܒܘܢܐ ܘܝܪ̈ܬܝܟ ܫܠܝܛܝܢ ܒܐܡܬܐ ܗܕܐ ܕܙܒܢܬ ܠܟ ܠܡܩܢܝܐ ܘܠܡܙܒܢܘ ܘܠܡܥܒܕ ܒܗ ܟܠ ܕܬܨܒܐ
>
> That from this day and forever you, Tiro, the buyer, and your heirs will have authority over this female slave whom I have sold to you, to keep or to sell or to do with her whatever you wish.[32]

30 Gropp, 2001, P1; Dušek, 2007, 108.
31 Yardeni, 1997, 123ff XḤev/Ṣe 50 + Mur 26.
32 Drjiver and Healey, 1999, P1.

Or in a tomb inscription from Mada"in Salih, the perpetuity phrase appears at the end of the ownership declaration rather than at the beginning:

> דנה כפרא די עבד תרצו הפרכא בר תימו לנפשה ולעידת אנתתה ברת עבדעבדנון ולעבדרבאל ותימו בנוהי ולילדהם ולאחרהם ואצדקהם מן יומא דנה עד עלם
>
> This is the tomb which Tarṣu the Hyparch,[33] son of Zaymu, made for him and for 'Aydat, his wife, daughter of Anb'rabel and Taymu, his sons, and for their children and or their descendants and their legitimate heirs from this day and forever.[34]

The second: Group B) the perpetuity phrase is abbreviated as לעלמא or עד עלם (forever). This method can be found in Aramaic inscriptions from Palmyra and Nabataean tomb inscriptions from Mada'in Salih.[35] In cession texts from Palmyra, the perpetuity phrase appears as the final formula in sale clauses:[36]

> די יהון חפרין ובנן מקברן היך די צבין להון ולבניהון ולבני בניהון לעלמא
>
> That they may dig and build tombs as they want for themselves and for their sons and for their descendants forever.[37]

Perpetuity language in late antiquity could be classified in the same manner. In Talmud Bavili, there is a section about the use of perpetuity phrases in the divorce process. This text explains how to express the formula:

> איבעיא להו בענן ודן או לא בענן ודן תא שמע דאתקין רבא בגיטי איך פלניא בר פלניא פטר ותריך ית אינתתיה מן קדמ דנא **מן יומא דנן ולעלם**
>
> The question was raised: Are the words 'and this' required or not? Come and hear: Rava laid down the formula of the GṬ (divorce bill) thus: 'So-and-so son of So-and-so dismissed his wife N that was his wife from before, **from this day and forever**.'[38]

---

33 Hackl et al., 2003, 335.

34 Healey, 1993, inscription 38; Hackl et al., 2003, 334f.

35 For Nabataean inscriptions from Mada'in Salih, see Healey, 1993, inscription 1 and inscriptions 2, 8, 9, 10, 11, 13, 19, 22, 23, 26, 32, 36, 38.

36 Cussini, 2010, 341; Cussini, 1995, 238.

37 PAT 0067; Kottsieper, 2004, 293.

38 TB, Gittin, 85b, 86a; see Bamberger, 2015, 73f.

It is worth noting that perpetuity language appears not only in legal texts but also in Aramaic and Syriac magic texts. Certain Aramaic and Syriac magic bowls named bills of divorce that borrowed perpetuity language from legal texts and used it in a semi-legal context.[39] For example, in Aramaic:

> [ד]פטרנא [י]ת֯כו֯ן֯ מ֯י֯נ֯הון בספר תרוכין וגט פיטורין ואיגרת ש֯יבוקין כדת משה וישראל מן יומ֯[א] ד[י]ן ו֯לעלם אמן֯ א֯מן
>
> [For] I release you from them by a document of divorce and a deed of release and a letter of dismissal, according to the Law of Moses and Israel, from th[i]s da[y] and forever. Amen, Amen.[40]

And the same occurs in Syriac magic bowls:

> ܘܟܬܒ ܥܠܝܗܘܢ ܕܬܦܢܝܬܐ ܥܠ ܟܠܗܘܢ ܫܐܕܐ ܘܕܝܘܐ ܘܣܛܢܐ ܘܠܠܝܬܐ ܘܠܐܛܒܐ ܕܐܝܬ ܒܒܝܬܗ ܕܕܐܕܒܗ ܒܪ ܐܣܡܢܕܘܟܬ ܬܘܒ ܟܬܒ ܥܠܝܗܘܢ ܕܬܦܢܝܬܐ ܕܠܥܠܡ
>
> He wrote against them a bill of divorce against all of them: demons and devils and Satans and Liliths and no-good-ones that are in the house of d'dbh son of 'smndwkt. Again, he wrote against them a bill of divorce that is forever.[41]

Regarding Greek documents from Egypt, the perpetuity language appears in the full version as Απο της εωεστωσες ημερας επι τον συμπαντα χρονον (from this day and forever), which is the translation of מן יומא דין ולעלם.[42]

In Iran, the perpetuity language was well known.[43] The MHD mentioned the abbreviations for property transfer. There are three terms for the perpetuity phrase in this book, including tā fraškart, which is an exact translation of

39 Bamberger, 2015a; 2015b; Morrigi, 2015, 87; the longer version appears more frequently in Aramaic magic bowls than the shorter version, although the perpetuity phrase occurs in various Syriac forms. The longest attested version of the phrase is ܡܢ ܗܫ ܘܥܕܡܐ ܠܥܠܡ ܥܠܡܝܢ (from now and forever and ever), see Moriggi, 2014, 243 and the glossary under the word 'lm'.

40 Shaked and Ford, 2013, 130 JBA 21.

41 Moriggi, 2014 bowl 5 and Moriggi, 2015, 87.

42 Blau 1912, 218f.

43 Recently, inscriptions written in the Elymaean (a dialect of Aramaic Language) were discovered in western Iran, which contain the shorter version of the perpetuity language; for more information, see Sims-Williams, 2015, 288f.

the Aramaic term עד לעלם.[44] However, for our purposes, the other equivalent for the Aramaic term, עד לעלם Jāwēdānag,[45] a cognate of the Bactrian word ιαοηδανο, is important. For this case, there are two possible explanations:

1. In a legal context, these two Middle Iranian words share a common ancestor, most likely Old Persian.
2. Given that Bactria was long a part of the Sasanian Empire, the word ιαοηδανο is a Pahlavi loan word in Bactrian.

The use of perpetuity language is also attested in some legal transactions from central Asia, such as Kharoṣṭhi,[46] Old Uyghur[47] and Tibetan[48] documents.

4 Opening Declaration: The Phrase (Pādixšāy)

The investiture clause in Bactrian conveyances employs two types of transfer declarations:

1. Simple declaration with the verb βο- ("to be"; in the texts "to belong")
2. Declaration with the verb παδαχþαν- (to have right, to have authority, be entitled)[49]

These two types are not mutually exclusive because some individual deeds include both types of transfer declarations, using one in the investiture clause and another in the reaffirmation of the investiture, although there are exceptions. Documents V and W use the verbs λαδο (to give) or οδο παραλαδο (to sell) instead of the verb βο- (to be), and document Nn expresses the transaction only with the verb παραλαδο (to sell), while in the familiar document Tt, the issuer declares he has vouchsafed and given (αχþαλ and λαυ) the addressee

44 On the perpetuity language in the MHD see Sheikh, 2022, 282f.

45 For example: ʾM YMMLLWNyt ʾYK-m ZNH BYTʾ pt mʾnsn' dʾšn' ʿL LK YHBWNt yʾwytʾnyk pt ḫwyšyh YHBWNt YHWWNyt; "If he said the house had been given by me for a dwelling to you, (then), it is given forever in the possession (of him i.e., the addressee or transferee)" MHD, 19, 2–3 Perikhanian, 1997, 64f. Furthermore, the perpetuity language was not only used in ownership rights; it also refers to the father's guardianship of his children: ʾB' srdʾryh y BRTH yʾwytʾnk' W ʾḤ ZK Yʾ ḤTH ʿd zyndkyh y BNPŠH BRʾ ŠLYTʾ YHBWNt;

"A father is entitled to transfer the guardianship over a daughter (to another person) forever, but a brother (is entitled to transfer) the guardianship over his sister to the end of his (own) life". (MHD, 28, 11–12. Perikhanian, 1997, 84f.).

46 Burrow, 1940, 419, 529; its authority is for a thousand years, as long as life (varṣasahasrami yavajio).

47 Yamada et al., 1993, 4ff. Sa01. may Alp Taš Sangun own this estate for thousand year and ten thousand days (ming yïl tümän kün-kä tägi).

48 Takeuchi, 1995, 159ff. doc. 6.

49 Sims-Williams, 2007, 250.

part of an immobile property. The other constituent elements of the investiture clause—perpetuity language and the heritability phrase—appear with both types. The delineation of rights occurs only with the παδαχϸαν-.[50]

5 Origin of the Phrase Pādixšāy

The Bactrian verb παδαχϸαν is the equivalent of the Aramaic word שליט.[51] This viewpoint is based on two factors. In the first example, two words serve the same function in legal texts. The Aramaic phrase שליט in the investiture clause of the papyri from Elephantine and Samira affirms the authority of a legal participant over some object involved in a legal transaction.[52] The verb παδαχϸαν serves the same purpose in Bactrian deeds. I have considered two examples from the Achaemenid period and compared them to Bactrian deeds showing how they served the same purpose. I compared an immobile transaction from Elephantine to a similar document from Bactria. More specifically, in an Aramaic deed from Elephantine on the sale of abandoned property, the issuer (seller) declares to the buyer that:

אנת ענניה בר עזריה שליט בביתא זך ובניך מן אחריך ולמן די צבית למנתן

> You, ʿAnaniah son of ʿAzariah, have right to [the] house and (so do) your children after you and anyone whom you desire to give (it) to.[53]

In a Bactrian land sale deed, the issuer recognizes the same rights for the addressee, but with additional details:

> ωσο παδαχϸανηιο τοο ζαροιωλο οδο τοο βρηδαγο οδο τοο σανδο οδο ταμαχαγγο βραδο πορο φροζανδανανο ασο ανδορονιγο ρωσο παρσο μαβαρο ζαμανο οδασο μωσο αβο ιαοηδανο ζοραγο ασιδαβο μασκο ναβισιδο χοαδο χοαρδο̣ οδο δδριγδο παρσο παραλαδο ναβαγο ωσταδο οιχαρηγανο κιρδο αλο ανδαρο ζ̇αμιγο μι̣γδο βαυαρο οδο βαγολαγγο κιρδο λαχμιγο οδο λαχϸατανιγο κιρδο αβο πορο οολοβαρο λαδο ναβανδο λογδο ναμαγγο αβαδο κιρδο ναρδδιγανο υιρτο νωιο νακανδο ασιδο υαρσο χοαδο ριμαδο σαγονδο χοβαοανδοαβο χιρσαγο βονο πιδαργανο πα̣δαχϸανινδο

50 For the delineation of rights, see below.
51 For the word שליט, see Hoftijzer and Jongeling, 1995, 1143f; Schwiderski, 2009, 787f.
52 Gropp, 1993, 31; for documents from Elephantine, see Porten, 1996, 166 n. 30.
53 TAD 3.4.

> Now you (sg.) have authority-you, Zar-yol, and you, Bredag, and you, Sand, and your (pl.) brothers, sons (and) descendants-from tomorrow (and) for (all) future time, and from now until eternity, (over) the property which is described herein, to have and to hold (it) yourselves, (and) afterwards to sell (it), to pawn (it), to put (it for) hire, to exchange (it) for another (a piece of) land, to make a monastery or temple, to make a place of burial or crematorium, to give (it) for a son's bride-price (or) with a daughter (as) a dowry, to cultivate (it), to leave (it) fallow, to dig a channel, whatever may suit yourselves, just as owners (customarily) have authority over what is purchased (and) ancestral estates.[54]

The second example of the same element can be found in movable deeds. Concerning a document from Wadi al-Daliyah, the issuer (seller) confirms the full right of the addressee (buyer) upon the slave he has sold to the buyer:

> [ויהונור ליהוחנן זך החסן עבד] יהוה לה ולבנוהי מן אחרוהי לעלמא שליט יהונור ליה[וחנן זך לעלמא]
>
> [And Yehonur took possession of the said Yehohanan. He will be slave] of his and of his sons after him in perpetuity. Yehonur has authority over the [said] Yeh[ohanan in perpetuity][55]

In a Bactrian document, the same declaration is made about the slave:

> οτο μισο παδοαχϸανηδο ασιδδηιο υαρσο κιρδο αριμαδο χοαδο δδριγδο παραλαδο ναβαγο ωσταδο λαϸνο αμβαγδο̣ αχρινο οιχρινο κιρδο πιδο γαοοανο πιδοκιϸ̣το
>
> And also, you have the right (to do) whatever it may suit you (sg.) to do, to keep (him) yourself, to sell (him), to pawn (him), to give (him as) a gift, to put (him for) purchase (or for) hire, to detain (him) for a misdeed, ...[56]

As we have seen, the verb παδαχϸαν and the word שליט play the same role in both traditions. In both cases, the issuer transfers full ownership rights to the new owner (the addressee), meaning the verb παδαχϸαν is the Bactrian equivalent of the Aramaic word שליט.

54 Doc. V.
55 Gropp, 2001, P 1.
56 Doc. P.

The other reason for the relationship between שליט and παδαχϸαν- is the Aramogram ŠLYTˀ in Pahlavi for the word Pādixšāy, which means "to have right" and "to be empowered",[57] and it serves the same function in a legal context as it does in Aramaic and Bactrian deeds. For example:

> ˀYK MNW YMLLWNyt ˀYK-m ZNH ẖwˀst' ˀywyn' ˁL LK MZBNWNt ˀywp LK YHBWNt' ˀDYN-š ˀy gwpt' YHWWNyt ˀYK ŠLYTˀ HWHwm ˁL LK MZBNWNt W YHBWNt'
>
> If one declares that, "I have sold and given you this property properly. Then he (has) said: *I am* ***empowered*** *upon to sell and give (it) to you.*[58]

In chapter two, the relationship between the terms זבן ו יהב in Aramaic and MZBNWN W YHBWN in Pahlavi was discussed. Now, the phrase šalliṭ is another Aramaic element in Pahlavi, indicating that Aramaic influenced Zoroastrian legal terminology. Below, I have examined how Aramaic influenced Bactrian and Pahlavi legal terminologies in more detail. Before beginning, let's consider the word שליט and how it was used in the ancient Near East, particularly in legal practice.

6 History of the Entitlement Phrase and the Word שליט

The word שליט first appears in Aramaic papyri from Elephantine in the investiture clause, a unique feature of Aramaic deeds, and does not appear in legal documents from Mesopotamia, where completion clauses are used instead.[59] Nevertheless, the verb šalāṭu exists in Akkadian from the early stages of the languages, e.g., in Old Assyrian and Old Babylonian texts.[60] The verb first started to appear during the Neo-Assyrian and Neo-Babylonian periods in the non-contest clause,[61] though its use in Neo-Assyrian deeds is extremely rare. For example:

> Ša ^{m}a-u-ú-a lu-u ŠEŠ.MEŠ-šú lu-u LÚ.šá-kan-šú lu-u me-me-ni-šú ina UGU MÍ.^{d}NIN.LÍL-ha-mat la i-šal-liṭ

57 Junker, 1955, 7; Mackenzie, 1971, 63; Greenfield, 1980, xxxiii Nyberg, 1988, 80.
58 MHDA, 22, 11–13; Perikhanian, 1997, 286f.
59 See Gross, 2008, 24f.
60 CAD, 17, 238f.
61 Kaufman, 1975, 98f; Greenfield, 1987, 37f CAD, 17.1, 239f.

> Auwa, his brothers, his prefect, or his relatives shall not dispose of Mullissu-hammat.[62]

In Neo-Babylonian deeds, on the other hand, the verb šalāṭu became a common feature of legal transactions in the non-contest clause. The non-contest clause is abbreviated as

> Mamma ina muḫḫi ul išallaṭ
>
> Nobody has right disposal over.[63]

Oelsner provided the following complete model of the non-contest clause in Neo-Babylonian:

> ul išallaṭ-ma PN_1 Object šuātu ana kaspi ana remūti ana nudunnî ana epēš ṣubûti ana mimma gabbi ana mamman šanamma gabbi elat (ana) PN_2 ul iddin U ul inamdin U ki iddin u ki iddan ul ušuzzu
>
> PN_1 has no authority on the said object for money, as [a] gift, as dowry, for using anyone or anything to anyone else except on PN_2 he did not give and he will not give it. And if he (already) has given if he will give it, they will not stand by him (not be a witness for that).[64]

The verb šalāṭu and its legal usage appear to have been borrowed by the Mesopotamians from the Aramaeans, the latter came from the west.[65] However, it is always formulated negatively in Neo-Babylonian documents, whereas the word שליט operates in both negative and positive forms in the Aramaic papyri from Egypt. As Gross demonstrates, the origins of the legal formula should not be confused with those of the terminology used in the formula. Rather than following Akkadian legal influences, the Aramaic investiture clause had deep roots in West Semitic legal traditions. The Akkadian influence would be "only a mere shift in the terminology of an already existing clause."[66] Therefore, it seems the positive formulation of שליט is an Aramaic innovation for the

62 Donbaz and Parpola, 2001, 119 doc. 164.
63 CAD, 17.1, 239.
64 Oelsner, 1995, 118. note 75.
65 Rabinowitz, 1961, 152.
66 Gross, 2008, 112.

investiture clause.[67] Furthermore, the positive formulation is used several times in the Aramaic section from the Book of Daniel. For example:

די שליט עלאה במלכות אנשא ולמן די יצבא

> That the Most High is sovereign over the kingdom of mortals; he gives it to whom he will.[68]

As Rabinowitz has suggested, this is an adaption of an Aramaic technical phrase.[69] After the Achaemenid period and into the Hellenistic, the entitlement clause became part of legal formularies in Aramaic and Nabataean deeds from Palestine, but the vocabulary changed and the word שליט was replaced with the verb רשי,[70] which means "permitted, authorized."[71] For example:

לעלם רשי אלעזר בזבן בתה דך אבניה ושריתא ודגריא כול די בה

> Forever is El'azar authorized with regard to the purchase of this house the stones, the beams, and the steps all that is within it.[72]

Nevertheless, these two words appear together as hendiadys in some deeds, particularly in some Nabataean texts. For example:

לעלם רשי ושלט יהו[דה זבנה ויר[תוהי בזב]נה דך למקנה ולמז[ב]נה ול[מ]עבד בה
כל די תצבה

---

67 Ibid., 111f; Botta claims that the investiture clause originated in Egypt, but his reasoning and evidence are inadequate and unconvincing, for more details, see Botta, 2006 and 2009; whereas Gropp assumes "the Akkadian clause was progressively transformed by Aramaic scribes into a positive investiture clause in conveyances," for further information, see Gropp, 1993, 35f.

68 Daniel, 4.17, 4.25, 4.32, 5.21; for שליט in a religious text from Qumran, see Genesis Apocryphon Machiela, 2009, 75 Col. 20.13:
די אנתה מרה ושליט על כולא ובכול מלכי ארעא אנתה למעבד בכולהון דין
"Because you are Lord and have authority over everything and over the kings of the earth having authority to e2nact judgment on all of them," see, Greenfield, 1980, xxxiii–xxxiv.

69 Rabinowitz, 1956, 20f.

70 Gross, 2008, 128; for the שליט in the Hellenistic period, see Rudman, 2001, 146ff.

71 Sokoloff, 2003, 80; Cook, 2015, 225.

72 Yardeni, 1997, 34ff. XḤev/Se, 8a.

> Forever Yehuda, the seller, and his heirs are authorized and empowered regarding that sale, to buy and to se[l]l, and to [d]o with it whatever you wish.[73]

Or

ורשיה ושליטה למעבד כל די תצבין

> And you are authorized and empowered to do whatever you wish.[74]

Or

רשיה ושליטה באתרי מתנתא דא

> You will be authorized and empowered in the properties of this gift.[75]

In some Aramaic corpora, this change did not occur. For instance, in the Palmyrene sessions, the word שליט was used in legal contexts as before.[76]

More examples from Syriac legal practice exist where the word ܫܠܝܛ appears in its original form with no changes. For example, the investiture clause of the slave sale deed reads:

ܕܡܢ ܝܘܡܢܐ ܘܠܥܠܡܐ ܬܗܘܐ ܐܢܬ ܬܝܪܘ ܙܒܘܢܐ ܘܝܪ̈ܬܝܟ ܫܠܝܛ
ܒܐܡܬܐ ܗܕܐ ܕܙܒܢܬ ܠܟ ܠܡܚܣܢܘ ܘܠܡܙܒܢܘ ܘܠܡܥܒܕ ܒܗ ܟܠ
ܕܬܨܒܐ

> That from this day and forever you, Tiro, the buyer, and your heirs will have authority over this female slave whom I have sold to you, to keep or to sell or to do with her whatever you wish.[77]

This tradition continued in Syriac legal practice, and more examples of the word ܫܠܝܛ can be found in the Syro-Roman Law Book. For instance:

73 Yardeni, 1997, 38ff. XḤev/Se, 9.
74 Yadin et al., 2002, 73ff. Yadin, 7.
75 Yadin, 2002, 73ff. Yadin 7.
76 PAT, No 1624; Inghot, 1962, 106f; Cussini, 1995, 240f.
77 Drijvers and Healey, 1999, P1.

ܘ ܫܠܝܛ ܠܗ ܕܬܟܬܘܒ ܘ ܬܬܠ ܠܝܪ̈ܬܘܬܗ. ܐܢ ܐܝܬ ܠܗ ܒܢܝܐ [ܠܒܢ̈ܝܗ.
ܐܢ ܕܝܢ ܠܝܬ ܠܗ ܒܢܝܐ] ܠܡܢ ܕܨܒܝܐ

> And she has authority to write (a testament), and give her inheritors if she has children. [If she has no children], whomever she wishes.[78]

Furthermore, during late antiquity, Aramaic magic bowls borrowed the investiture clause and used it as a semi-legal context in the hendiadys form as ראשא שליטא:

דאם תיהויין ראשא שליטא בנפשיכי לכל אינש דיתצבין

> Also, that if you may are authorized and empowered over yourself to any man that you wish.[79]

Notably, the magic bowls were written in Mesopotamia, whereas the Aramaic documents are from the Judean desert in Palestine. The fact that the Aramaic deeds date from the 2nd-century CE while the Magic bowls date from later indicates that the Palestinian tradition influenced the Jewish community in Mesopotamia or that they shared common origins.

It cannot be said with certainty how the word שליט was translated into Greek because no Greek document from Bactria has been discovered. However, the Aramaic and Greek legal corpora from the Hellenistic period, as well as other Aramaic texts translated into Greek, reveal that Greek translators used the word κυριευω and its derivations as an equivalent of the Aramaic wordשליט .[80] Thus, terms for the entitlement phrase and how it was imported into Bactrian can be reconstructed as follows:

> שליט (Aramaic) – κυριευω(Greek) – παδαχþαν (Bactrian)

---

78 Selb and Kaufhold, 2002, Band 2. §31 (§87a Absätze 4,6–10); for the other version, see Selb, 1964, 117.

79 Shaked and Ford, 2013, 236 Bowl 53 and bowls 50–52 and 54 and 56. It modeled exactly the Jewish marriage clause from Murabba'at

אתי רשיא בנפשכי למ[ה]ך למהי אנתא לכול גבר יהודי די תצבין

> "You are authorized over yourself and go and become a wife of any Jewish man that you wish" (Mur, 19).

See also Bamberger, 2015a, 76f.

80 Muraoka, 2010, 72.

7 The Phrase שליט in Negative Form

I have already discussed how the entitlement phrase in Aramaic corpora and Bactrian deeds is similar. We have seen that the word שליט in the entitlement phrase has a positive connotation. Now, it's important to consider the word שליט in its negative form to determine how it served the same purpose in both traditions. The negative form of the verb šalāṭu was used in the non-contest clause of Neo-Assyrian texts and especially Neo-Babylonian legal documents.[81] However, in the case of Aramaic legal papyri from the Achaemenid period, the word שליט has more functions than the verb šalāṭu in Mesopotamian legal documents for the negative formulation in investiture and warranty clauses. In fact, by using a negative formulation, the issuer denies any rights to something or someone.

The negative formulation of the word שליט appears in a withdrawal clause of Aramaic papyri from Elephantine:

> לא איתי לי בר וברה אחרנן אח ואחה ואנתה ואיש אחרן שליט בארקא זך להן אנתי ובניכי עד עלם
>
> I have no other son or daughter, brother or sister, or woman or [an]other man (who) has [a] right to that land but you and your children forever.[82]

Similarly, negative formulations can be found in the Wadi al-Daliyah papyri:

> [לא שליטן··· ו··· או מן א]חרי זנה בנן ואחן זילנ[א]
>
> PN and PN do not have authority, nor will sons and relatives of ours hereafter.[83]

In terms of its legal import, this clause in the papyri from Wadi al-Daliyah parallels the withdrawal clause known from Aramaic conveyances of Elephantine, though its formulation differs. The variation is in the withdrawal clause, with

---

81 Oelsner, 1997, 310.

82 TAD B2.3; Porten, 1996, 168, notes 31–2; moreover, in Aramaic papyri from Elephantine, the word שליט occurs also in the warranty clause of a gift deed in negative form, for example, להן ביתא זנך לא שליט אנת לזבנה ולמנתן רחמת לאחרנן להן בניך מן מבטחיה ברתי המו שליטן בה אחריכם
"But this house you do not have the right to sell it or to give (it) lovingly to others but it is your children from Mibtahiah my daughter (who) has the right to it after you (both)". TAD, B2.4.

83 Gropp, 2001, P 4, 6–7.

Aramaic conveyances from Elephantine using the verb רחק (to withdraw)[84] rather than לא שליט.[85] The withdrawal clause in Bactrian documents serves the same purpose:

> οτο ναπαδοαχϸανιμο αζο οιημο οδο ναζο βαγορημαρηγο οδο ναιαμαχο φροζανδανο κιδο πιδο μασκο ναβιχτιγο αγγαργο μισο σαγισο χοανδο οδο οισαρδο αβζιιενδδηιο
>
> And I, Wyem, do not have (any) authority (over it), nor I, Bag-re-mareg, nor (any of) our descendants who might continue to claim or argue (over) anything else in respect of the property described herein.[86]

Furthermore, the referents of the withdrawal clause are expanded in two late Bactrian texts:

> ακιδο ναυο παδαχϸανινδο υαρσο κισο ιειο αγγαραγο ασιδαβο μασκο ναβισιδο κισο ασφαγο ζαροιωγο οδο ναυο ασφαγο βρηδαγο οδο ναυο ασφαγο σανδο οδο ναυο ασο ταμαχαγγο βραδο πορο φροζανδαναν[ο] αχσαδο οδο ναυο πιδοκιϸτο οδο ναυο ζιδο οδο ναυο πωστιγο αζγαδο καβογγο οδο ναυο νωγο ναυο χιρσοβωστιγο οδο ναυο ναβαγοβωστιγο οδο ναυο οιχαρηγανοβωστιγο
>
> So that no-one (else) has authority (over) this property which is described herein, (neither) to dispute (it) with you, Zar-yog, nor with you, Bredag, nor with you, Sand, nor with your (pl.) brothers, sons (and) descendants, nor to withhold (it), nor to seize (it), nor to produce a contract-(neither) an old nor a new (one), neither a purchase contract, nor a pawn-contract, nor a hire-contract.[87]

Regarding the formulation of the withdrawal in Bactrian, it seems the Aramaic withdrawal clause in Achaemenid Bactria differed from other Aramaic legal texts, implying it played the role of the withdrawal clause in the Aramaic papyri from Elephantine, but with terminology from papyri in Wadi al-Daliyah.

---

84 Schwiderski, 2009, 754; Cross, 1996.

85 Gross, 2008, 119f; Muffs noted that the Aramaic שלט (šlṭ) and Akkadian qerēbu (to come close/to have a claim) are functional equivalents, and both are antonyms of rêqu/rḥq, whereas in later Neo-Assyrian and Neo-Babylonian documents, šalāṭu completely replaces qerēbu in the non-contest clause; the same situation is also reflected in Elephantine usage, see Muffs, 2003, 178.

86 Doc. J.

87 Docs. V, W.

8 The Delineation of Rights

As I have discussed, the issuer confers on the new owner full power over the property and declares the right to do whatever is desired. This expression occurs in six deeds.[88] Its length and content vary from each document; some are shorter, and others are longer. More specifically, consider two examples of movable property, namely slave sale deeds. The new master has the right to do whatever with the slave under a slave sale deed:

> οτο μισο παδοαχþανηδ̣ο ασιδδηιο υαρσο κιρδο αριμαδο[89]
>
> And also, you (pl.) have the right (to do) whatever it may suit you (sg.) to do

For some documents, the issuer explains in more details about the delineation of rights:

> οδο ζινο κιδο οαραγο ναμο παδαχþανηιο αβο χανο δδριγδο παρσο παραλαδο αμβαγαδο πιδο γαοανο πιδοκιþτο πιδο σπασο παδαχ̣νωρο κιρδο σογγο υαρσο χοαδο ρημαδο
>
> And you have the right to keep the woman whose name (is) Warag in the house, (or) afterwards to sell (her), to give (her) away, to detain (her) for a misdeed, (or) to make (her) the recompense (of freedom in return) for service, just as may suit yourselves.[90]

Alternatively, the essential elements are fixed and common. The central term in the entire set of documents is the verb ρημ- (to be pleased),[91] which is the Bactrian equivalent of the Aramaic verb צבי (to desire).[92] The verb צבי, along with the verb רחם, reveal how full power is conferred on the new owner (the addressee) in Aramaic papyri from Elephantine:[93]

88 Docs. J, L, P, T, V, W.
89 Doc P.
90 Doc. T.
91 Sims-Williams, 2007, 260.
92 Schwiderski, 2009, 707; Hofijzer and Jongling, 1995, 957f.
93 Gross, 2008, 114f; Porten and Szubin, 1983, 36f.

ולמן די צבית למנתן

And to whomever you desire you may give (him).[94]

Though the frequency of using רחם in Aramaic papyri from Elephantine is greater than צבי, the verb צבי is more common for the delineation of rights during the Hellenistic period and thereafter.

Notably, the verb צבי is preserved not only in Aramaic papyri from Elephantine but also in documents from the Neo-Babylonian period. In certain documents, the verb ṣebû,[95] the Akkadian equivalent of צבי, has the same meaning and function as צבי, and is used to delineate rights. For example, in a manumission document:

> SAL la-qip-ti u DUMU.MEŠ-e-šú LÚ.DUMU.MEŠ DÚ.MEŠ šú-nu ina il-ki EN-ú-tu šá ina UGU [Id]UTU.NUMUN.DÙ SAL la-qip-ti u DUMU.MEŠ-e-šú za-ku-ú a-šar ṣi-ba-a-ta SAL la-qip-tum u DUMU.MEŠ-e-šú a-na É LÚ DUMU.DÙ-[i] ta-šap-par
>
> Lāpītum and her sons are free citizens. Lāpītum and her sons are clear of responsibility for performing the ilku-service rest upon Šamaš-zēr-ibni. Insofar as she may wish, Lāpītum may send her sons to a family of free citizens.[96]

During the Hellenistic period, the verb צבי was used for the delineation of rights in Aramaic documents from the Judean Desert. For example:

> לעלם רשי ושלט יהו[דה זבנה ויר[תוהי בזב]נה דך למקנה ולמז[ב]נה ול[מ]עבד בה כל די תצבה מן יומה דנן [לעלם]
>
> Forever is Yehu[dah], the purchaser, entitled and empowered, and [his] he[irs with regard to] this [pur]chase to acquire, and to sell, and to do with it whatever you desire from this day [and forever].[97]

In Syriac, the verb ܨܒܐ serves the same purpose i.e., in a Syriac slave sale deed, the buyer has full authority to do whatever he wishes with the slave girl:

94 TAD B2.11; for more details, see Schwiderski, 2009, 706f.

95 CAD, 16, 120 ṣebû; I believe the use of this verb in Neo-Babylonian legal documents demonstrates the influence of Aramaic legal terminology on Akkadian, even though the verb ṣebû was already used in Akkadian texts, but not in this context.

96 Weisberg, 2003, 67f text 37; Holtz, 2001, 248ff.

97 Yardeni, 1997, 38ff. XḤev/Se 9; Sokoloff, 2003, 75.

ܕܡܢ ܝܘܡܢܐ ܘܠܥܠܡܐ ܬܗܘܐ ܐܢܬ ܬܝܪܘ ܙܒܘܢܐ ܘܝܪ̈ܬܝܟ ܫܠܝܛ
ܒܐܡܬܐ ܗܕܐ ܕܙܒܢܬ ܠܟ ܠܡܚܣܢܐ ܘܠܡܙܒܢܘ ܘܠܡܥܒܕ. ܒܗ ܟܠ
ܕܬܨܒܐ

That from this day and forever you, Tiro, the buyer, and your heirs will have authority over this slave female whom I have sold to you, to keep or to sell or to do with her whatever you wish.[98]

Moreover, the Nabataean inscriptions are another example of the verb צבי used within a legal context. According to a tomb inscription at Madaʾin Salih, the owner gave the tomb to his wife as a gift and granted her full ownership:

דנה כפרא די עבד תימאלהי בר חמלת לנפשה ויהב כפרא דנה לאמה אנתתה ברת
גלהמו מן זמן שטר מוהבתא די בידה די תעבד בה כל די תצבא

This is the tomb which made Taymallahi son of Himlat for himself. And he gave this tomb to amah, his wife, daughter of Glhmw, from the date of this deed of gift which is in her hand she might do with it whatever she desires.[99]

In a Palmyrene text, the word שליט and the verb צבי, serve different functions, but they are used within the same context in other Aramaic corpora:

ולא יהא שליט לה למרח לעלוה על רבועתא מדען ואן צבא די יעבד בסטרא דידה
חולוה מדען יהוא בנא או כתל די חורא או חמרין ירח לעליהון בה בשטרא

And he does not have the right to enlarge his room in any way. And if he wants to make in his own side something unconsecrated, he must build either a wall of limestone or a wall made of plaster or clay which he may enlarge on that side.[100]

In the above-mentioned passage from the Syro-Roman Law book about the investiture clause, the verb צבי is used for approving the full right of the owner.

98 Healey and Drijvers, 1999, P 1; Goldstein, 1990, 48; in a Greek deed from Dura-Europos, the seller confirms the buyer's rights in detail as follows:

"Which the price the seller has received from the buyer, and he has transferred to him the land to have it as owner securely for all time, to acquire and to employ, to sell and to administer, in such fashion as he pleases (δι[οι]κειν τροπο ως αν αιρηθαι)" see Welles, 1959, 134ff P. 26.

99 Healey, 1993, inscription 27 and inscriptions 5, 7, 27.

100 PAT, 1624; Cussini; 1995, 240ff; Cussini, 2015, 45f; Kottsieper, 2004, 294.

Another example of using the Aramaic model, עבד כל די יתצב (PN does whatever he desires) in a religious context, is the Hebrew phrase כל אשר־חפץ עשה (he does whatever he pleases)[101] in the Old Testament.[102]

Additionally, there are more examples of the verb צבי in semi-legal and non-legal contexts. For example, in a semi-legal context, many Aramaic incantation bowls present themselves as a bill of divorce to the demons attaching themselves to the clients or their households in various ways.

In this example, the scribe declares that he is writing a divorce bill from a demon for the female client and then she will have authority and power over any man she wishes:

> דאם תיהוין ראשאה ושליטא בנפשיכי לכל אינש דיתצבין דיכתבית ליכי גיטא גיט פיטורין מן הדא אימי בת קאקי
>
> In order that if you may have authority and power over yourself to any man that you wish, for, I have written to you a deed of divorce (and) a deed of release from this Immi daughter of Qaqa.[103]

9 In Iranian Languages

In legal contexts, the verb kāmistan or kām also means "to will or to wish" which has the same meaning in Pahlavi, and is written as Aramogram YSBHN-.[104] This verb appears frequently in the MHD, either with or without ŠLYTʾ. An example with ŠLYTʾ:

> ʾMT GBRʾ 2 kʾnynʾ hwʾstk'-1 ʿL GBRʾ-1 MZBNwd pšt' ʿBYDWNd ʾYK drwst' YHSNNym wʾhrʾm gwpt' ʾYK drwst' dʾršnyh MN KLʾ MNW YSBHNyt BʾYHWNst' ŠLYTʾ:
>
> If two men jointly sell a thing to one person and make the (following) agreement: "we shall preserve (it) intact", then, Vahrām has said that he

101 For example, Ps 115.3 ואלהינו בשמים כל אשר־חפץ עשה "Our God is in the heavens; he does whatever he pleases," for more detail, see Hurvitz, 1982.

102 For other religious contexts, see Greenfield, 1987; in the Islamic legal tradition, the delineation of rights frequently appears in transactions with the verb ش ي أ (to wish, to will, to desire), see Frantz-Murphy, 1989, 98.

103 Shaked & Ford, 2013, bowls, 50–4.

104 Nyberg, 1988, 88.

(the buyer) has the right to demand the preservation of the thing from whichever (of them) he wishes.[105]

The delineation of rights is found not only in Bactrian and Pahlavi legal terminologies; the Sogdian slave sale deed contains this phrase as well, and like Pahlavi, the verb k'm't 'krty is equivalent to צבי in Aramaic:

> wβyw šmny y'nsy'n xwty 'PZYšy 'xw BRY 'PZY 'xw npyšn 'PZY 'xw pδy 'PZY ZKh 'wzyh pr k'm'kw x'w't rnp'tw βynt't pr'yδ't np'kw 'wsty't r'tw βxš't prβxš't wn'tw wyspy 'cwtyšn "δprmw k'm't 'krty
>
> Accordingly, the monk Yansyan himself and his sons, grandsons, family, and descendants may at hit her, abuse her, bind her, sell her off, pledge her, give and offer her as a gift, and do whatsoever they may wish to [do to her].[106]

In summation, two common elements of entitlement clauses in the Aramaic legal corpora that did not undergo change are שליט and צבי. These two terms are certainly reflected either as an Aramogram, in Pahlavi, or translated into local languages, Bactrian and Sogdian.

10 Heritability Phrase

The heritability phrase occurs in the investiture, warranty, and withdrawal clauses. Usually, the issuer confirms a right or obligation that will outlive the parties in the document. Therefore, in an investiture clause, the rights of ownership continue beyond the lifetime of the addressee mentioned in the conveyance and pass to the children. Moreover, in a warranty clause, a no-contest or a withdrawal, where we also have found these same references to heirs, the legal obligations of the issuer continue even after death and pass to the children and their descendants.[107] In all documents, regardless of type, the heritability phrase in Bactrian contracts is usually recorded as βραδο πορο φραζινδδινανο (brothers, sons (and) descendants). Following a brief history of the heritability phrase, I have addressed the question below of why it includes brothers as well as sons in Bactrian deeds.

105 MHD, 6, 13–14; Perikhanian, 1997, 38f.
106 Yoshida, 2003, 160.
107 Yaron, 1960a, 258.

11 History of the Heritability Phrase

The heritability phrase serves a similar function to perpetuity language because both permanently affirm the rights of the new owner. Yaron has suggested that the heritability phrase does not appear in Assyrian or Babylonian documents.[108] Instead, the heritability phrase first appears in legal deeds from Ugarit in Ugaritic as **w l bnh** (and to his sons) and in Akkadian **u ištu qāti mārīšu** (and to his sons).[109] This phrase is similar to the Biblical phrase (לך ולזרעך אחריך),[110] and in Aramaic conveyances it's a common feature.

In the investiture clause after the rights of the addressee,[111] Aramaic papyri from Elephantine include the formula ובניכי אחריכי "and your sons after you."[112] The Aramaic papyri from Wadi al-Daliyah employ the same phrase:

עבד יהוה לה ולבנוהי מן אחרוהי לעלמא

He will be a slave of his and of his sons after him in perpetuity.[113]

Throughout Aramaic deeds from the Hellenistic period, the heritability phrase is spelled ירתהן (heirs)[114] rather than ובניכי אחריכי. Notably, the same phrase appears in the Syriac slave sale deed:

ܐܢܬ ܬܝܪܘ ܙܒܘܢܐ ܘܝܪܬܟܝ

You, Tiro, the buyer, and your heirs.[115]

---

108 Yaron, 1960b, 386.

109 Marquez Rowe, 2006, 249ff.

110 נָתַתִּי לְךָ וּלְזַרְעֲךָ אַחֲרֶיךָ אֵת אֶרֶץ מְגֻרֶיךָ אֵת כָּל-אֶרֶץ כְּנַעַן לַאֲחֻזַּת עוֹלָם וְהָיִיתִי לָהֶם לֵאלֹהִים "And I will give to you, and to your offspring after you, the land where you are now an alien, all the land of Canaan, for a perpetual holding; and I will be their God." Gn, 17:8; for more detail, see Yaron, 1960b, 386; Porten, 2003, 66; Gross, 2008, 100 n 33; Both elements (perpetuity language and the heritability phrase appear in e.g., Gen. 13:15; 17:7–10; 17:19; 48:4; Lev. 25:43; Deut. 12:28; Josh. 14:9; and 1 Chr. 28:8. The heritability phrase alone appears in Gen. 9:9; 18:19; 35:12; Deut. 4:40; 12:25; and 2 Sam. 7:12 (= 1 Chr. 17:11). Cf. also Exod. 28:43; 29:29.

111 Botta, 2009, 57f.

112 TAD B2.3:9 Porten, 2003, 66.

113 Gropp, 2001, Pap.1; ibid., 38 n 27.

114 Gross, 2008, 131.

115 Drijvers and Healey, 1999, P. 1.

On the contrary, the cession inscriptions from Palmyra use the old formula בני rather than ירתהן. In a Palmyrene cession inscription, full right is ceded to the addressees and their son and descendant: ולבניהון ולבני בניהון.[116]

The heritability phrase is expressed in Nabataean tomb inscriptions from Mada'in Salih as וילדה ואחרה (their sons and their descendants):

> דנה קברא די עבד כהלן אסיא בר ואלן לנפשה וילדה ואחרה אצדק באצדק עד עלם
>
> This is the tomb which Kahlan the Physician, son of Wa'lan, made for himself and his children and descendants by hereditary title forever.[117]

As we have seen, almost all deeds have sons and descendants of the addressee as the heirs, whereas Bactrian deeds have brothers as the heirs alongside children.[118] This decision is due to the practice of fraternal polyandry, a system where brothers share a single wife, which was prevalent in Greater Khurasan.[119] Therefore, mentioning brothers in contracts as heirs seems plausible. Later, except in rare cases,[120] the hereditary phrase is omitted in legal documents from the eastern borders of Islamic lands.

---

116 PAT, 0067; Kottsieper, 2004, 293.

117 Healey, 1993, inscriptions 16, 19.

118 Interestingly, in two Nabataean inscriptions, the owner of the tomb concedes the right to the sons and brothers of the owner as ברה ואחוהי (his son and brothers):

> דנה כפרא די עבד חלפו בר קסנתן לנפשה ולשעידי ברה ואחוהי מה די יתילד לחלפו דנה מן דכרין ולבניהם ואחרהם אצדק באצדק עד עלם
>
> "This is the tomb which Halafu son of Qosnatan made for himself and for Su'aydu, his son, and his brothers, whatever male children may be born to this Halafu, and for their sons and their descendants by hereditary title forever," see, Healey 1993, inscription 24, 36.

119 Crone says: "fraternal (or adelphic) polyandry is a system whereby brothers inherit the property of their parents without dividing it up, cultivate it in common, and share a wife, whose sons will jointly take over the family property in their turn. The system allows the property to pass intact from one generation to the next and seems to be attested particularly where cultivation is difficult (as in hill agriculture) and/or where the men would spend long periods away from home, conscripted as laborers by the state, forced to work for feudal lords, or seeking income away from home as mercenaries or traders; the environment was usually such that it was wise to keep the population small, encouraging female infanticide," see Crone, 2012, 393; in chapter 17 Crone offers a detailed explanation of both the general history of polyandry and its history in Bactria.

120 For example, in a gift deed from Azerbaijan, the donor declares the land belongs to the addressee and his descendants as نسلا بعد نسل عقبا بعد عقب "generation after generation descendant after descendant," see Sheikh Ol-Hokamai, 1384/2005, 563, 570.

12 Contingency or Final Clauses

Contingency clauses protect the addressee (the buyer or donee) from any future challenges to the validity of transactions, whether they are made by the issuer (seller or donor) or by a third party. The final clauses are divided into two parts: no-contest and warranty clauses.

13 No-Contest (Withdrawal) and Warranty Clauses

Even after a transaction was complete, the addressee still faced the potential risk of legal challenges to the validity of the acquisition. As a result, the issuer has the responsibility to uphold and defend the addressee's rights of ownership against any future challenges. I refer to the responsibility of the "issuer" because he is the only one under the obligation of defense if one receives consideration in exchange for the property. Challenges by the issuer and his family are barred by the no-contest clause, while challenges by third parties are covered by the defense clause. However, this definition falls short of the mark. In certain documents, the non-contest and defense clauses are consolidated, becoming one clause and even in one conveyance the defense clause is omitted, as we will see below. Accordingly, there are two types of documents for protecting the rights of the addressee:

1. Shorter version: documents that only include a no-contest clause and a penalty clause (No-contest clause)
2. Longer version: documents containing no-contest, defense, and penalty clauses (Warranty clause)

In the shorter version, the issuer declares that in the future he and his family will protect and recognize the agreement and will not raise any charge against the new owner and if they do, they will pay the fine. Example:

> οδο καλδανο αστηιο μαπορσο ζοριγο αλο αζο þαροοανι(νδο) χοαδο αλο μανο βραδο αλο μανο πορο αλο μανο φορζινδο κιδανο αλαφαγο ιαμþοσπαλο αλο αλο ταο βραδο αλο αλο ταοι πορο αλο αλο ταοι φορζινδ̣ο πιδο μασκο ναβιχτογο ζαμιγο αλο πιδο ιαβο σιδο οαρο ναυαγγο χοανδο ο̇ισαρδο αβζιηιο ταδοιηιο ι̣χοανδο οδο οισαρο μαοαοαρηιο οτο λαηιο μισο αβινδαμο αβο þαυογανο γαζνο ζ̇αροζιδγο διναρο κ' οιστο οδο δαφρηλο φαρο παδαρλογο

> And if in the future[121] there should be (anyone)—whether I, Shar-wanind myself, or my brothers, or my sons, or my descendants-who might

121 In other documents, "from tomorrow (or) at (any) future time." For the history of this phrase in Akkadian and Aramaic documents, see Rabinowitz, 1955, 59f Muffs, 2003, 183f.

continue to claim (or) argue with you, Yamsh-spal, or with your brothers, or with your sons, or with your descendants, concerning the land described herein or concerning the water which (is) adjacent thereto, then his claim and argument shall not be valid, and also he shall pay a penalty to the royal treasury of twenty dinars of struck gold, and the Same to the opposite party.[122]

14 Warranty Clause

Aside from the no-contest clause assuring the addressee against any claims, the warranty clause imposes a two-part obligation on the issuer, namely defending the addressee in court against the third-party claim and compensating him in the event of an unsuccessful defense. The two parts of this obligation could be referred to as the "defense clause" and the "eviction clause." The defense clause is divided into two parts:

15 The Protasis

The obligation of the issuer is invoked whenever anyone makes a claim against the addressee, disputing his title:

> οτο καλδο ανδαρισο κισο ασταδο κιδο μασκο ναβιχτιγο αγγαργο πιδοκαρλαδο οταβο τωμαχο αβο λαδο οδαβο ραζογολο οιηλαδο
>
> And if there should be anyone else who might withhold the property described herein, and might take you to court and to the royal tribunal.

16 The Apodosis

The apodosis normally requires the issuer to protect the addressee against any allegations:

> ταδαζο οιημο οδαζο βαγορημαρηγο οδο ιαμαχο φροζανδανο αβο λαδο λαδο þοαμο οτο αβηβινδο κιραμο ασο <ι̣> παδοιαρλιγο

122 Doc. C; the warranty or peace clause is written in this format with docs. aa, ab, and in five settlements (docs. N, O, R, Uu, X). The issuer (the defendant) assures the addressee (the plaintiff) in these documents that he and his family will not damage or injure him and his family in the future.

Then I, Wyem, and I, Bag-re-mareg, and our descendants shall go to lawsuit (after) lawsuit and shall cause (the property to be) detached from the opposite party.[123]

17 Eviction Clause[124]

In this part, the issuer declares that he will pay a fine if he fails to waive claims and defend the addressee against the third party. For example:

οδαλδο αβο λαδο λαδο ναϸοαμο οτο αβηβινδο νακιραμο ασο παδοιαρλιγο {οδαλδο} {αβο λαδο λαδο ναϸοαμο οτο αβηβινδο νακιραμο ασο παδοιαρλιγο} ταδο δαραφηλο ταοανο τωζαμο σαγονδαβο μασκο ναβισιδο

And if we do not go to lawsuit (after) lawsuit and do not cause (the property to be) detached from the opposite party, then we shall pay the same fine as is written herein.[125]

As mentioned above, the no-contest and warranty clauses are combined in some documents, which can be divided into two groups: the first with, and the second, without the defense clause. Documents in the first group, include the defense and eviction clauses, and the issuer must pay a fine if he fails to defend the addressee against a third party as specified in the warranty:[126]

α̣κιδο πιδο μ̣α̣σκο ναβιχτι̣γο ζαμιγο αβαφαγο βραμα̣ρζο κισο ηβαδο ιωλαδο οισηραδο λαδο̇ χοιναδο λαστανο κιραδο τ̣αδασο οισπο̇ παδαρλιγανο αβηβινδο-κιριμο οδο αβηβινδο νακιρανο οδαβο λαδο̇ λαδο ναϸοοανο ταδο ταο̣ανο τωζανο αβο γαζνο γωζαναγγο ϸαυοζιδαγο δδιναρο ν′ οδο δδιναρο φαροφα̇γο βραμαρζο τωζανο οδο ταοαγ̣γ̣ο̣ β̣ραδο ζαδακο φορζανδανο τωζανο

Whoever may dispute with you, Bramarz, concerning the (piece of) ground described herein, (or) may fight, argue, invoke the law (or) cause litigation, I shall cause (this property to be) detached from every opponent; and if [I do] not cause (this property to be) detached (from the

123 Doc. J.

124 A provision in the event of non-defense by the vendor, see Yaron, 1958, 17f.

125 Docs. J, L', V, W; the position of the warranty and defense clauses has shifted in two recent documents, i.e., the defension clause comes first, followed by the warranty clause.

126 Docs. Nn, P.

opposite party) and do not go to lawsuit (after) lawsuit, then I shall pay a fine to the treasury of Goz(g)an of fifty dinars of gold struck by the king and I shall pay fifty dinars to you, Bramarz, and I shall (likewise) pay (it) to your brothers, children (and) descendants.[127]

However, in the other group, whomever files a claim against the addressee is required to pay the fine himself. For example:

> οδαλδο ασταδ̣ο μαπαρσο ζαμανο αλο αζο οηϸολαδο χοαδο οδαλο μανο πορο οδαλο μανο φροζινδανο οδαλο ανδαρισο κισο κιδο αλο φρωδοκο αλιιο αλο πορα-νανο σιγισο χοηναδο οισηραδο ταδιιο ι χοανδο οδο οισαρο ναοαραδο οτο λ̣α̣υαδο αβ̣ινδ{α̣}αμο φαρο υαστ̣αμογαρανο διναρο οιστο οδο φρηλο φα̣ρο ιπαδαρλ̇ιγανο
>
> And if in the future there should be (anyone)—whether I, Wesh-lad myself, or my sons, or my descendants, or anyone else who might claim or argue with Froduk or with his sons (over) anything, then his claim and argument shall be invalid,[128] and he shall pay a penalty (to their) excellencies of twenty dinars, and the Same to the opponents.[129]

The final clauses of early Mesopotamian contracts only contained a no-contest clause[130] while Old Babylonian warranty clauses are shorter and simpler; in the most common form, both parties swear by the name of the gods or the king that they will not raise any claim against each other in the future:

> u$_4$-kúr-šè lú lú-ra gù nu-gá-gá-a mu ^{d}Za-ba$_4$-ba$_4$ ^{d}Marduk ù Am-mi-ṣa-du-qá ša-ri in-pà-dè-meš
>
> They have sworn by the name of the gods Zababa and Marduk and by the name of the king Ammiṣaduqa that in the future they will not raise any claim against each other.[131]

127 Doc. Nn.

128 For further details, see the Greek papyri from Dura-Eurpos; "and he makes no claim ... of the lots and the vines within them ... in no manner and on no excuse, but if he did, [his claim would be invalid (ακυρον)]", Welles, 1959, P 17 and P 31–2.)

129 Docs. aa, ab, T, Tt, U; in doc. U, the third person is introduced as οδαλο ανδαρο ρωβιιο οδαλο βαμοιανιιο μαρδο ("and or the other men of Rob or of Bamyan").

130 Kienast, 1982, 28ff.

131 Wilcke, 1982, 427ff, doc. MLC 2656.

In certain examples, only one of the parties (usually the seller) swears that he will not bring any claim against the other in the future:

> ud kur$_2$-še$_3$ ^{Id}EN.ZU-i-din-nam ^{geš}kiri$_6$-še$_3$ inim nu-um-ĝa$_2$-ĝa$_2$-a mu lugal-bi in-pad$_3$
>
> He (= Sîn-iddinam) has sworn by the name of the king that in the future Sîn-iddinam shall not raise a claim concerning (this) orchard.[132]

Later, during the first millennium BC the warranty clause in northern and southern Mesopotamia has been expanded to include more information about avoiding future lawsuits:

> ⸢tu-a-ru de⸣-nu DUG$_4$.DUG$_4$ la-áš-šú man-nu šá ina ur-kiš ina ma-te-ma i-za-qu-pa-a-ni lu-u ^{m}TI.LA—KAM-eš lu-u DUMU-MEŠ-šú lu-u DUMU—DUMU-MEŠ-šú TA ^{m}mu-DI—15 denu DUG$_4$.DUG$_4$ ub-ta-ú-ni 10 MA.NA KUG.UD 01 MA.NA KUG.GI [ina] ⸢bur⸣-ki ^{d}IŠ.TAR a-ši-bat ⸢URU⸣.arba-ìl.KI i-šá-⸢kan⸣ [kas]-⸢pu⸣ a-na 10-[MEŠ-te] [a]-⸢na⸣ EN-[MEŠ]-⸢šú GUR⸣-[ra] ina ⸢de-ni⸣-šú DUG$_4$.⸢DUG$_4$⸣-[ma] la ⸢i⸣-laq-[qi]
>
> Any revocation, lawsuit, or litigation is void. Whoever in the future, at any time, lodges a complaint, whether Balaṭu-ereš or his sons or his grandsons and seeks a lawsuit or litigation against Mušallim-Issar shall pla[ce] 10 minas of silver (and) one mina of gold [in] the lap of Ištar residing in Arbela, [and shall return the mon]ey tenfold to its owners. He shall cont[est] in his lawsuit and not succeed.[133]

In Aramaic conveyances from Elephantine, the former owner promises that he and his family will not file any claims against the new owner, but if anyone does, they will defend him. For example:

> לא אכהל אנה ענניה ארשנכי עלדברה דין אף לא יכהל בר לי וברה אח ואחה יגרנכי
> בשם ביתא זך והן אנה גריתכי דין בשם ביתא זך אנה אחוב ואנתן לכי כסף כרשן

132 Spada, 2018, 57.

133 Kwasman and Paropla, 1991, 7 Doc. 6 and Guarantee phrase in slave sale deeds ibid. Doc. 6.
be-⸢en-nu⸣ [ṣib]-⸢tú⸣ a-na 01 me UD-me sa-ar-tú a-na kàl UD-MEŠ-te
(Guaranteed against) epileptic [sei]zures for 100 days (and against) fraud forever) For the final clauses in Neo-Assyrian see Krecher, 1980, 521f and in Neo-Babylonian documents see Oelsner, 2009, 36ff.

2ˉ3 הו חמשה באבני מלכא כסף ר 2 לכרש 1 ולא דין והן גבר אחרן יגרנך דין ינתן לכי
כסף כרשן 20 וביתא אפם זילכי

I shall not be able, I, ʾAnaniah, to bring suit against you on account of it moreover, son of mine or daughter, brother or sister shall not be able to institute suit against you in the name of that house. And if I institute suit against you in the name of that house, I shall be obligated and I shall give you silver, 5 karsh, that is five by the stone (weight)s of the king silver 2 q(uarters) to 1 karsh, without suit. And if another person institute against you suit, he shall give you silver, 20 Karsh. And the house likewise is yours.[134]

However, the warranty clause in Wadi al-Daliyah papyri is similar to the Mesopotamian model:[135]

הן אנה חנניה בר ב[י]דאל [דינן אעבד עמך יהונור והן גבר אחרן דינן יעבד עמך]
יהונור ועם בניך מן אחריך אנה חנניה ובני מן אחרי [אמרק אנתן לך או אשנה
באסרא זנה זי הקימת] עמך אנת יהונור במליא אלה[ואמר]לך א[נ]ת יהונור [כזי
ליהוחנן זנה עבדא לא זבנת לך וכספא ש 20ˉ10ˉ3ˉ2] לא מקבל אנה מנך אף כספא
ש 20ˉ10ˉ3ˉ2 זי יהב[ת לי יהונור אנה חנניה אהתיב אנתן לך אנת יהונור] ואחר חיב
אנה חנניה אשלם [א]נתן לך אנת יהונור [ובניך מן אחריך כסף מנן 3 3 1 לקבל אסרא
זנה תהחסן] זי לא דינן ולא חובן כסף מנן 3ˉ3ˉ1 ליהוחנן זך לא [שליט אנה חנניה
ושליט אנת יהונור ובניך] מן אחריך לקבל זנה אסרא <זי> הקימו ביניהם

If I, Ḥananiah son of Be[y]adʾel [enter into litigation with you, Yehonur, or if someone else enters into litigation with you,] Yehonur, or with your sons after you, I, Ḥananiah, and my sons after me [will clear (the slave of adverse claims and) give (him back) to you. Or if I renege on this bond, which I concluded] with you, you Yehonur, in these terms, [and say to you-y[o]u, Yehonur, [as follows: "Yehoḥanan, this slave, I did not sell you, and the sum of 35 shekels] I have not received from you", then, the sum of 35 sheliels, which [you, Yehonur,] gave [me, I, Ḥananiah, will return to you-you, Yehonur.] And afterwards, I, Ḥananiah, am (still) liable; [I] will pay you-you Yehonur, [and your sons after you 7 silver minas as stipulated in this bond. You may take possession of 7 silver minas without litigation and without liabilities. Over the said Yehohanan [I, Ḥananiah,] do not

134 TAD B3.5 Porten, 1996, 218.
135 Gropp, 2001, 24ff.

> [have authority. But you, Yehonur, and your sons] after you [have authority] as stipulated in this bond <which> they concluded between them ...[136]

The structure of the warranty clause in Bactrian documents is more akin to those from Elephantine than Wadi al-Daliyah. In Pahlavi, the situation is similar to the Bactrian format; the warranty clause cited in the MHD is both an abbreviated version and conceptual translation of the warranty clause attested in the Elephantine legal papyri:

> ˀMT YMLLWNyt ˀYK Lˀ ptkˀrm ˀwgwn ˁBYDWNm ˀYK ptˀ-c dstwbryh y L ˀYŠ Lˀ ptkˀryt' W HT ywdtr ˁBYDWNm tˀyywˀn YHBWNm
>
> If he makes (this) declaration: "I shall not bring suit, and I shall arrange that no one brings suit on my instruction and empowering either, and if I act otherwise, I shall pay the fine."[137]

Regarding, formulation and terminology, the warranty clauses in Sogdian and Khotanese documents differ from those in Bactrian examples. Therefore, they have not been discussed here.

18 Penal Provision (*Duplum* and *Fiskalmult*)

The final section of the eviction clause is a penal provision including two elements: the fined amount and the recipients. The fined amount is doubled in Bactrian deeds, which means if the issuer fails to meet obligations, he must pay twice as much (*in duplum*).[138] The second element is that the issuer pays a fine to the addressee and the state of an equal amount (Fiskalmult)[139] (Table 13).

---

136 Gropp, 2001, P1.

137 Perikhanian, 1997; MHDA 17. 4–5; interestingly, Porten gives a similar brief account of the guarantee clause in Aramaic legal papyri, "I shall not be able to sue you; penalty if I sue; the property is still yours," see Porten, 1996, 81.

138 For more about *duplum* or *stipulatio duplae*, see Berger, 1911, 131f; Taubenschlag, 1955, 326.

139 Berger, 1911, 31ff; 93ff.

TABLE 13

Doc	Fine	Penalty	Place Fiskalmult	Opposite παδαρλογο	Measure	Price
A	ταοανο		ϸαογανο γαζνο	+	20 ζαροζιδγο διναρο	
C		αβινδαμο	ϸαυογανο γανζο	+	20 ζαροζιδγο διναρο	
F	ταοανο		γαζνο βρηδαγανο	+	50 ζαροζιδαγο δ̣ι̣ναρο	25 dinarii!?
J	ταοανο		αβο γαζνο αβο ϸαυαγανο	+	20 ζαροζιδαγο δδιναρ	8 dinarii
L	ταοανο		γαζνο ϸα̣υογανο	+	40 ζαροζιδαγο δδιναρο	20 dinarii
N	ταοανο		ρωβοχαραγγο γαζνο	+	1000 ζαρο δδιναρο	
Nn	Ταοοανο		γαζνο γωζαναγγο	+	50 ζαρο ϸαυοζιδαγο δδιναρο	25 dinarii
O	ταοοανο		γαζνο γωζογανοχοηοαγγο	+	50 ζαροζιδαγο δδιναρο	
P			uncomplete	+		
Q	τα̣οοανο		λαδοβα̣ρο αβο γαζνο	+	80 δδραχμο παρσαγγο	Forty dirhams
R	ταοανο		σκαγογωζογαναγγο γαζνο	+	100 Δραχμο καοοαδο	
S	ταοανο		γαζνο λαδοβαραγγο	+	100 δδραχμο κοοαδο	
T	ταοανο̣		γαζανο βρηδαγανο	+	100 ζαροζιδαγο δδιναρο	
Tt	ταοοανο		γαζνο λαδοβαραγγο	+	500 δδραχμο κοοαδο [π]α̣ν̣ζοσαδο	
U	ταοοανο̣		γαζνο βρηδαγανο	+	100 ζαροζιδαγο δδιναρο 500 δδραχμο (opposite)	Not cash
Uu	ταοανο		γαζανο λαδοβαραγγο		500 Δραχμο κο̣αδο	
V	ταοανο		γαζνο βρηγανο	+	300 δδραχμο σιμιγγο ϸιζγο ωδαγο ο̣ιζινδ-διγο υαρηιοσαδο	150 dirhams

TABLE 13 (*cont.*)

Doc	Fine	Penalty	Place Fiskalmult	Opposite παδαρλογο	Measure	Price
W	ταοανο		γαζνο βρηγανο	+	120 δ̣δραχμο ταζαγο σιμιγγο þιζγο ωδαγο οιζινδδιγο σαδο ρʹ οιστο κʹ	60 dirhams
X	ταοανο		γαζανο βρηδαγανο	+	100 ζαρζιδαγο Διναρο σαδο ρʹ	
Y	ταοοανο		-	-	100 ζαροζιδ̣αγο δδιναρο	
aa	-		γ̣αζ[νο] αβο þηγαν̣ο	+	ζαρ̣ο πανζο̣ dinarii	
ab	-	αβ̣ινδ{α̣}αμο	υαστ̣αμογαρανο	+	20 διναρο οιστο	Maybe 10 dinarii
ad	...		...	+	100 ζαροζιδ̣αγο διναρ̣ο̣ σ̣αδο ρʹ	50 dinarii?

19 *Duplum*

This element is clearly expressed in some documents. The seller declares in slave sale deed that he will pay the fine *in duplum*:

> ταδο α' β' τωζαμο
>
> Then we shall pay (at the rate of) two (to) one.[140]

Alternatively, through a loan contract, the borrower can agree if the loan and its interest are not paid on time, he and his family must pay *in duplum*:

> ο̣[δο]φ̣[α]ρ̣ο α' β' τωζαμο
>
> Then we (borrowers) shall pay (at the rate of) two (to) one.[141]

140 Doc. P.
141 Doc. Q.

Another option is a loan receipt when the receiver of the money promises that if the borrower files a claim against the lender, he (the receiver) must pay twice as much:

> ταδαζο νανηβανδο ι ιωγο πιδο λοο τωζανο
>
> Then I, Nane-band, shall pay (at) the (rate of) two to one.[142]

20 *Duplum* in History

Duplum is a Latin word meaning double. In Roman legal terminology *Actiones in duplum* is "actions in which the defendant is condemned to pay double damages or price paid by the plaintiff when he purchased the object in dispute."[143]

Retribution in *duplum* has a long history in legal practices specifically in the ancient Near East.[144] A few examples have been discussed below. In the early dynastic and Sargonic periods, if a seller breached the contract, he was obliged to repay the purchaser(s) double the price. It was also the standard penalty for loan default.[145] A severe contractual penalty for default in the Neo-Sumerian period was to pay double the loan.[146] Breach of contract by the buyer was penalized with a payment equal to the purchase price in the Old Assyrian period, but if the seller breached the contract, he was penalized with a double payment.[147] In the Old Babylonian period, Hammurabi declares in his law code that if the bride's father refuses to give his daughter in marriage, he must restore double the terḫatum (bride-price) and other payments received.[148] In the Middle Babylonian period, the penalty for breaching a contract was double payment.[149] Furthermore, in the sale of persons and animals, the contract requires the seller to pay twice if the sale item is "vindicated," or

142 Doc.M.

143 Berger, 1953, 446.

144 For a history of *duplum* in ancient Mesopotamia see Limet, 1969, Dombradi, 2000a; 2000b.

145 Wilcke, 2007, 96.

146 Lafont and Westbrook, 2003, 214.

147 Veenhof, 2003, 464, 472; Hertel, 2013, 257, 261f.

148 Westbrook, 2003c, 387; the text states: "if a man has brought a gift to his bride's father's house, and after he has given the bride-price the father of the girl has said, I shall not give you my girl, he shall double the quantity of any gift he has brought to make recompense (*mimma mala ibbablušum uštašannāma utâr*)," LH 160; 124; for details on *šunušû*, see Richardson, 2000, 310.

149 Slanski, 2003, 493.

successfully claimed by a third party.[150] *Duplum* is recorded in the Hittite law as well. In marriage contract cases, the bride's parents might have unilaterally annulled the contract, and now they must restore double the betrothal payment received from the groom.[151] Another example of paying a fine with *duplum* occurred in the late Bronze Age city of Emar, northern Syria, through a document concerning the redemption of a slave. The slave's father or uncle has first priority in redemption; if they fail to free the slave, they must pay twice as much.[152] Later, in Neo-Assyrian legal documents, the divorce clause of a marriage contract states that if the husband divorces his wife due to her hatred for him, he must pay her to double the dowry.[153]

In the Old Testament, two people who disagree about ownership of an animal, a piece of cloth, or other lost property, must "approach God," and the person found guilty must pay twice as much.[154] *Duplum* fines from the aforementioned ages and regions are uncommon in legal documents.

Duplum was not mentioned in Achaemenid Aramaic deeds. Penalties in Aramaic papyri from Elephantine were in multiples of five,[155] whereas in Aramaic papyri from Wadi al-Daliyah, the penalty amount for breach of contract varied by each deed.[156] However, during the Hellenistic period and thereafter, this element appears frequently in documents from Palestine to Bactria.[157]

Avroman documents provide the earliest evidence of *duplum* from the Hellenistic period in the Near East.[158] This element can also be found in Greek deeds from the Judean Desert,[159] while retribution in *duplum* from Dura-Europos was first introduced during the Roman period. Previously, in Dura-Europos under the Arsacid dynasty, the fined amount in the penalty clause was fixed to a certain sum,[160] but after the Romans seized the city, some changes

---

150 Ibid., 509.

151 Haase, 2003; for other examples, see Haase 2011, 62.

152 Westbrook, 2003d, 667; 686; Fijalkowska, 2007, 21.

153 Radner, 2003, 896; 903.

154 Exod. 22:8; Proppt, 2006, 249.

155 Porten, 2011, 154 n16.

156 Gropp, 2001, 27f.

157 Taubenschlag postulated that retribution in *duplum* was first introduced in Egypt during the Roman period, and earlier during the Ptolemaic period, fines were paid in *simplum*, see Taubenschlag, 1955, 349f; however, this does not seem to be accurate because retribution in *duplum* was a special feature for sales of immovable property in Greek deeds dating to the Ptolemaic period, see Keenan et al., 2014, 301.

158 See below, section Fiskalmult.

159 Lewis, 1989, 40; Oudshoorn, 2007, 124; Lewis believes that retribution in *duplum* was known to Jewish law from Exodus and thereafter.

160 See Welles, 1959, P. 18–20.

in legal practice occurred, including the payment of fines in *duplum*.[161] In contrast to Greek documents, in Aramaic documents from the Judean Desert, fines were not paid in *duplum*. Lewis believes that retribution in duplum was used under the Nabatean kings.[162] However, Oudshoorn rightly noted that Lewis' suggestion about duplum in Nabataean papyri 2–3 is not accurate;[163] the text does not mention that the fine will be doubled:

> והן אנה אביׄעדׄן דא א······ ואשנ{נ}א מן דנה [די] ל[א ברשא] אׄחׄובׄ לך אׄנׄתׄ ארכלס
> [דנ]ה ··כׄלׄ דׄמׄיׄ זבניא אלה ובׄכׄלׄכׄל די אבעא ויׄתׄב[עא] בשמי עליך בׄהׄמׄ ולמראנא
> רבאל מלכא כות
>
> And if I, this (same) 'Abbcadan, will ..., or will deviate from this (agreement) [with]ou[t authority] then I shall owe to you, [this] (same) Archelaus, the entire price of these purchases, and for all and everything that I may claim, or that may be clai[med] in my name against you regarding them. And, as well, to our lord, Rab'al.[164]

21 *Fiskalmult*

The *Fiskalmult*, or paying fines for breach of contract to the sovereign or state treasury, is the second element of the penal provision. This feature can be found in some Hellenistic Greek and Aramaic documents from various areas, with the first in legal documents from Ptolemaic Egypt.[165] However, the earliest evidence originated in the Seleucid territories from Avroman. An example is document A, when the seller agrees to defend the buyer against any future

161 See Welles, 1959, P. 25–6; however, this *duplum* differs from that in Bactria. If the seller fails to defend the buyer against any claims (defence) in Dura-Europos, he must pay the fine in *duplum* as well as other losses:
Εαν δε μη καθαροποιησῃ βλαβη δε τι ο Ηλιοδωρος δια ταυτα εκτι σειν αυτωι παν ο αν γενηται αυτωι βλαβος διπλουν κια επιτιμον αργυριου δραχμας πεντακοσιασ
"If he does not establish a clear title, and Heliodorus suffers any loss, in consequence, he will pay to him double the amount of whatever loss has occurred and an additional penalty of 500 drachmae" (Welles, 1959, P. 26.)

162 Lewis, 1989, 40.

163 Oudshoorn, 2007, 124 n. 93.

164 P. Yadin 2. Thus, Healey's suggestion about duplum in p. Yadin 2 is wrong, see Healey, 2013, 172.

165 Berger, 1911, 31ff; 93ff; for Greek deeds, see Cowley and Markesh, 2001, 106f; for Demotic documents, see Felber, 1997, 186f.

claims, and if he fails, he must pay the *duplum* price plus an additional fine to the new owner (the buyer), as well as the same amount to the king:

> Ες ται ακυρος και προσαποταεισει εν ελαβεν τειμην διπλην και αλλας επιτειμου δραχμας Σ και τω βασιλει τας ισας
>
> He shall lose his rights and pay double the price he received and an additional fine of 200 drachmae and to **the King** an equal sum.[166]

This phrase appears frequently in Greek deeds from Dura-Europos and Palestine, specifically, the element appears in Greek deeds before and after Roman sovereignty, but the formulation changed due to differences in administration between the two systems; εις δε το βασιλικον τας ισας (and the same amount to the crown) in the Parthian Period[167] or τω φυσκω τας εισας (a similar amount to the Fiscus),[168] and τω ειροτατω ταμιειω (and an equal sum to the most sacred treasury)[169] in the Roman period.[170] In the Aramaic deeds from the Judean Desert the phrase occurs in some documents as ולמראנא קיסר כות (and for our lord, Caesar, as well)[171] or ולמראנא רבאל מלכא כות (and for our lord Raba'al, the king, as well).[172] This type of penalty is recorded not only in papyri transactions, but also in the Nabataean tomb inscriptions from Mada'in Salih. For example:

> ומן יעבד כעיר מה די עלא כתיב פאיתי עמה לדושרא אלהא בחרמא די עלא לדמי מגמר סלעין אלף חרתי ולמראנא חרתת מלכא כות
>
> And whoever does other than what is written above shall be liable to the god Dushara regarding the inviolability referred to above, for the full price of a thousand Haretite Sela's and to our lord king Haretat for the same amount.[173]

166 P. A, B Avoraman, Minns, 1915.

167 P. 19–22, 24 Dura-Europos, Welles, 1959.

168 sury of the prince or emperor; Gradner et al., 2009, 712.

169 P. 32; in ancient Rome, the name aerarium (in full, "*aerarium stabulum*," treasure-house) was given to the public treasury; Gradner et al., 2009, 65.

170 Welles, 1959, 16.

171 P. Yadin 8; for a new edition with commentary of this text, see Newman, 2006.

172 P. Yadin 2–4; Yadin et al., 2002, 247ff; Newman assumes in P. Yadin 5, a fragmentary Greek document, the phrase και καισαρι ωσαυτως (and for Caesar as well) is a part of the penalty clause. Newman, 2004, 250.

173 Healey, 1993, inscription 1, and inscriptions 12, 19, 34, 36, 38; Healey, 1994, 211 note 19.

This penalty is recorded in Greek tomb inscriptions from Lycia; the delinquent was liable for prosecution for ασεβεια (impiousness), which involved a fine, and were to pay damages to the treasury as well.[174]

In summary, it seems that the penalty clause in Bactrian documents was established during the Hellenistic period in the form containing *duplum* and *Fiskalmult*. Prior to that, the penalty amount and its recipients were most likely similar to stipulations in Aramaic deeds from the Achaemenid era.

22 *Clausula Salvatoria* and Validity Clause

I've discussed how the issuer was fined for failing to defend the addressee against any claim made by him, his family, or a third party. After the fine was paid, the addressee would have unhindered possession of the property, and the conveyance would remain valid. In legal parlance, this is known as *clausula salvatoria* or the status quo ante (the state in which before).[175]

In any type of document, especially in transactions and settlements, this clause is always recorded alongside the validity clause.[176] For example:

> οτο ιϑασο παρσο τογδο ταοανο πιτανοβωστιγο μολραγο χοζο οαοαρο αβοδηιο σαγονδαβο μασκο ναβισιδο
>
> And so, after the fine has been paid, may (this) guarantee-contract, (this) sealed document, be (considered) good and valid as (it) is written herein.[177]

On the history of *clausula salvatoria*, Skaist believes, based on the evidence, that it first appeared in 14th-century BCE in Akkadian documents from Ugarit. Later, there is sufficient evidence for the *clausula salvatoria* in Neo-Assyrian legal deeds, although the clause is never developed in Neo-Babylonian conveyances.[178] The device appears frequently in Aramaic papyri from Elephantine, and it's distinguished in conveyance deeds by the words (adverbs) אפם

174 Arkwright, 1911, 271.

175 Blackwell, 2008, 470; Garner et al., 2009, 1543.

176 The *clausula salvatoria* in Bactrian deeds, much like the *clausula salvatoria* in Greek deeds from Dura-Europos, serves two functions simultaneously, similarly to *clausula salvatoria* and the validity clause; for more information, see the section on the Validity Clause.

177 Doc. N; however, the *clausula salvatoria* is omitted in three of the sale deeds; doc. L concludes with the fine clause, while docs. aa and ab reach the conclusion with the names of the witnesses and the scribe.

178 Skaist, 1983, 37f.

(still, nonetheless, as well)[179] אם (also, furthermore)[180] תוב (again, moreover).[181] The word אפם occurs far more frequently than the others in documents:

הן כליתך אנתן לך כסף כרשן 5 באבני מלכא כסף צריף ואגרא זך אפם

> If I restrain you, I shall give you silver, 5 Karsh by the stone-weights of the king, pure silver and that wall is yours as well.[182]

In certain cases, the word אם replaces the usual אפם:

זי יגרנכי דין ו<ד>בב אנה ואח ואחה קרב ורחק בעל דגל ובעל קריה ינתן לכי כסף כרשן 10 ובית אם דילכי

> Whoever will institute against you suit or (pro)cess—I, or brother or sister, near or far, member of a detachment or member of a town—shall give you silver, 10 karsh and (the) house is likewise yours.[183]

In any case, whenever the validity of the conveyance was challenged, the contestant was required to pay a penalty, and the conveyance remained valid.[184] From the Hellenistic period onwards, the *clausula salvatoria* formed part of the penalty clause in Greek legal practice, and it appears at the end of the document before the names of witnesses as

> χωρις του μενειν κυρια τα προγεγραμμενα or και μηδεν ησσον μενειν κυρια τα προγεγραμμενα

179 Schwiderski, 2009, 76.

180 Ibid., 50.

181 Ibid., 828.

182 TAD, B2.1; TAD B2.2, 2.3, 2.9, 2.10; 3.5, 3.9, 3.13; 5.5, 3.13; for further details, see Porten, 1996, 155 n.19.

183 TAD, B2.7, 3.4, 3.10, 3.11; for further details, see Porten, 1996, 155 n.19; only in one document the word תוב (again, moreover) occurs instead of אפם / אם
וזי יגרנכי במנתא זכי זי יהבן לכי ינתן לכי כסף כרשן 3־2 ומנתכי זילכי תוב
"And whoever shall institute (suit) against you in (regard to) that share which we gave you shall give you silver, 5 Karsh, and your share is yours furthermore" see TAD, B 5.1; Porten, 1996, 256 n.11; despite the fact that the terms differ, there does seem to be no legal distinction between them.

184 Rabinowitz, 1956, 50.

> Consequently, the agreement remains in effect, or what has previously been stated remains in effect.[185]

This clause is inserted in conveyances, e.g., land leases, sales, etc.[186] The clause is recorded in Greek deeds from Dura-Europos as follows:

> Και την συγγραφην ταυτην ειναι και ουτως κυριαν
>
> And to hold this contract as valid nevertheless[187]

Even in Bactria, the *clausula salvatoria* was used before the Hellenistic period; most likely, the *clausula salvatoria* in Bactrian deeds follows a Greek pattern established during the Hellenistic period.

23 Validity Clause

Almost all Bactrian legal documents conclude with a validity clause. As previously stated, the phrase μολραγο χοζο οαοαρο αβοδηιο σαγονδαβο μασκο ναβισιδο (the sealed document, be (considered) good and valid as (it) is written herein) serves as both the *clausula salvatoria* and validity clause together. In the second role, the phrase provides absolute dependability to the document.

Skaist thoroughly examined the validity clause and its history and function throughout the Near East from ancient times to the early Middle Ages in a study on the Talmudic closing formula כל שריר וקיים.[188] I will not summarize the article here, instead, I will examine some texts he has ignored or that have since been published. The validity clause in Bactrian deeds, contains four words—the first three, in descending order of frequency, are οαοαρο, χοζο and word παρμανο (autoreactive), and they can occur with or without other words preceding them. The fourth word, οηζο (potent), appears only in three later deeds (Table 14).

185 See Berger, 1911, 47ff.

186 Taubenschlag, 1955, 300, n 46.

187 Welles, 1959; Dura 17, 18, 19, 20, 21, 22, 25, 26, 27, 31; remarkably, the word ουτως much like the words תוב / אם /אפם and μηδεν ησσον in Greek documents from Egypt serve the same purpose, namely to return to the previous state.

188 Skaist, 1980.

TABLE 14

Document	Good	Potent	Valid	Authoritative
C	χοζο	–	Οαοαραδο	–
F	χοζο	–	Οαοαρηιο	–
J	χοζο	–	οαοαρο	–
L		–	–	–
N	χοζο	–	οαοαρο	
N‘	–	–	οαοαρο	Παρμανο
Nn	χοζο	–	οαοαρο	–
O	χοζο	–	οαοαρο	–
Q	–	–	οοοαρο	Παρμανο
R	χοζο	–	οοοαρο	–
S		–	οαοαρο	Παρμανο
T	χοζο	–	οαοαρο	Παρομανο
T‘	–	–	οαοαρο	–
U‘	χοζο	–	οοοαρο	Παρμανο
Uu	–	–	–	Παρμανο
Uv	χοοζο		οο'οαρο	
V	χοζο	οηζο	οαυοοαρο (οδο)	Παρμανο
W	χοζο	οηζο	οαυοαρο	Παρμανο
X	χοζο	οοηζο		Παρμανο
X‘	–	–	–	Παρμανο
aa	–	–	–	–
ab	–	–	–	–
ad	χοζο		οαοαρο	–

In addition to the validity clause in Aramaic papyri from Elephantine and Greek deeds from Ptolemaic Egypt, there is further evidence for the validity clause in the Dura-Europos Greek deeds. As noted above, the *clausula salvatoria* in Greek deeds from Dura-Europos serves two functions and can also be considered a validity clause.

In the Aramaic deeds from the Judean Desert the word קים[189] means valid, and two documents are close to this word:

189 Sokoloff, 2003, 77.

וקים לקבלדך

It (document) is valid accordingly,[190]

or

קתרא דנן יהוא קים

This "tie" shall be valid.[191]

The validity clause, שריר וקיים (firm and established)[192] according to Talmudic tradition, must be written at the end of the document. This rule is mentioned in the Talmud Bavli, as follows:

וניחוש דלמא זייף ותב מאי דבעי ו חתימי סהדי דכתיב ביה שריר ו קיים וניחוש דלמא כתב מאי דבעי והדר כתב שריר וקיים חד שריר וקיים כתבינן תרי שריר וקיים לא כתבינ

But let us be concerned perhaps [the holder of the document] will falsify and write whatever he wishes—having witness signed already signed—? that "firm and established" are written into (the end) of [a bound document But let us be concerned that perhaps [the holder of the document] may write whatever he wishes and then write firm and established a second time we write "firm and established" once we do not write "firm and established" twice.[193]

The Talmud Yerushalmi expresses the same rule in the form קיים שריר וברור:

שייר סקעת הגט כול. מהו שייר. אמר רבי יוסי בר ביבון. כגון קיים שריר וברור

190 Yadin, 2002, 142ff; Yadin 42.

191 Yadin, 2002, 150ff; Yadin 43; for a Nabataean tomb inscription from Mada'in Saleh.
מן די ינפק בידה כתב מן יד כמכם או כליבת ברתה בכפרא הו פקים
"Who produces a document in his handwritten by Kamkam or her daughter with regards the tomb this document is valid," see Healey, 1993, inscription 16.

192 The same combination of שריר וקים appears at the end of the main text of magic bowls from Mesopotamia. For example, דין קמיעה [יהוי] שריר וקים ([may] this Amullet[be] firm and established), see Shaked and Ford, 2013, Bowls, 7:14; for more examples, see Shaked & Ford, 2013, Bowls 25:11, 40:6, 55: 14, 61, 7; Levene, 2014, (VA.2423:16, VA.2424:15, VA.2417:13,) M102:14, M163:28, 30.

193 TB Baba Barṭa, 160a.

> "If some of the text remained" etc. What does "remained" mean? Rebbi Yose ben Rebbi Baibon said, e.g., "true, valid, and clear."[194]

Two similarities exist between the validity clause in Talmudic texts and Bactrian examples. Firstly, the clause is placed at the end of documents, before the names of the witnesses, as well as their signatures and seals. Secondly, unlike Greek documents from Egypt and Dura-Europos, complementary terms are used in the formulation of the clause in these two traditions.[195] Nonetheless, the development of this clause within these two traditions has a different history. The Talmudic formula is a synthesis of two earlier traditions; the first word, קים, occurs in Aramaic documents from the Judean Desert (Palestine), while the second, is attested in Syriac legal literature[196] and the Palmyrene tax tariff (Mesopotamia).[197]

The vocabulary of the formula in Bactrian, on the other hand, is a mix of Iranian and Indian terms; the word οαυοαρο in the validity clause is the Bactrian version of the Pahlavi word wābar:

> ˀywk' GBRˀ MNW pšt' ˁBYDWNyt ˀYK YHWWNt' y ZNH MNDˁM rˀd pt mwdr y wˀprykˀn GBRˀ nˀmk' YHYTYWNm ˁMT pt mwdr y ˁLH MNW pt gwkˀyyh mwdr y pt' wˀprykˀnyh MKBLWNt YKˁYMWNyt nˀmk' YHYTYWNyt hwp'

> A (decision is this): A man makes a contract, in as following: "I will bring a document with the seal of a trustworthy man." If he brings a document with the seal of the one bearing witness, the document will be accepted as valid. It (the decision) is lawful.[198]

---

194 TY, Giṭṭin, 9. Halakha 9 Guggenheimer, 2007, 397; the formula at the end of documents is mentioned as affirming the validity, which appears at the end of almost all known Jewish documents from the Gaonic period and thereafter, see Friedmann, 1980, 478f.

195 The validity clause in Egypt often is η συγγραφη ηδε κυρια εστω πανταχε επιφερομενη (this document is valid wherever produced), see Pringsham, 1950, 138f; Wolff, 1978, 145f.

196 See ܫܪܝܪܐ in Sokoloff, 2009, 1607f and ܫܛܪܐ ܫܪܝܪܐ (valid document) in Sachau, 1914, 188 §5.

197 Skaist, 1980, XLIII; Skaist suggested that in the tariff of Palmyra שריר is the Aramaic equivalent of κυρια in the Greek version of the text; see Shifman, 2014, and in Glossaries שרר (to decree, affirm) & κυροω (to confirm).

198 MHD, 93.11–14, and 34.15–35.1. Moreover, the word χοζο in Bactrian is equated with the word xub (good) in Pahlavi, providing the same function in legal contexts where it means "lawful." For example:

> Pt gwpt' y dstwrbˀn ˀwgwn npšt' ˀYK ywkhy putscytˀ ˀMT zyndk' ˀB' šwd ˁBYDWNyt hwp

Whereas, the other term, παρμανο, is a Sanskrit loan word, **pramāṇa-**, which is attested in other eastern middle Iranian languages as well (Sogdian and Khotanese, see below).

The validity clause can also be found in two other Middle Iranian legal formularies: Sogdian and Khotanese. In Sogdian, two documents contain this clause; one is in a slave sale contract from Turfan as:

> rty ZNH δ'ypwsty ... wyspy n'βyh šwyn'k prm''n
>
> And this slave girl sale contract is for all the people valid and authorative.[199]

And the other occurs in the marriage contract from Mount Mug:

> ZNH n'm'k ... wyspy n'ßy prm'n ZY šw'm'k
>
> This contract ... is authorative and valid for all the people.[200]

Both documents use the same terms for the validity clause: prm'n and šw'm'k. while in Khotanese legal documents only the word pramāṇa- appears as follows:

> ttī ṣä pīḍakä prąmāṃ khu hā darmapuñä haṃguṣṭä viśtä
>
> This contract is authorative when darmapuña places his finger on it.[201]

Apart from differences in formulation, the common feature among these three middle Iranian languages are the presence of the Sanskrit loan word pramāṇa-. This term is found in the Kharoṣṭhi documents[202] and ancient Indian legal terminology.[203] Undoubtedly, the Sanskrit term entered eastern Middle Iranian legal terminologies via Indian administration in Central Asia. However, it is

---

"According to the declaration of the authorities of law the following is written, if an epikleros-daughter (yō hē pasčaēta) will marry during her father's lifetime, (this marriage) is lawful" (MHD, 22.1–2 Perikhanian, 1997, 68f.)

199 Yoshida, 2003, 160 my translation is based on Yakubovich's commentary. see Yakubovich, 2006, 328.

200 Doc. 4 in Livshitz, 2008.

201 Skjaervo, 2017, 458f.

202 For an example of the word pramana, see doc. 568 (CKD 568) parmana yavajiva (its authority is as long as life) for more examples see https://gandhari.org/dictionary/pramana.

203 Monier-Williams, 1899, 685 Column 3; furthermore, it is an important term in Indian philosophy, see Cush et al., 2008, 625f; for Buddhism, see Buswell and Lopez, 2014, 660f.

unclear when this occurred.[204] In any case, the origin of the clause is clearly Greek, not Indian.

The synonymous and complementary words and phrases in the validity clause serve a common purpose and are suitable for making any relevant point of a legal event certain and explicit through linguistic dissection.[205] According to an examination of the penalty and validity clauses, the final form of the warranty clause in Bactria was completed during the Hellenistic period.

204 For more information of the validity clause in eastern Iranian languages. See Sheikh, 2019.

205 See Chapter 2, the section *Figurae per adiectionem*.

Conclusion

Legal practices in the languages and societies throughout the ancient Near East changed and evolved over time. In this regard, Bactrian deeds reflect some of these changes and developments. Hereupon, this study has demonstrated the differences and similarities between Bactrian and other traditions in the region. We can follow these changes and developments throughout history by using documents to retrace their trajectories. The structure of legal documents in Bactrian was established during the Achaemenid period, and while some changes occurred in the Hellenistic period, it remained mostly stable. Later, in the Kushan and Sasanian periods, Bactrians made minor changes to documentary forms but did not alter the overall structure.

Based on these developments and changes, the history of the Bactrian legal formulary could be divided into three phases: Achaemenid, Hellenistic, and Kushano-Sasanian. It appears that the structure was similar to other Aramaic legal documents from the Achaemenid Empire. However, some elements in Bactrian documents not attested in Aramaic documents from other satrapies of the Persian Empire, including the *clausula salvatoria* and nail press instead of sealing, were borrowed from the Mesopotamian tradition. Structures changed in some places in the Hellenistic period. The declaration clause was changed from indirect to direct subjective, and the Greek form of declaration, homologia, was introduced, and in other Near Eastern lands. The witnesses are mentioned in the first lines; however, it is likely that the inclusion of their names was introduced later, in the time of the Kushans. Furthermore, the final version of the validity clause was incorporated into legal terminology in the Sasanian period. Simultaneously, a financial penalty in double (*duplum*) for breach of contract was introduced, payable to both the state (*Fiskalmult*) and the offended party. During this time, double copies became common throughout the Near East. Despite the fact that this practice died out in the eastern territories of the Roman Empire in the 4th-century CE, Bactrians continued to use the format until the Islamic formulary succeeded and it vanished forever. Some amendments and developments are introduced after the Bactrian language became the official idiom in Bactria during the 2nd century CE, e.g., the cause clause, location in an official place, title, naming the witnesses in the first lines by name, and adding complementary words and phrases to the text to make the content of the contract more explicit.

In the first half of the 8th-century, Muslims conquered the region, significantly changing the legal norms, and eventually, the formulary. They also would introduce the Greek legal formulary from Egypt but with certain

 | DOI:10.1163/9789004519985_006

changes based on their beliefs. Additionally, dropped terms and clauses from earlier times sometimes arise in a fossilized form of contracts.[1] The Bactrian legal formulary is a synthesis of several traditions, ranging from Mesopotamian to Greek. Although my research focused on the micro-level (specific terminology), demonstrating how closely the Bactrian tradition was related to others, namely Aramaic and Greek, when examined on a macro level (the level of legal ideas),[2] the potential for further connections and affinities between Bactrian and other legal traditions is certain.[3]

1 For the satisfaction clause, see Frantz- Murphy, 1988, 106.

2 I borrow these two terms, micro level and macro level, from Wells, 2012, 127.

3 Numerous studies have been conducted on the relationship between cuneiform and Jewish traditions. For example, see Westbrook and Wells, 2009; Greengus, 2011; Levine, 2002; 2004; Holtz, 2001.

Appendix

Structure of the Bactrian legal formulary and historical backgrounds of its elements

Element	Tradition
Date-Formula at Beginning	Aramaic
Title	Bactrian
Place	Aramaic and Greek
Witness at the first line	Bactrian
Declaration	Aramaic Subjective indirect in the Achaemenid period+
Subjective	Greek and Aramaic in Hellenistic Period subjective direct
Volition clause	Mesopotamian
Cause clause	Bactrian
Description of property	Mesopotamian
	From east Aramaic
Clausula salvatoria	Mesopotamian
Full price	Mesopotamian
Satisfaction clause	Mesopotamian
Entitlement clause	Aramaic
Non-contest clause	Aramaic
Warranty clause	Aramaic
Fine in *duplum*	Greek
Fiskalmult	Greek
Validity clause	Greek Final version
Double copies	Greek (Mesopotamian)
complements	Bactrian
signature	Greek
Nail press	Mesopotamian

 | DOI:10.1163/9789004519985_007

Bibliography

Abdelaziz, Mehdi: 2010. "Les formules juridiques dans les contrats nabatéens". In: Démare-Lafont and Lemaire, 2010, 321–336.

Al-Bīrūnī, Abū-Reyhān Muhammad bin Ahmad: 1380/2001. Al-Āṯār Al-Bāqīya. Edited by Parviz Azkāei. Tehran: Mirās-e Maktub.

Altman, Amnon: 2012. *Tracing the Earliest Recorded Concepts of International Law: The ancient Near East (2500–330 BCE)*. Leiden: M. Nijhoff Publishers.

Arkwright, W: 1911. "Penalties in Lycian Epitaphs of Hellenistic and Roman Times". *JHS* 31: 269–275.

Arnaud, Daniel: 2013. "Textes du Levant (Supplément)". *Aula Orientalis* 31: 5–15.

Avigad, Nahman: 1986. *Hebrew bullae from the time of Jeremiah: remnants of a burnt.* Jerusalem: Israel Exploration Society.

Bagnall, Roger: 2009. *Everyday Writing in the Graeco-Roman East.* Berkley: University of California Press.

Baker, Heather D.: 2004. *The archive of the Nappāḫu family.* Vienna: Instituts für Orientalistik.

Bamberger, Avigail Manekin: 2015a. "Jewish Legal Formulae in the Aramaic Incantation Bowls". *Aramaic Studies* 13: 69–81.

Bamberger, Avigail Manekin: 2015b. "Naming Demons: The Aramaic Incantation Bowls and Gittin". http://thegemara.com/naming-demons-the-aramaic-incantation-bowls-and-gittin/.

Baums, Stefan: 2018. "A new Gāndhārī document from Niya". In: *Reading Slowly: A Festschrift for Jens E. Braarvig*. Edited by Lutz Edzard, Jens W. Borgland and Ute Hüsken. 59–70. Wiesbaden: Harrassowitz Verlag.

Beckman, Gary: 1988. "Three Tablets from the Vicinity of Emar". *JCS* 40: 61–8.

Beckman, Gary: 1996. *Texts from the Vicinity of Emar in the Collection of Jonathan Rosen.* Padova: SARGON.

Beckman, Gary: 1997. "Real Property Sales at Emar". In: Young et al., 1997, 95–120.

Beckman, Gary: 2017. "Zeuge (witness). B. Bei den Hethitern. *RlA* 15: 259–60.

Bellotto and Simonetta Ponchia (eds): 2009. *Witnessing in the Ancient Near East: I testimoni nella documentazione del Vicino Oriente antico*. Padova: SARGON.

Benjamin, Craig: 2018. *Empires of Ancient Eurasia. The First Silk Roads Era, 100 BCE–250 CE*. Cambridge: Cambridge University Press.

Benoit, P., J. T. Milik and R. de Vaux: 1961. *Les grottes de Murabbaʿât.* Oxford: Clarendon Press. (Avec des contributions de G. M. Crowfoot)

Berger, Adolf: 1911. *Die Strafklauseln in den Papyrusurkunden.* Leipzig: Teubner.

Berger, Adolf: 1953. *Encyclopedic dictionary of Roman law.* Philadelphia: American Philosophical Society.

Berges, Dietrich: 1993. "Tonsiegel aus dem karthagischen Tempelarchiv". *Mitteilungen des Deutschen Archäologischen Instituts, Römische Abteilung* 100: 245–68.

Bilabel, F. 1924: "Zur Doppelausfertigung ägyptischer Urkunden". *Aegyptus* 5: 153–73.

Bilabel, F. 1925: "Zur Doppelausfertigung ägyptischer Urkunden". *Aegyptus* 6: 93–113.

Blackman, Philip (ed. and trans.): 1951–6. *Mishnayoth*. London: Mishna Press.

Blackwell, Amy Hackney: 2008. *The Essential Law Dictionary*. Naperville, Il: Sphinx Publishing.

Blau, Ludwig: 1912. "Zur demotischen und griechischen Papyrusurkunde". In: *Judaica: Festschrift zu Hermann Cohens siebzigstem Geburtstage*, 207–26. Berlin: Bruno Cassirer.

Bordreuil, Pierre, and Pardee, Dennis: 2009. *A manual of Ugaritic*. Winona Lake: Eisenbrauns.

Botta, Alejandro (ed.): 2013. *In the Shadow of Bezalel: Aramaic, biblical, and ancient Near Eastern studies in honor of Bezalel Porten*. Leiden: Brill.

Botta, Alejandro: 2006a. "The Legal Function and Egyptian Background of the שליט Clause: A Reevaluation". *Maarav* 13: 193–209.

Botta, Alejandro: 2006b. "רחק in the Bible, a Re-evaluation". *Biblica* 87: 418–20.

Botta, Alejandro: 2008a. "A Reevaluation of the use of זבן and יהב in Elephantine". *Antiguo Oriente* 6: 99–108.

Botta, Alejandro: 2008b. "How long does an eternal covenant last? עולם in the Light of Aramaic-Egyptian Legal Documents". *The Bible translator* 59: 158–63.

Botta, Alejandro: 2009. *The Aramaic and Egyptian legal traditions at Elephantine*. London: T&T Clark.

Botterweck, G.J. and H. Ringgren (eds.): 1977–2004. *Theological Dictionary of the Old Testament*. Grand Rapids, MI: William B. Eerdmans.

Boussac, Marie-Francoise and Antonio Invernizzi (ed.): 1996. *Archives et sceaux du mondehellénistique: Archivi e sigilli nel mondo ellenistico*. Athens: École Française d'Athène.

Boyer, G: 1939. "Ṣupur x kima kunnukišu". In: *Symbolae ad iura Orientis antique pertinentes Paulo Koschaker dedicatae*. Edited by J.G. Friedrich, J. Lautner and J. Miles, 208–18. Leiden: Brill.

Boyer, G.: 1955. "La Place des textes d'Ugarit dans l'Histoire de l'Ancien Droit oriental". In: Nougayrol, 1955, 283–308.

Bregstein, Linda: 1996. "Seal use in fifth century B.C. Nippur, Iraq: A study of seal selection and sealing practices in the Murašû Archive". In: Boussac and Invernizzi, 1996, 53–63.

Briant, Pierre: 2002. *From Cyrus to Alexander: a history of the Persian Empire*. Winona Lake: Eisenbrauns.

Müller-Kessler, Christa: 2017. "Zauberschalen und ihre Umwelt: Ein Überblick über das Schreibmedium Zauberschale". In: *Zauber und Magie im antiken Palästina und seiner Umwelt*. Edited by J. Kamlah, R. Schäfer and M. Witte, 59–93. Wiesbaden: Harrassowitz.

Brinkman, J.A: 1980–3. "Kudurru". *RlA* 7: 267–74.

Brinkman, J.A: 1989. "A Legal Text from the Reign of Erība-Marduk (c. 775 B.C.)". In: *Dumu-e2-dub-ba-a: studies in honor of Åke W. Sjöberg*. Edited by Hermann Behrens, Darlene Loding and Martha T. Roth, 37–47. Philadelphia: Occasional Publications of the Samuel Noah Kramer Fund.

Brown, Keith and Jim Miller: 2013. *The Cambridge Dictionary of Linguistics*. Cambridge: Cambridge University Press.

Pfeiffer, Robert H. and E.A. Speiser: 1936. *One hundred new selected Nuzi texts*. New Haven: American schools of Oriental Research.

Burrow, Thomas: 1934. "Iranian Words in the Kharoṣṭhi Documents from Chinese Turkestan". *BSOAS* 7: 509–16.

Burrow, Thomas: 1940. *A Translation of the Kharoṣṭhi documents from Chinese Turkestan*. London: The Royal Asiatic Society.

Buswell Jr., Robert E. and Donald S. Lopez Jr.: 2014. *The Princeton dictionary of Buddhism*. Princeton: Princeton University Press.

Butts, Aaron M.: 2011. "Old Syriac documents". In: *Gorgias encyclopedic dictionary of the Syriac heritage*. Edited by Sebastian P. Brock, Aaron M. Butts and George Anton Kiraz, 314–17. Piscataway: Gorgias Press.

Cheung, Johnny: 2007. *Etymological dictionary of the Iranian verb*. Leiden: Brill.

Cheung, Johnny: 2009. "Two Notes on Bactrian". In: *Exegisti monumenta Festschrift in Honour of Nicholas Sims-Williams*. Edited by Werner Sundermann, Almut Hintze and François de Blois, 51–58. Wiesbaden: Harrassowitz.

Choksy, Jamshid: 1988. "Loan and sales contracts in ancient and early medieval Iran". *Indo-Iranian Journal* 31:91–218.

Coogan, Michael D. (ed.): 2010. *The New Oxford Annotated Bible (New Revised Standard Version with the Apocrypha)*. Oxford: Oxford University Press.

Cook, Edward M.: 2015. *Dictionary of Qumran Aramaic*. Winona Lake: Eisenbrauns.

Cotton, H.M., W.E.H. Cockle and F.G.B. Millar: 1995. "The Papyrology of the Roman Near East: A Survey". *The Journal of Roman Studies* 85: 214–235.

Cotton, Hannah M. and Ada Yardeni: 1997. *Aramaic, Hebrew and Greek Documentary Texts from Naḫal Ḫever and Other Sites*. Oxford: Clarendon Press.

Cotton, Hannah: 2003 "Diplomatics or External Aspects of the Legal Documents from the Judaean Desert: Prolegomena". In: *Rabbinic Law in Its Roman and Near Eastern Context*. Edited by Catherine Hezser, 49–61. Tübingen: Mohr-Siebeck.

Cowley, James and Klaus Maresch: 2001. *Urkunden des Politeuma der Juden von Herakleopolis: (144/3–133/2 v. Chr.)*. Wiesbaden: Westdeutscher Verlag.

Crone, Patricia: 2012. *The nativist prophets of early Islamic Iran*. Cambridge: Cambridge University Press.

Cross, F.M.: 1996. "A Papyrus Recording a Divine Legal Decision and the Root rḫq in Biblical and Near Eastern Legal Usage". In: *Texts, Temples, and Traditions: A Tribute to Menahem Haran.* Edited by Michael V. Fox, Victor Avigdor Hurowitz, Avi M. Hurvitz, Michael L. Klein, Baruch J. Schwartz and Nili Shupak, 311–20. Winona Lake: Eisenbrauns.

Cuq, Édouard: 1931. "Les actes juridiques susiens". *RA* 28: 47–71.

Cuq, Édouard: 1932. "Le droit Élamite d'après les fouilles de Suse". *RA* 29: 149–82.

Cush, Denise, Catherine Robinson and York Michael: 2008. *Encyclopedia of Hinduism.* London: Routledge.

Cussini, Eleonora 2009 "Witnesses in Aramaic Legal Documents and Inscriptions". In: Bellotto and Pochia, 2009, 191–224.

Cussini, Eleonora: 1995. "Transfer of Property at Palmyra". *ARAM* 7: 233–250.

Cussini, Eleonora: 2010. "Legal Formulary from Syriac Documents and Palmyrene Inscriptions: An Overview". In: Démare-Lafont and Lemaire, 2010, 337–55.

Cussini, Eleonora: 2013. "The Career of Some Elephantine and Murashu Scribes". In: Botta, 2013, 39–52.

Cussini, Eleonora: 2016. "Reconstructing Palmyrene Legal Language". In: *The World of Palmyra.* Edited by A. Kropp and R. Raja, 42–52. Copenhagen: Det Kongelige Danske Videnskabernes Selskab.

Czajkowski, Kimberley: 2017. *Localized Law: The Babatha and Salome Komaise Archiv.* Oxford: Oxford university press.

Czajkowski, Kimberley: 2020. "Law and Administration at the Edges of Empire: The Case of Dura-Europos". In: *Law in the Roman Provinces.* Edited by Kimberley Czajkowski and Benedict Eckhart, 115–33. Oxford: Oxford University Press.

Dalley, Stephanie: 1986. "The God Ṣalmu and the Winged Disk". *Iraq* 48: 85–101.

De Blois, François: 1985. "Freemen and Nobles in Iranian and Semitic Languages". *JRAS* 117: 5–15.

De Blois, François: 1996 (1998). See Sims-Williams and De Blois, 1996 (1998).

De Blois, François: 2006. "Du nouveau sur la chronologie bactrienne post-hellénistique: l'ère de 223–224 ap. J.-C". *Comptes rendus des séances de l'Académie des Inscriptions et Belles-Lettres* 150: 991–7.

De Blois, François: 2013. "Bactria, Bāxδī-, Balx". In: *Commentationes iranicae: Vladimiro f. Aaron Livschits nonagenario donum natalicum.* Edited by Sergei Tokhtasev and Pavel Lurje, 268–271. St. Petersburg: Nestor-Historia.

Deimel, P.: 1924. "Die Vermessung der Felder bei den Sumerern um 3000 v. Chr". *Or* 4: 1–43.

Dekiere, Luc: 1995. *Old Babylonian real estate documents from Sippar in the British Museum. Part 3: Documents from the reign of Samsu-Iluna.* Ghent: University of Ghent.

Demare-Lafont, Sophie and Andre Lemaire: 2010. *Trois millenaires de formulaires juridiques.* Genève: Droz.

Demare-Lafont, Sophie: 2010. "Éléments pour une diplomatique juridique des textes d'Émar". In: Demare-Lafont and Lemaire, 2010, 43–84.

Démare-Lafont, Sophie: 2018. "Kauf (achat). B. 1. und II. Nach altbabylonischen und mittelbabylonischen Quellen". *RlA* 16: 399–403.

Dietrich, Manfried, Oswald Loretz, and Joaquín Sanmartín: 2013. *Die keilalphabetischen Texte aus Ugarit, Ras Ibn Hani und anderen Orten*. Münster: Ugarit.

Djelani Davary, Golam: 1982. *Baktrisch: ein Wörterbuch auf Grund der Inschriften, Handschriften, Münzen und Siegelsteine*. Heidelberg: Julius Gross Verlag.

Dombradi, Eva: 2000a. "Studien zu mitḫārum/mitḫāriš und die Frage des Duplums: I. Zum semantischen Feld von mitḫārum in juristischem Kontext". *ZA* 90: 40–69.

Dombradi, Eva: 2000b. "Studien zu mitḫārum/mitḫāriš und die Frage des Duplums: II. Poenaler Zweck oder sozio-ökonomisch motivierte Regulierung des Vertragsbruchs?". *ZAR* 6: 16–34.

Donbaz, Veysel and Simo Parpola: 2001. *Neo-Assyrian legal texts in Istanbul*. Saarbrücken: Saarbrücker Drükerei und Verlag.

Donbaz, Veysel: 1982. "A Middle Babylonian Legal Document Raising Problems in Kassite Chronology". *JNES* 41: 207–12.

Doty, L. Timothy: 1978. "The Archive of the Nanâ-iddin Family from Uruk". *JCS* 30: 65–90.

Drijvers, Han J.W. and John F. Healey: 1999. *The Old Syriac inscriptions of Edessa and Osrhoene*. Leiden: Brill.

Duan, Qing: 2014. "Puñadatta's Contract of Sale of an Estate". *Annual Report of the International Research Institute for Advanced Buddhology at Soka University XVII*: 349–63.

Duan, Qing: 2015. *Xinjian manuscripts preserved in the national library of China: Khotanese remains. Part I. Shang hai: Zhong xi shu ju* (In Chinese).

Duan, Qing; Shixin Hou and Da Li: 2016. "In the case of the proverb: Xinjiang Uygur Autonomous Region. Museum Collection Early Tang: case study". *Tang research* 22: 371–400 (In Chinese).

Durkin-Meisterernst, Desmond: 2004. *Dictionary of Manichaean Middle Persian and Parthian*. Turnhout: Brepols.

Dušek, Jan: 2007. *Les manuscrits araméens du Wadi Daliyeh et la Samarie vers 450–332 av. J.-C.* Leiden: Brill.

Dušek, Jan: 2009. "The Satisfaction and the Payment-Receipt Clauses in the Aramaic Legal Tradition: Between Egypt and Levant". In: *My Things Changed Things*. Edited by P. Maříková Vlčková – J. Mynářová – Martin Tomášek, 87–99. Prague: Charles University in Prague.

Dušek, Jan: 2010. "Formulaires juridiques dans les contrats du wadi Daliyeh". In: Démare-Lafont and Lemaire, 2010. 279–316.

Dušek, Jan: 2011. "Protection of Ownership in the Deeds of Sale: Deeds of Sale from the Judean Desert in Context". In: *The Dead Sea Scrolls in Context*. Edited by A. Lange, E. Tov and M. Weigold, 857–79. Leiden: Brill.

Dušek, Jan: 2013. "Aramaic in the Persian period". *Hebrew Bible and Ancient Israel* 2: 243–264.

Dušek, Jan: 2020. "The Importance of the Wadi Daliyeh Manuscripts for the History of Samaria and the Samaritans". *Religions* 11(2): 63. https://doi.org/10.3390/rel11020063.

Ebeling, E. and B. Meissner (ed.): 1928–2018. *Reallexikon der Assyriologie und Vorderasiatischen Archäologie*.

Eisser, Georg: 1939. "Beiträge zur Urkunden lehre der altassyrischen Rechtsurkunden vom Kültepe". In: *Symbolae ad iura Orientis antique pertinentes Paulo Koschaker dedicatae*. Edited by J.G. Friedrich, J. Lautner and J. Miles, 94–125. Weimar: Böhlau.

Elman, Yaakov: 2014. "Commercial Law in Rome and Ctesiphon: Roman Jurisconsults, Rabbis and Sasanian Dastwars on Risk". In: *Rabbinic traditions between Palestine and Babylonia*. Edited by Ronit Nikolsky and Tal Ilan, 250–83. Leiden: Brill.

Erdal, Marcel: 1984. "The Turkish Yarkand Documents". *BSOAS* 47: 260–301.

Eshel, Esther, Hanan Eshel and Ada Yardeni: 2011. "A Document from Year 4 of the Destruction of the House of Israel". *Dead Sea discoveries* 18: 1–28.

Eshel, Hanan: 2000. "Murabbaat, Wadi: Written Material". In: *Encyclopedia of the Dead Sea Scrolls*. Edited by L.H. Schiffman and J.C. VanderKam, 583–6. New York: Oxford University Press.

Eshel, Hanan: 2011. "A Survey of the Refuge Caves and Their Legal Documents". In: *Halakhah in light of epigraphy*. Edited by Albert I. Bamgarten, Hanan Eshel, Ranon Katzoff and Shani Tzoref, 103–53. Göttingen: Vandenhoeck and Ruprecht.

Esler, Philip F.: 2017. *Babatha's orchard: the yadin papyri and an ancient Jewish family tale retold*. Oxford: Oxford University Press.

Faist, Betia: 2012. "Der neuassyrische Kaufvertrag im Spannungsfeld zwischen Formular und konkretem Fall". *ZAR* 18: 209–19.

Faist, Betina et al.: 2004. "Bibliografía de los estudios de Emar". In: *UF*.

Fales, F.M.: 1990. "The Rural Landscape of the Neo-Assyrian Empire". *State Archives of Assyria Bulletin* 4/2: 81–142.

Fales, F.M.: 2000. "The Use and Function of Aramaic Tablets". In: *Essays on Syria in the Iron Age*. Edited by G. Bunnens, 89–124. Leuven: Peeters.

Fales, F.M.: 2010. "New Light on Assyro-Aramaic Interference: The Assur Ostracon". In: *Camsemud 2007: Proceedings of the 13th Italian Meeting of Afro-Asiatic Linguistics: Held in Udine, May 21st–24th, 2007*. Edited by Frederick Mario Fales and Giulia Francesca Grassi, 189–204. Padova: SARGON.

Fauth, Wolfganf: 1979. "Sonnengottheit (DUTU) und königliche Sonne". *UF* 11: 227–63.

Feissel, Denis and Gascou, Jean: 1989. "Documents d'archives romains inédits du Moyen Euphrate (IIIe s. ap. J.-C.)". *Comptes rendus des séances de l'Académie des Inscriptions et Belles-Lettres* 133: 535–61.

Feissel, Denis and Jean Gascou: 1995. "Documents d'archives romains inédits du Moyen Euphrate (IIIe s. après J-C)". *Journal des savants* 1: 65–119.

Feissel, Denis and Jean Gascou: 2000. "Documents d'archives romains inédits du Moyen Euphrate [III. Actes divers et Lettres (P. Euphr. 11 à 17)]". *Journal des savants* 2: 157–208.

Felber, Heinz: 1997. *Demotische Ackerpachtverträge der Ptolemäerzeit: Untersuchungen zu Aufbau, Entwicklung und inhaltlichen Aspekten einer Gruppe von demotischen Urkunden*. Wiesbaden: Harrassowitz.

Felföldi, Szabolcs: 2011. Information and Secrecy on the Silk Road. Methods of Encryption of Legal Documents in Inner Asia (3th–4th century CE). In: *Integrated information: International Conference on Integrated Information Kos, Greece September, 29–October, 3 2011*. Edited by Georgios A. Giannakopoulos and Damianos P. Sakas, 102–105. Piraeus, Greece.

Feliu, L., J. Llop, A. Millet Albà and J. Sanmartín J.: 2013: *Time and History in the Ancient Near East Proceedings of the 56th Rencontre Assyriologique Internationale, Barcelona, July 26–30, 2010*. Winona Lake: Eisenbrauns.

Fijalkowska, Lena: 2007. "La propriété immobilière à Emar en Syrie, du XIVème au XIIème siècle av. J.-C". *Revue internationale des droits de l'antiquité* 54: 13–26.

Fijalkowska, Lena: 2014. *Le droit de la vente à Emar*. Wiesbaden: Harrassowitz.

Fischer, Leopold: 1910. "Die Urkunden in Jer 32:11–14 nach den Ausgrabungen und dem Talmud". *Zeitschrift fur die alttestamentliche Wissenschaft* 30: 136–42.

Fischer, Leopold: 1912. *Beiträge zur Erklärung der talmudischen Urkunden*. Frankfurt am Main: Buch druckerei Louis Gaide.

Follmer, Martha: 2020. "Aramaic as Lingua Franca". In: *A companion to ancient Near Eastern languages*. Edited by Rebecca Hasselbach-Andee, 373–99. Hoboken: Wiley Blackwell.

Fonrobert, Charlotte Elisheva and Martin S. Jaffee: 2007. *The Cambridge Companion to the Talmud and Rabbinic literature*. Cambridge: Cambridge University Press.

Frantz-Murphy, Gladys: 1988. "A Comparison of the Arabic and Earlier Egyptian Contract Formularies, Part III: The Idiom of Satisfaction". *JNES* 47: 105–12.

Frantz-Murphy, Gladys: 1989. "A Comparison of the Arabic and Earlier Egyptian Contract Formularies, Part V: Formulaic Evidence". *JNES* 48: 97–107.

Friedman, Mordechai A.: 1980. *Jewish Marriage in Palestine: A Cairo Geniza Study*. 2 vols. Tel-Aviv: The Jewish Theological Seminary of America.

Gadd, C.J.: 1926. "Tablets from Kirkuk". *RA* 23/2–4: 49–161.

Gagon, Traianos and Peter van Minnen: 1994. *Settling a dispute: toward a legal anthropology of late antique Egypt*. Ann Arbor: University of Michigan Press.

Garner Bryan, A.: 2009. *Black's Law Dictionary*. St. Paul, MN: Thomson Reuters.

Gautier, J.-É.: 1908. *Archives d'une famille de Dilbat au temps de la première dynasţie de Babylone*. Cairo: Institut français d'archéologie orientale.

Geiger, Gregor: 2017. "Die Doppelurkunden aus der Judäischen Wüste: Das Verhältnis vom oberen (inneren) und unteren (äusseren) Text". *Revue de Qumran* 29: 247–79.

Gelb, Ignace J. et al.: 1956–2010. *The Assyrian Dictionary of the Oriental Institute of the University of Chicago*. Chicago: Chicago University Press.

Geller, Markham J. and Herwig Maehler (ed.): 1995. *Legal Documents of the Hellenistic World*. London: The Warburg Institute, University of London.

Geller, Markham J.: 2011. "Review of Botta, 2009". In: *JJS* 62: 150–51.

Gemoll, W.: 2006. *Griechisch-deutsches Schul- und Handwörterbuch*. München: Oldenbourg.

Gharib, B.: 1995. *Sogdian dictionary: Sogdian – Persian – English*. Tehran: Farhangan Publications.

Gholami, Saloumeh: 2009. "Ergativity in Bactrian". *Orientalia Suecana* LVIII: 132–41.

Gholami, Saloumeh: 2014. *Selected Features of Bactrian Grammar*. Wiesbaden: Harrassowitz.

Gignoux, Philippe: 2009. "Les comptes de monsieur Friyag: quelques documents économiques en Pehlevi". In: *Sources pour l'histoire et la geographie du monde iranien (224–710) [Res Orientales, XVIII]*. Edited by Rika Gyselen, 115–142. Bures-sur-Yvette: Groupe pour l'Étude de la Civilisation du Moyen-Orient.

Gignoux, Philippe: 2012. "Une Aarchive Post-Ssasanide du Tabaristan (I)". In: *Objets et documents inscrits en Pārsīg [Res Orientales, XXI]*. Edited by Rika Gyselen, 29–96. Bures-sur-Yvette: Groupe pour l'Étude de la Civilisation du Moyen-Orient.

Gnoli, Gherardo: 2002. "The 'Aryan' language". *JSAI* 26: 84–90.

Goddeeris, Anne: 2009. *Tablets from Kisurra in the collections of the British Museum*. Wiesbaden: Harrassowitz.

Goldschmidt, Lazarus: 1935–1937. *Babylonischer Talmud*. Den Haag: Nijhoff.

Goldstein, Jonathan A.: 1990. *Semites, Iranians, Greeks, and Romans: studies in their interactions*. Atlanta: Scholars Press.

Greenfield, Jonas C.: 1980. "The Genesis Apocryphon: Observations on Some Words and Phrases". In: Sarfatti et al., 1980, xxii–xxix

Greenfield, Jonas C.: 1987. "The Verb Sallaṭa in the Qur'ān in the Light of Aramaic Usage". *JSAI* 9: 36–41.

Greengus, Samuel: 1986. *Studies in Ishchali documents*. Malibu: Undena Publications.

Greengus, Samuel: 2011. *Laws in the Bible and in early rabbinic collections: the legal legacy of the ancient Near East*. Eugene: Cascade Books.

Grenet: 1988. See Leriche and Grenet, 1988.

Grenet, Frantz: 2005. "An Archaeologist's Approach to Avestan Geography". In: *Birth of the Persian Empire*. Edited by Vesta Sarkhosh Curtis and Sarah Stewart, 29–51. London: Tauris.

Grohmann, Adolf: 1936. *Legal texts with twenty-four plates*. Cairo: Egyptian Library Press.

Gronke, Monika: 1982. *Arabische und persische Privaturkunden des 12. und 13. Jahrhunderts aus Ardabil (Aserbeidschan)*. Berlin: Schwarz.

Gronke, Monika: 1984. "La rédaction des actes privés dans le monde musulman médiéval: théorie et pratique". *Studia Islamica* 59: 159–74.

Gronke, Monika: 1986. "The Arabic Yārkand Documents". *BSOAS* 49: 454–507.

Gropp, Douglas M.: 1993. "The Origin and Development of the Aramaic Šallīṭ Clause". *JNES* 52: 31–6.

Gropp, Douglas M.: 2000. "The Wadi Daliyeh Documents Compared to the Elephantine Documents". In: Schiffman, Tov and VanderKam, 2000, 826–35.

Gropp, Douglas M.: 2001. *Wadi Daliyeh II: The Samaria Papyri from Wadi Daliyeh*. Oxford: Clarendon Press.

Gropp, Douglas M.: 2003. "The Samaria Papyri and the Babylonio-Aramean Symbiosis". In: Schiffman, 2003a, 23–51.

Gross, Andrew D.: 2008. *Continuity and innovation in the Aramaic legal tradition*. Leiden: Brill.

Gross, Andrew D.: 2010. "The Judean Desert Documents as a Regional sub-tradition in Aramaic common law". In: *The Dead Sea scrolls at 60*. Edited by Lawrence H. Schiffman and Shani Tzoref, 99–114. Leiden: Brill.

Gross, Andrew D.: 2012 (2014). "Hebrew in the Age of Revolution" *Maarav* 19: 37–63.

Gross, Andrew D.: 2013a. "Emar and the Elephantine Papyri". In: Botta, 2013, 333–49.

Gross, Andrew D.: 2013b. "The Aramaic Law of Sale Considered from the Papyrological and Rabbinic Evidence". In: Hagedorn and Kratz, 2013, 129–64.

Guggenheimer, Heinrich W.: 2005–. *The Jerusalem Talmud*. Berlin: De Gruyter.

Gulak, Asher: 1935. *Das Urkundenwesen im Talmud*. Jerusalem: Rubin Mass.

Gurney, O.R.: 1983. *The Middle Babylonian legal and economic texts from Ur*. London: British School of Archaeology in Iraq.

Gzella, Holger: 2015. *A cultural history of Aramaic: from the beginnings to the advent of Islam*. Leiden: Brill.

Haase, Richard: 1967. "Anmerkungen zum ugaritischen Immobilienkauf". *ZA* 58: 196–210.

Haase, Richard: 2003. "The Hittite Kingdom". In: Westbrook, 2003a, 619–56.

Haase, Richard: 2011. "Die Entscheidungssammlung von Ḫatti, das Rechtsleben eines Hethiters in seinem Königreich (1650 bis 1180 v. Chr.) betreffend". *ZAR* 17: 33–74.

Hackl, Johannes: 2018."Kauf. B. III. Neubabylonisch". *RlA* 15: 403–11.

Hackl, Ursula, Bruno Jacobs and Dieter Weber (ed.): 2010. *Quellen zur Geschichte des Partherreiches*. Göttingen: Vandenhoeck and Ruprecht.

Hackl, Ursula, Hanna Jenni and Christoph Schneider: 2003. *Quellen zur Geschichte der Nabatäer*. Göttingen: Vandenhoeck and Ruprecht.

Hagedorn, Anselm C. and Reinhard Gregor Kratz: 2013. *Law and religion in the Eastern Mediterranean: from antiquity to early Islam*. Oxford: Oxford University Press.

Haig, Geoffrey: 2015. "Ergativity in Iranian". www.academia.edu/15321950/Ergativity_in_Iranian.

Haim, Ofir: 2019a. "What is the 'Afghan Genizah'? A short guide to the collection of the Afghan Manuscripts in the National Library of Israel, with the edition of two documents". *Afghanistan* 2: 70–90.

Haim, Ofir: 2019b. "Acknowledgment Deeds (*iqrārs*) in Early New Persian from the Area of Bāmīyān (395–430 AH/1005–1039 CE)". *JRAS* 29: 415–46.

Hansen, Valerie: 1995. *Negotiating daily life in traditional China: how ordinary people used contracts, 600–1400*. New Haven: Yale University Press.

Harris, Rivkah: 1975. *Ancient Sippar: a demographic study of an Old-Babylonian city (1894–1595 B.C.)*. Istanbul: Nederlands Historisch-Archeologisch Instituut te Istanbul.

Harris, Susan Rebecca: 1983. *Land conveyance in Old Babylonian Larsa*. University of Michigan. Diss.

Healey, John F.: 1993. *The Nabataean tomb inscriptions of Mada'in Salih*. Oxford: Oxford University Press.

Healey, John F: 1994. "Sources for the Study of Nabataean Law". *New Arabian Studies* 1: 203–14.

Healey, John F.: 2005. "The Writing on the Wall: Law in Aramaic Epigraphy" In: *Writing and Ancient Near Eastern Society*. Edited by Piotr Bienkowski, Christopher Mee and Elizabeth Slater, 127–141. New York: T&T Clark.

Healey, John F.: 2008. "Some Lexical and Legal Notes on a Syriac Loan Transfer of 240 CE." In: *Malphono w-Rabo d-Malphone*. Edited by George A. Kiraz, 211–226. Piscataway: Gorgias Press.

Healy, John F.: 2009. *Aramaic inscriptions and documents of the Roman period*. Oxford: Oxford University Press.

Healey, John F.: 2013. "Fines and Curses: Law and Religion among the Nabataeans and their Neighbours". In: Hagedorn and Kratz, 2013, 165–86.

Heirman, Ann and Stephan Peter Bumbacher: 2007. *The Spread of Buddhism*. Leiden: Brill.

Hengstl, Joachim: 1978. *Griechische Papyri aus Ägypten als Zeugnisse des öffentlichen und privaten Lebens*. Darmstadt: Wissenschaftliche Buchgesellschaft.

Henning, Walter B.: 1964 (1965). "The Choresmian documents". *Asia Minor* 10: 166–79.

Hertel, Thomas Klitgaard: 2013. *Old Assyrian Legal Practice*. Leiden: Nederland Instituutt voor het Nabije Oosten.

Heuhnergard, John: 1983. "Five tablets from the vicinity of Emar". *RA* 77: 11–43.

Hezser, Catherine: 2001. *Jewish literacy in Roman Palestine*. Tübingen: Mohr Siebeck.

Hillers, Delbert and Cussini, Eleonora: 1996. *Palmyrene Aramaic Texts*. Baltimore: The Johns Hopkins University Press.

Hoftijzer, Jacob and Karel Jongeling: 1995. *Dictionary of the North-West Semitic Inscriptions*. Leiden: Brill.

Holtz, Shalom: 2001. "To Go and Marry Any Man That You Please: A Study of the Formulaic Antecedents of the Rabbinic Writ of Divorce". *JNES* 60: 241–58.

Holtz, Shalom: 2009. *Neo-Babylonian Court Procedure*. Leiden: Brill.

Horowitz, Wayne: 1998. *Mesopotamian cosmic geography*. Winona Lake: Eisenbrauns.

Huart, Clément: 1914. "Trois actes notariés arabes de Yârkend". *JA* 4: 607–27.

Humbach, Helmut: 1966–67. *Baktrische Sprachdenkmäler*. 2 Bände. Wiesbaden: Harrassowitz.

Humbach, Helmut: 2002. "Review Sims-Williams, 2000". *BSOAS* 65: 415–18.

Humbach, Helmut and Klaus Feiss: 2012. *Herodotus's Scythians and Ptolemy's Central Asia: semasiological and onomasiological studies*. Wiesbaden: Reichert.

Humbach, Helmut and Sussane Ziegler: 1998. *Ptolmy, Geography, book 6: Middle East, Central and North Asia, China*. Wiesbaden: Reichert.

Hunt, A.S. and C.C. Edgar: 1932. *Non-literary papyri. Private affairs*. Cambridge: Harvard University Press.

Hurvitz, Avi: 1982. "The History of a Legal Formula". *Vetus Testamentum* 32: 257–67.

Inghot, Harald: 1962. "Palmyrene Inscription from the Tomb of Malkū". *Me'langes de l'universite' Saint Joseph* 38: 99–119.

Jalilivand Sadafi, Sheyda: 2014. *Die Altbabylonischen Kaufurkunden aus Susa*. Tübingen. Diss.

Jas, Remko: 1996. *Neo-Assyrian judicial procedures*. Helsinki: Neo-Assyrian text corpus project.

Jastrow, Marcus: 1901. *A dictionary of the Targumim, the Talmud Babli and Yerushalmi, and the Midrashic literature*. New York, Berlin.

Jenni. Ernst: 1997. " עולם ʿôlām Eternity". *TDOT* 2: 852–862.

Jirku, Anton: 1923. *Altorientalischer Kommentar zum Alten Testament*. Leipzig: Deichert.

Joannes, Francis: 2010. "Les formulaires juridiques néo-babyloniens". In: Démare-Lafont and Lemaire, 2010, 261–78.

Junker, Heinrich F.J.: 1955. *Das Frahang i Pahlavīk in zeichengemäßer Anordnung*. Leipzig: Harrassowitz.

Jursa, Michael: 2005. *Neo-Babylonian legal and administrative documents*. Münster: Ugarit.

Kaufhold, Hubert: 2005. "Die syrische Rechtsliteratur". In: *Nos sources: arts et littérature syriaques*. Edited by Ray Jabre Mouawad, 211–35. Antélias: Centre d'Etudes et de Recherches Orientales.

Kaufman, Stephen. A: 1975. *The Akkadian Influences on Aramaic*. Chicago: University of Chicago Press.

Keenan, James G., J.G. Manning and Uri Yiftach-Firanko: 2014. *Law and legal practice in Egypt from Alexander to the Arab conquest*. Cambridge: Cambridge University Press.

Kessler, Karlheinz: 1999. "Ein Einbruch in ein Bīt Šutummu eines Tempelbäckers". In: *Munuscula Mesopotamica: Festschrift für Johannes Renger*. Edited by Barbara Böck, Eva Cancik-Krischbaum and Thomas Richter, 245–57. Münster: Ugarit.

Khan, Geffrey: 2014. *Arabic documents: from early Islamic Khurasan*. Berlin: Freie Universität Berlin.

Khan, Geoffrey: 2019. "The Opening Formula and Witness Clauses in Arabic Legal Documents from the Early Islamic Period". *JAOS* 139: 23–39.

Khwājah Mohammad Mirzā and Sāqi, Nabi: 1388/2009. *Barghā yi az yak fasl* (*Asnād tārikhi ye Ghur*). Kabul: Enteshārāt e Sa'id.

Kienast, Brukhart: 1982."Verzichtklausel und Eviktionsgarantie in den ältesten sumerischen Kalifurkunden". *ZA* 72: 28–41.

Kienast, Brukhart: 1980."Die altbabylonischen Kaufurkunden aus Alalaḫ". *Die Welt des Orients* 11: 35–63.

Kienast, Brukhart: 1979. "Rechtsurkunden in ugaritischer Sprache". *UF* 11: 432–52.

Kienast, Brukhart: 2015. *Das altassyrische Eherecht: eine Urkundenlehre*. Wiesbaden: Harrassowitz.

Klima, Josef: 1960. "Untersuchungen zum elamischen Erbrecht". *ArOr* 28: 5–54.

Koch, Christoph: 2008. *Vertrag, Treueid und Bund*. Berlin: Walter de Gruyter.

Koffmahn, Elisabeth: 1968. *Die Doppelurkunden aus der Wüste Juda: Recht und Praxis der jüdischen Papyri des 1. und 2. Jahrhunderts n. Chr.* Leiden: Brill.

Koschaker, Paul: 1928. *Neue keilschriftliche Rechtsurkunden aus der El-Amarna-Zeit*. Leipzig. Hirzel.

Koschaker, Paul: 1931. *Über einige griechische Rechtsurkunden aus den östlichen Randgebieten des Hellenismus*. Leipzig: Hirzel.

Koshurnikov, S.G. and N. Yoffee:1986. "Old Babylonian Tablets from Dilbat in the Ashmolean Museum". *Iraq* 48: 117–30.

Kottsieper, Ingo: 2004. "Hebräische, aramäische und phönizische Texte". In: *Texte aus der Umwelt des Alten Testaments Band 1: Texte zum Rechts- und Wirtschafts*. Edited by Bernd Janowski and Gernot Wilhelm, 249–294.Gütersloh: Gütersloher Verlagshaus.

Kottsieper, Ingo: 2013. "Aramäische Archive aus achämenidischer Zeit und ihre Funktion." In: *Archives and Archival Documents in Ancient Societies*. Edited by Michele Faraguna, 175–200. Triest: Edizioni Università di Trieste.

Kraus, F.R.: 1953. "Nippur und Isin nach altbabylonischen Rechtsurkunden". *JCS* 3: 1–228.

Kraus, F.R.: 1955. "Provinzen des neusumerischen Reiches von Ur". *ZA* 51: 45–75.

Krebrenik, Manfred: 2006–8. "Richtergot(heiten)". *RlA* 7: 344–61.

Krecher, Joachim, Claus Wilcke, Karl Hecker, Guillaume Cardascia, Herbert P.H. Petschow, Richard Haase and Burkhart Kienast: 1980. "Kauf". *RlA* 6: 490–541.

Krückmann, Oluf: 1931. *Babylonische Rechts- und Verwaltungs-Urkunden aus der Zeit Alexanders und der Diadochen*. Weimar: Hof-Buchdruckerei.

Kümmel, Hans Martin: 1989. "Ein Kaufvertrag aus Ḫana mit mittelassyrischer līmu-Datierung". *ZA* 79: 191–200.

Kunkel, Wolfgang: 1936. "Zur Gräko-Ägyptischen Doppelurkunde". In: *Studi in onore di Salvatore Riccobono nel XL anno del suo insegnamento*, 415–433. Palermo: Arti Grafiche Castiglia.

Kutscher, E.Y.: 1954. "New Aramaic Texts". *JAOS* 74: 233–48.

Kwasman, Theodore and Simo Parpola: 1991. *Legal transactions of the Royal Court of Nineveh; Pt. 1*. Helsinki: Helsinki University Press.

Lafont, Bertrand and Raymond Westbrook: 2003. "Neo-Sumerian Period (Ur III)". In: Westbrook, 2003a, 183–226.

Lafont, Sophie: 2003. "Middle Assyrian Period". In: Westbrook, 2003a, 521–63.

Lambert, W.G.: 2011. "Another Boundary Stone of Merodachbaladan I". *AfO* 52: 16–21.

Landsberger, Bruno: 1937. *Materialien zum sumerischen Lexikon: Vokabulare und Formularbücher*. Roma: pontificium istitutum biblicum.

Lane, Edward William: 1863–1893. *An Arabic-English Lexicon*. 8 vols. London and Edinburgh: Williams and Norgate.

Lauinger, Jacob: 2012. "Esarhaddon's Succession Treaty at Tell Tayinat: Text and Commentary". *JCS* 64: 87–123.

Lauinger, Jacob: 2015. *Following the Man of Yamhad: Settlement and Territory at Old Babylonian Alalah*. Leiden: Brill.

Lauinger, Jacob: 2020. "The Jurisdiction of Legal Transactions at Middle Bronze Age Alalah". In: *Alalakh and its Neighbours*. Edited by K. Aslıhan Yener and Tara Ingman, 55–71. Leuven: Peeters.

Leriche, Pierre and Frantz Grenet: 1988. "Bactria". *EIr* 3: 339–44.

Leriche, Pierre: 2007. "Bactria, Land of a Thousand Cities". In: *After Alexander: Central Asia before Islam*. Edited by Joe Cribb and Georgina Herrmann, 121–153. Oxford: Oxford University Press.

Lerner, Judith and Nicholas Sims-Williams: 2011. *Seals, sealings and tokens from Bactria to Gandhara*. Wein: Verlag der Österreichischen Akademie der Wissenschaften.

Levene, Dan: 2013. *Jewish Aramaic Curse Texts from Late-Antique Mesopotamia*. Leiden. Brill.

Levine, Baruch A.: 1975. "On the Origins of the Aramaic Legal Formulary at Elephantine". In: *Christianity, Judaism, and other Greco-Roman Cults: Studies for Morton Smith at Sixty*. Edited by Jacob Neusner, 3: 37–54. Leiden: Brill.

Levine, Baruch A.: 2002. "On the Role of Aramaic in Transmitting Syro-Mesopotamian Legal Institutions" In: *Ideologies as Intercultural Phenomena*. Edited by A. Panaino, and G. Pettinato, 157–66. Milan: Università di Bologna and IsIao.

Levine, Baruch A.: 2003. Prolegomenon to 2003 reprint of Muffs 1969.

Levine, Baruch A.: 2004. "The Jewish Ketūbbāh as a 'Dialogue Document': The Continuity of a Cuneiform Tradition". In: *Schools of Oriental Studies and the Development of Modern Historiography*. Edited by A. Panaino and A. Piras, 169–81. Milan: Università di Bologna and Islao.

Levine, Baruch A.: 2013. "Time in Ancient Israel: Hebrew 'ôlām, Past and Future" in: Feliu et al., 2013, 159–68.

Lewenton, Ursula: 1970. *Studien zur keilschriftlichen Rechtspraxis Babyloniens in hellenistischer Zeit*. Münster Universität. Dissertation.

Lewis, Nephtali: 1989. *The documents from the Bar Kokhba period in the cave of letters: Greek papyri*. Jerusalem: Israel Exploration Society.

Liddell, Henry George and Scott, Robert: 1996. *A Greek-English Lexicon*. Oxford: Clarendon Press.

Lieberman, Saul: 5748/1988. *The Tosefta*. New York: The Jewish theological Seminary of America.

Limet, Henri: 1969. "La clause du double en droit néo-sumérien". *Or* 38(4): 520–2.

Lipinski, Edward: 2000. *The Aramaeans*. Leuven: Peeters.

Lipinski, Edward: 2002. "New Aramaic Tablets". *BiOr* 59: 245–259.

Lipinski, Edward: 2010. *Studies in Aramaic inscriptions and onomastics*. Leuven: Uitgeverij Peeters en Departement Oriëntalistiek.

Lipinski, Edward: 2013. "The Aramaeans in the West (13th–8th centuries)". In: *Arameans, Chaldeans, and Arabs in Babylonia and Palestine in the first millennium B.C.* Edited by Angelika Berlejung and Michael P. Streck, 123–147. Wiesbaden: Harrassowitz.

Lippert, Sandra: 2012. *Einführung in die altägyptische Rechtsgeschichte*. Berlin: LIT.

Liverani, Mario: 1990. "The shape of Neo Sumerian fields". *Bulletin on Sumerian agriculture* 5: 147–86.

Liverani, Mario: 1996. "Reconstructing the Rural Landscape of the Ancient Near East". *Journal of the Economic and Social History of the Orient* 39: 1–41.

Liverani, Mario: 1997. "Lower Mesopotamian Fields: South vs. North". In: *Ana šadî Labnāni lū allik*. Edited by Beate Pongratz-Leisten, Hartmut Kühne and Paolo Xella, 219–227. Münster: Ugarit.

Livshitz, Vladimir A.: 1984. "Dokumenty". In: *Toprak-kala. Dvorets (Toprak-kala. The palace), Trudy Khorezmskoi arkheologohnograjicheskoi ekspeditsii*. Edited by Iu. A. Rapoport and E.E. Nerazik, 14: 251–86 Moskva: Izdatel'stvo Nauka.

Livshitz, Vladimir A.: 2008. *Sogdiyskaya ėpigrafika Srednej Azii i Semireč'ya*. St Petersburg: Filologicheski'i fakultet; Sankt-Peterburgskogo universiteta.

Livshitz, Vladimir: 2010. "The Avroman Parchment III in Parthian". *Anabasis (Studia classica et orientalia)* 1: 159–74.

Livshits, Vladimir A.: 2015. *Sogdian epigraphy of Central Asia and Semirech'e*. London: School of Oriental and African Studies.

Loewenstamm, Samuel E.: 1956. "Notes on the Alalakh Tablets". *Israel Exploration Journal* 6: 217–25.

Loewenstamm, Samuel E.: 1980. *Comparative studies in biblical and ancient oriental literatures*. Kevelaer: Butzon and Bercker.

Lundbom, Jack R.: 2004. *Jeremiah 26–31*. The Anchor Bible. Garden City: Doubleday.

MacGinnes, John: 1993. "Two Achaemenid Tablets from the Fitzwilliam Museum, Cambridge". *Iraq* 55: 149–53.

Machiela, Daniel A.: 2009. *The Dead Sea Genesis Apocryphon*. Leiden: Brill.

Mackenzie, David Neil: 1971. *A concise Pahlavi dictionary*. Oxford: Oxford University Press.

Mackenzie, David Neil: 1987. "Avroman". *EIr* 3: 111–12.

Mackenzie, David Neil: 1994. "Dates and Dating". *EIr* 7: 124–6.

Shaki, Mansour: 2011. "Judicial and legal systems ii. Parthian and Sasanian judicial Systems". *EIr* 15: 177–80.

Macuch, Maria: 1981. *Das sasanidische Rechtsbuch Mātakdān i hazār dātistān: (Teil II)*. Wiesbaden: Steiner.

Macuch, Maria: 1993. *Rechtskasuistik und Gerichtspraxis zu Beginn des siebentenJahrhunderts in Iran: die Rechtssammlung des Farroḫmard i Wahrāmān*. Wiesbaden: Harrassowitz.

Macuch, Maria: 2009. "Mādayān ī Hazār Dādestān". *EIr* www.iranicaonline.org/articles/madayan-i-hazar-dadestan.

Macuch, Maria: 2010. "Legal Constructions of Identity in the Sasanian Period". In: *Iranian Identity in the Course of History*. Edited by Carlo G. Cereti, 193–212. Roma: Istituto italiano per l'Africa e l'Oriente.

Macuch, Maria, Dieter Weber and Desmond Durkin-Meisterernst: 2010. *Ancient and Middle Iranian studies*. Wiesbaden: Harrassowitz.

Madan, Dhanjishab Medherjibhai: 1911. *The complete text of the Pahlavi Dinkard*. Bombay: Fort Printing Press.

Maidman, Maynard: 1994. *Two hundred Nuzi texts from the Oriental Institute of the University of Chicago*. Winona Lake: Eisenbrauns.

Mairs, Rachel (ed.): 2021. *The Graeco-Bactrian and Indo-Greek world*. London; New York: Routledge.

Malul, Me'ir: 1988. *Studies in Mesopotamian legal symbolism*. Kevelaer: Butzon and Bercker.

Marquez Rowe, Ignacio: 2006. *The royal deeds of Ugarit: a study of ancient Near Eastern diplomatics*. Münster: Ugarit.

Mason, Steve: 2016. *A history of the Jewish war A.D. 66–74*. Cambridge: Cambridge University Press.

Mattila, Raija: 2002. *Legal Transactions of the Royal Court of Neneveh, Part II*. Helsinki: Helsinki University Press.

Matuš, Lubor: 1950. "Les contrats de vente d'immeubles provenant de Larsa". *ArOr* 18/4: 11–67.

Mauer, Gerlinde: 1979. *Das Formular der altbabylonischen Bodenpachtverträge*. München: Univ., Diss.

Mayer, Walter: 2001. *Die Ausgrabungen in Tall Munbāqa-Ekalte. Bd. 2: Die Texte*. Saarbrücken: Saarbrückener Druckerei und Verlag.

Minns, Ellis H.: 1915. "Parchments of the Parthian Period from Avroman in Kurdistan". *JHS* 35: 22–65.

Mercer, Samuel A.B.: 1913. "The Oath in Cuneiform Inscriptions. The Oath in Babylonian Inscriptions of the Time of the Hammurabi Dynasty". *The American Journal of Semitic Languages and Literatures* 29/2: 65–94.

Messina, Vito: 2009. "Witnesses and Sealers of Seleucid Mesopotamia. A Comparison between the Seal Impressions from Uruk and Those from Seleucia on the Tigris". In: Bellotto and Ponchia, 2009, 175–90.

Meyer, Elizabeth A.: 2007. "Diplomatics, Law and Romanisation in the Documents from the Judaean Desert". In: *Beyond Dogmatics Law and Society in the Roman World*. Edited by J.W. Cairns and P.J. du Plessis, 52–82. Edinburgh: Edinburgh University Press.

Meyer, Elizabeth A.: 2004. *Legitimacy and Law in the Roman World*. Cambridge: Cambridge University Press.

Minorski, V.: 1942. "Some Early Documents in Persian (I)". *JRAS* 74: 181–94.

Minovi, Mojtaba: 1345/1966. "Qabāle ye Fārsi az qarn e sheshom". *Farhang e Irān zamin* 14: 287–8.

Mitteis, L.: 1912. *Grundzüge und Chrestomathie der Papyruskunde. Bd. 2: Juristischer Teil. Hälfte 1*. Leipzig: Teubner.

Moazami, Mahnaz: 2014. *Wrestling with the Demons of the Pahlavi Widewdad*. Leiden: Brill.

Monier-Williams, Monier: 1899. *A Sanskrit-English dictionary*. Oxford: Clarendon Press.

Moore, Ellen Whitley: 1975. *Neo-Babylonian business and administrative documents*. Aalen: Scientia-Verlag.

Moriggi, Marco: 2014. *A Corpus of Syriac incantation bowls: Syriac magical texts from late antique Mesopotamia*. Leiden: Brill.

Morrigi, Marco: 2015. "Jewish Divorce Formulae in Syriac Incantation Bowls". *Aramaic Studies* 13: 82–94.

Muffs, Yuchnan: 1992. *Love and Joy: Law, Language and Religion in Ancient Israel*. Cambridge: Harvard University Press.

Muffs, Yuchnan: 2003. *Studies in the Aramaic legal papyri from Elephantine*. Leiden: Brill.

Muraoka, Takamitsu: 2009. *A Greek-English lexicon of the Septuagint*. Leuven: Peeters.

Muraoka, Takamitsu: 2010. *A Greek-Hebrew/Aramaic two-way index to the Septuagint*. Leuven: Peeters.

Naveh, Joseph and Jonas Greenfield: 1984. "Hebrew and Aramaic in the Persian period". In: *The Cambridge history of Judaism*. Edited by W.D. Davies and L. Finkelstein, 115–129. Cambridge: Cambridge University Press.

Naveh, Joseph and Shaked, Shaul: 2012. *Aramaic documents from Ancient Bactria: (fourth century BCE.)*. London: The Khalili Family Trust.

Neumann, Hans: 2003. "Recht im antiken Mesopotamien". In: *Die rechtskulturen der Antike*. Edited by Ulrich Manthe, 55–123. München: Beck.

Newman, Hillel I.: 2004. "The Documents from the Bar Kokhba Period in the Cave of Letters: Hebrew, Aramaic and Nabataean-Aramaic Papyri". *Scripta Classica Israelica* 23: 239–254.

Newman, Hillal I.: 2006. "P.Yadin 8: A Correction". *JJS* LVII: 330–35.

Niedorf, Christian: 2008. *Die mittelbabylonischen Rechtsurkunden aus Alalaḫ (Schicht IV)*. Münster: Ugarit.

Nougayrol, Jean: 1955. *Le Palais royal d'Ugarit, publié sous la direction de Claude F.-A. Schaeffer, vol. 3: Textes accadiens et hourrites des archives est, ouest et centrales, avec des études de G. Boyer et E. Laroche*. Paris: Imprimerie Nationale.

Nyberg, Samuel: 1988. *Frahang-i pahlavīk: from the posthumous papers of Henrik Samuel Nyberg by Bo Utas*. Wiesbaden: Harrassowitz.

Oelsner, Joachim: 1978. "Zur neu- und spätbabylonischen Siegelpraxis". In: *Festschrift Lubor Matouš*. Edited by B. Hruška and G. Komoroczy, Bd. 2: 167–86. Budapest.

Oelsner, Joachim: 1995. "Recht im hellenistischen Babylonien: Tempel – Schuldrecht – Sklaven – allgemeine Charakterisierung" In: Geller and Maehler 1995, 106–48.

Oelsner, Joachim: 1996. "Siegelung und Archivierung von Dokumenten im hellenistischen Babylonien". In: Boussac and Invernizzi 1996, 101–12.

Oelsner, Joachim: 1997. "Neulspätbabylonische und aramäische Kaufverträge" in: *Ana šadî Labnāni lū allik. Beiträge zu altorienta- lischen und mittelmeerischen Kulturen. Festschrift für Wolfgang Röllig*, 307–14. Neukirchen-Vluyn: Kevelaer.

Oelsner, Joachim: 2002. "Frühneubabylonische Rechtsurkunden: die Schlußklauseln". In: *Ex Mesopotamia et Syria Lux. Festschrift für Manfried Dietrich zu seinem 65. Geburtstag*. Edited by O. Loretz, K.A. Metzler and H. Schaudig, 527–44. Münster: Ugarit.

Oelsner, Joachim: 2009. "Bemerkungen zu den neu- und spätbabylonischen Kauffomularen". *ZAR* 15: 31–55.

Oelsner, Joachim, Bruce Wells and Cornelia Wunsch: 2003. "Mesopotamia. Neo-Babylonian Period". In: Westbrook, 2003a, 911–74.

Olmo Lete, Gregorio Del and Juaquin Sanmartin: 2015. *A dictionary of the Ugaritic language in the alphabetic tradition*. Leiden: Brill.

Opificius, R.: 1957–71."Gottessiegel". *RlA* 3: 576–80.

Oppenheim, Leo: 1936. "Der Eid in den Rechtsurkunden aus Susa". *Wiener Zeitschrift für die Kunde des Morgenlandes* 43: 242–62.

Oudshoorn, Jacobine G.: 2007. *The relationship between Roman and local law in the Babatha and Salome Komaise archives.* Leiden. Brill.

Palme, Bernhard: 2009. "The Range of Documentary Texts: Types and Categories". In: *The Oxford handbook of papyrology.* Edited by Roger Bagnall, 358–94. Oxford: Oxford University Press.

Panaino, Antonio: 1990. "Calendar". *EIr* 4: 658–68.

Pardee, Denis: 2008. "Review Muffs, 2003". *JNES* 67: 311–12.

Parpola, Simo and Gernot Wilhelm: 2011–13. "Staatvertrag". *RlA* 13: 38–49.

Paulus, Sussane: 2014. *Die babylonischen Kudurru-Inschriften von der kassitischen bis zur frühbabylonischen Zeit.* Münster: Ugarit.

Payne, John A.: 1998. "Ergative Construction". *EIr* 8: 555–8.

Perikhaian, Anahit: 1983. "Iranian Society and Law". In: *Cambridge History of Iran: The Seleucid, Parthian and Sasanian Periods.* Edited by Ehsan Yarshater, 3(2): 627–80. Cambridge: Cambridge University Press.

Perikhanian, Anahit: 1997. *The book of a thousand judgements.* Costa Mesa, CA: Mazda Publishers.

Petschow, Herbert: 1939. *Die neubabylonischen Kaufformulare.* Leipzig: Weicher.

Petschow, Herbert: 1965. "Die neubabylonische Zwiegesprächsurkunde und Genesis 23". *JCS* 19: 103–20.

Pfeiffer, Robert Henry and E.A. Speiser: 1936. *One hundred new selected Nuzi texts.* New Haven: American Schools of Oriental Research.

Podany, Amanda H.: 2002. *The land of Hana: kings, chronology, and scribal tradition.* Bethesda: CDL Press.

Podany, Amanda H.: 2016. "The Conservatism of Hana Scribal Tradition". In: *Cultures and Societies in the Middle Euphrates and Habur Areas in the Second Millennium BC: Scribal Education and Scribal Traditions.* Edited by Shigeo Yamada and Daisuke Shibata, 69–98. Wiesbaden: Harrassowitz.

Podany, Amanda H.: 1997. "Some Shared Traditions between Ḫana and the Kassites". In: Young et al., 1997, 416–432.

Porten, Bezalel: 1969. *Archives from Elephantine: the life of an ancient Jewish military colony.* Berkeley: University of California Press.

Porten, Bezalel: 1981. "Structure and Chiasmus in Aramaic Contracts and Letters". In: *Chiasmus in Antiquity: Structures, Analyses, Exegesis.* Edited by John W. Welch, 169–82. Hildesheim: Gerstenberg Verlag.

Porten, Bezalel: 1992. "Aramaic-Demotic Equivalents: Who is the Borrower and Who the Lender?". In: *Life in a Multi-Cultural Society: Egypt from Cambyses to Constantine and Beyond.* Edited by J. Johnson, 259–264. Chicago: Oriental Institute of the University of Chicago.

Porten, Bezalel (ed.): 1996. *The Elephantine papyri in English: three millennia of cross-cultural continuity and change.* Leiden: Brill.

Porten, Bezalel: 1997. "Egyptian Aramaic Texts". In: *The Oxford Encyclopedia of Archaeology in the Near East.* Edited by Eric M. Meyers, 3: 213–219, 5: 393–410. Oxford: Oxford University Press.

Porten, Bezalel: 2000. "Boundary Descriptions in the Bible and in Conveyances from Egypt and the Judean Desert". In: Schiffman et al., 2000, 852–61.

Porten, Bezalel: 2003. "Elephantine and the Bible". In: Schiffman, 2003a, 51–84.

Porten, Bezalel (ed.): 2011. *The Elephantine papyri in English: three millennia of cross-cultural continuity and change.* 2nd rev. Ed. Atlanta: Society of Biblical Literature.

Porten Bezalel and Ada Yardeni: 1986–1999. *Textbook of Aramaic documents from ancient Egypt.* 4 Vols. Winona Lake: Eisenbrauns.

Postgate, John: 1976. *Fifty Neo-Assyrian legal documents.* Warminster: Aris & Phillips.

Postgate, John: 1997. "Middle Assyrian to Neo-Assyrian: the Nature of the Shift". In: *Assyrien im Wandel der Zeiten.* Edited by Helmut Waetzoldt and Harald Hauptmann, 159–68. Heidelberg: Heidelberger Orientverlag.

Powell, Marvin: 1984. "Late Babylonian Surface Mensuration". *AfO*: 31: 32–66.

Powell, Marvin: 1987–1990. "Maße und Gewichte". *RlA* 7: 457–530.

Powell, Marvin: 1992. "Weights and Measures". In: *The Anchor Bible Dictionary.* Editor-in-Chief David Noel Freedman, 6: 897–908. New York: Doubleday.

Preuss, H.D.: 1999. " עולם ʿôlām". *TDOT* X: 530–545.

Pringsham, Fritz: 1950. *The Greek law of sale.* Weimar: Böhlau.

Propp, William H.C.: 2006. *Exodus 19–40: a new translation with introduction and commentary.* New York: Doubleday.

Rabinowitz, Jacob J.: 1955. "Meaning of the Phrase מחר או יום אחרן in the Aramaic Papyri". *JNES* 14: 59–60.

Rabinowitz, Jacob J.: 1956. *Jewish Law: Its Influence on the Development of Legal Institutions.* New York: Bloch Publishing Company.

Rabinowitz, Jacob J.: 1958. "Some Notes on an Aramaic Deed of Sale from the Judean Desert". *Biblica* 39: 486–487.

Rabinowitz, Jacob J.: 1961. "Neo-Babylonian legal documents and Jewish law". *JJP* XIII: 137–139.

Radner, Karen: 1997. *Die neuassyrischen Privatrechtsurkunden als Quelle für Mensch und Umwelt.* Helsinki: Neo-Assyrian Text Corpus Project.

Radner, Karen: 1999. *Ein neuassyrisches Privatarchiv der Tempelgoldschmiede von Assur.* Saarbrücken: Saarbrücker Druckerei und Verlag.

Radner, Karen: 2003. "Neo-Assyrian Period". In: Westbrook, 2003a, 883–910.

Raffaelli, Enrico G.: 2014. *The Sīh-rōzag in Zoroastrianism.* London: Routledge.

Renger, Johannes: 1967. "Götternamen in der altbabylonischen Zeit". In: *Heidelberger Studien zum Alten Orient: Adam Falkenstein zum 17. September 1966*, 137–171. Wiesbaden: Harrassowitz.

Renger, Johannes: 1977. "Legal Aspects of Sealing in Ancient Mesopotamia". In: *Seals and sealing in the ancient Near East*. Edited by Gibson McGuire and Robert D. Biggs, 75–88. Malibo: Undena Publications.

Renger, Johannes: 2008. "Law and Legal Custom during the Old Babylonian Period". In: *Diritti del mondo cuneiforme*. Edited by Mario Liverani and Clelia Mora, 183–207. Pavia: IUSS Press.

Rezakhani, Khodadad: 2010. "Balkh and the Sasanians. The Economy and Society of Northern Afghanistan as Reflected in the Bactrian Economic Documents". In: Macuch et al., 2010, 191–204.

Rezakhani, Khodadad: 2017. *ReOrienting the Sasanians: east Iran in late antiquity*. Edinburgh: Edinburgh University Press.

Richardson, M.E.J.: 2000. *Hammurabi's laws: Text, Translation and Glossary*. London; New York: T&T Clark.

Richter, Thomas: 2004. *Untersuchungen zu den lokalen Panthea Süd- und Mittelbabyloniens in altbabylonischer Zeit*. Münster: Ugarit.

Richter, Thomas and Lange, Sarah: 2012. *Das Archiv des Idadda: die Keilschrifttexte aus den deutsch-syrischen Ausgrabungen 2001–2003 im Königspalast von Qaṭna*. Wiesbaden: Harrassowitz.

Ritner, Robert K.: 2002. "Third Intermediate Period Antecedents of Demotic Legal Terminology". In: *Acts of the Seventh International Conference of Demotic Studies*. Edited by K. Ryholt, 343–59. Copenhagen: Museum Tusculanum Press.

Roth, Martha: 1989. *Babylonian Marriage Agreements 7th–3rd Centuries B.C.* Neukirchen-Vluyn: Neukirchener Verlag.

Roth, Martha: 1997. *Law collections from Mesopotamia and Asia Minor*. Atlanta: Scholars Press.

Rouault, Oliver: 1984. *Terqa final reports*. Malibu: Undena publications.

Roushan-Zamir, Mehdi: 2537/1978. *Tārik̲-e Siyāsi wa Niẓāmi-ye Dudmān-e Ġuri*. Tehran: Enteshārāt-e Dānishgāh-e Milli-ye Irān.

Rubensohn, Otto: 1907. *Elephantine-Papyri*. Berlin: Weidmann.

Rudman, Dominic: 2001. *Determinism in the book of Ecclesiastes*. Sheffield: Sheffield Academic Press.

Rupprecht, Hans-Albert: 1994. *Kleine Einführung in die Papyruskunde*. Darmstadt: Wissenschaftliche Buchgesellschaft.

Rupprecht, Hans-Albert: 1995. "Sechszeugenurkunde und Registrierung". *Aegyptus* 75: 37–53.

Sachau, Eduard (ed.): 1907. *Syrische Rechtsbücher. Bd. 1: Leges Constantini Theodosii Leonis*. Berlin: Reimer.

Sachau, Eduard (ed.): 1914. *Syrische Rechtsbücher. Bd. 3: Corpus juris des persischen-Erzbischofs Jesubocht. Erbrecht oder Canones des persischen Erzbischofs Simeon. Eherecht der Patriarchen Mâr Abhâ*. Berlin: Reimer.

Salonen, Erkki: 1967. *Glossar zu den altbabylonischen Urkunden aus Susa*. Helsinki: Societas Orientalis Fennica.

San Nicolo, Mario: 1928. "Ein neubabylonischer Rückschenkungsvertrag aus dem Jahre 523 v. Chr.". *ZSSR* 48: 575–78.

San Nicolo, Mario: 1929."Einiges aus den neubabylonischen Rechtsurkunden". *ZSSR* 49: 24–54.

San Nicolo, Mariano: 1931. *Beiträge zur Rechtsgeschichte im Bereiche der keilschriftlichen Rechtsquellen*. Oslo: Aschehoug & Co.

San Nicolo, Mario: 1974. *Die Schlussklauseln der altbabylonischen Kauf- und Tauschverträge*. München: Beck.

San Nicolo, Mario and Arthur Ungnad: 1929–1937. *Neubabylonische Rechts- und Verwaltungsurkunden*. Leipzig.

Sand, Ephraim: 2002. "Two Dialogue Documents in the Bible: Genesis Chapter 23:3–18 and 1 Kings Chapter 5: 15–25". *ZAR* 8: 88–130.

Sarfatti, Gad B., Pinijas Artzi, Jonas C. Greenfield (ed.): 1980. *Studies in Hebrew and Semitic Languages Dedicated to the Memory of Prof. Eduard Yechezkel Kutscher*. Ramat-Gan: Bar-Ilan University Press.

Scarborough, Matthew J.C.: 2021. "Bactrian χþονο '(calendar) year, (regnal) year'". *JRAS* 31: 1–9.

Scarcia, Gianroberto: 1963. "A preliminary report on a Persian legal document of 470/1078 found at Bāmiyān". *EW* 14: 73–86.

Scarcia, Gianroberto: 1966. "An Edition of the Persian Legal Document from Bāmiyān". *EW* 16: 290–295.

Scheil, Jörg-Michael: 1995. *Die chinesischen Vertragsurkunden aus Turfan*. Stuttgart: Steiner.

Scheil, Vincent: 1930–33. *Actes juridiques susiens. 3 vols. Mémoires de la Mission archéologique de Perse 22–4*. Paris: E. Leroux.

Schiffman, Lawrence H.: 2003a. *Semitic papyrology in context: a climate of creativity*. Leiden: Brill.

Schiffman, Lawrence H.: 2003b. "Witnesses and Signatures in the Hebrew and Aramaic Documents from the Bar Kokhba Caves". In: Schiffman, 2003a, 165–86.

Schiffman, Lawrence H.: 2005. "Reflections on the Deeds of Sale from the Judaean Desert in Light of Rabbinic Literature" In: *Law in the Documents of the Judaean Desert*. Edited by Ranon Katzoff and David Schaps, 185–203. Leiden: Brill.

Schiffman, Lawrence H., Emanuel Tov and James C. VanderKam: 2000. *The Dead Sea Scrolls: Fifty Years after their Discovery*. Jerusalem: Israel Exploration Society.

Schindel, Nikolaus: 2011. "The Era of the Bactrian Documents: A Reassessment". *Gandhāran Studies* 5: 1–10.

Schmitt, Rüdiger: 2009. *Die altpersischen Inschriften der Achaimeniden*. Wiesbaden: Reichert.

Schmitt, Rüdiger: 2014. *Wörterbuch der altpersischen Königsinschriften*. Wiesbaden: Reichert.

Schönbauer, Ernst: 1918."Zur Entwicklung der Doppel-Urkunde in Ptolämischer Zeit". *ZSSR* 39: 224–247.

Schorr, Moses: 1913. *Urkunden des altbabylonischen Zivil- und Prozessrechts*. Leipzig: Heinrich.

Schramm, Wolfgang: 2010. *Akkadische Logogramme*. Göttingen: Universitätsverlag.

Schulz, Fritz: 1922."Die Lehre vom erzwungenen Rechtsgeschäft im antiken römischen Recht". *ZSSR* 43: 171–261.

Schwiderski, Dirk: 2009. *Die Alt-und reichsaramaischen inschriften/the old and imperial aramaic inscriptions. Band. 1: Konkordanz*. Berlin: De Gruyter.

Seidl, Erwin: 1962. *Ptolemäische Rechtsgeschichte*. Glückstadt: Augustin.

Selb, Walter and Hubert Kaufhold: 2002. *Das syrisch-römische Rechtsbuch. 3 Bände*. Vienna: Verlag der Österreichischen Akademie der Wissenschaften.

Selb, Walter: 1964. *Zur Bedeutung des syrisch-römischen Rechtsbuches*. München: Beck.

Shaked, Shaul and James Nathan Ford: 2013.*Jewish Babylonian Aramaic bowls*. Leiden.

Shaki, Mansour: 1392/2013. "Hoquq dar Irān-e Bāstān". *Dāerat ol-Maʕāref-e bozorg-e Eslāmi*. Chief editor: Kāzem Mūsavī-ye Bojnūrdī, 21: 102–11. Tehran: Markaz-e Dāerat ol-Maʕāref-e bozorg-e Eslāmi.

Shaki, Mansour: 1992. "Class System: iii. In the Parthian and Sasanian Periods". *EIr* 5: 652–58.

Shaki, Mansour: 1993. "Contracts". *EIr* 6: 22–224.

Sheikh, Hossein: 2019. "Die Kyria-Klausel in den ost-mitteliranischen Sprachen". In: *Unter dem Bodhi-Baum, Festschrift für Klaus Röhrborn anlässlich des 80. Geburtstags überreicht von Kollegen, Freunden und Schülern*. Edited by Zekine Özertural and Gökhan Şilfeler. 371–379. Göttingen: Vandenhoeck & Ruprecht Verlag.

Sheikh, Hossein: 2021. "From Mesopotamia to Khotan: Payment clauses in Eastern Middle Iranian languages and their historical backgrounds". *DABIR* 8: 118–136.

Sheikh, Hossein: 2022. "Aramaic Legal Terminology in the Sasanian Law-Book Mādayān ī Hazār Dādestān: Some remarks on Late Antique Legal *termini technici*". *Sasanian Studies | Sasanidische Studien* 1: 277–290.

Sheikh Ol-Hokamai, Emad Ol-Din: 1384/2005. "Kohantarin mubāyaʿa-nāma-ye fārsi dar Irān". In: *Pazhuhishhā-ye Īrānshināsī. J. 16 Sotūde-nāme* [2]. Edited by Iraj Afshar, 559–570. Tehran: Bonyād-e Moqūfāt-e Doktor Mahhmud Afshār.

Sheikh Ol-Hokamayi, Emad Ol-Din: 1388/2009. "Do sanad az nāhiye ye Balkh dar sadeha ye 6 va 7". *Gozāresh e Mirās e Maktub* 31–2: 23–6.

Shifman, Ilia Sholeimovich: 2014. *The Palmyrene Tax Tariff*. Oxford: Oxford University Press.

Simonetti, Cristina: 2013. "The Importance of Time in Old Babylonian Juridical Texts". In: Feliu et al., 2013, 503–08.

Sims-Williams, Nicholas: 1988. "Bactrian Language". *EIr* 3: 344–49.

Sims-Williams, Nicholas: 1989. "Bactrian Language". In: *Compendium Linguarum Iranicarum.* Edited by Rüdiger Schmitt, 230–35. Wiesbaden: Reichert.

Sims-Williams, Nicholas: 1997 (2000). "Four Bactrian Economic Documents". *BAI* 11: 3–15.

Sims-Williams, Nicholas: 1997. *New light on ancient Afghanistan: the decipherment of Bactrian.* London. [Corrected reprint in: *The Silk Road: Key papers. Part I: The Pre-Islamic Period.* Edited by V. Hansen, 1: 95–114. Leiden 2012.]

Sims-Williams, Nicholas: 1997–8 (1998). "A Bactrian deed of manumission". SRAA V: 191–211.

Sims-Williams, Nicholas: 1998. "Further notes on the Bactrian inscription of Rabatak, with an Appendix on the names of Kujula Kadphises and Vima Taktu in Chinese". In: *Proceedings of the Third European Conference of Iranian Studies (Part 1, Old and Middle Iranian Studies).* Edited by Nicholas Sims-Williams, 1: 79–92. Wiesbaden: Reichert.

Sims-Williams, Nicholas: 2000. *Bactrian documents from Northern Afghanistan, Vol. I: Legal and economic documents.* London: Nour Foundation.

Sims-Williams, Nicholas: 2001(2005). "Bactrian legal documents from 7th- and 8th-century Guzgan". *BAI* 15: 9–29.

Sims-Williams, Nicholas (ed.): 2002. *Indo-Iranian Languages and Peoples.* Oxford: Oxford University Press.

Sims-Williams, Nicholas: 2003 (2007). "A Bactrian quarrel". *BAI* 17: 9–15.

Sims-Williams, Nicholas: 2004 (2008). "The Bactrian inscription of Rabatak: a new reading". *BAI* 18: 53–68.

Sims-Williams, Nicholas: 2005 (2009). "Before the quarrel: a Bactrian purchase contract". *BAI* 19: 191–98.

Sims-Williams, Nicholas: 2006/2007. "News from Ancient Afghanistan". *The Silk Road* 4/2: 5–10.

Sims-Williams, Nicholas: 2007. *Bactrian documents from Northern Afghanistan, Vol. 2: Letters and Buddhist texts.* London: Nour Foundation.

Sims-Williams, Nicholas: 2010. *Bactrian Personal Names.* Vienna: Verlag der Österreichischen Akademie der Wissenschaften.

Sims-Williams, Nicholas: 2011. "Differential object marking in Bactrian". In: *Topics in Iranian linguistics.* Edited by Agnes Korn, Geoffrey Haig, Simin Karimi und Pollet Samvelian, 23–38. Wiesbaden: Reichert.

Sims-Williams, Nicholas: 2011 (2012). "The Bactrian era of 223 C.E. some numismatic considerations". In: *Proceedings of the Symposium on Ancient Coins and the Culture of the Silk Road, edited by the Shanghai Museum Shanghai,* 62–74. Shanghai: the

Shanghai Museum Shanghai. [上海博物館編《絲綢之路古國錢幣暨絲路文化國際學術研討會論文集》上 海書畫出版 社.]

Sims-Williams, Nicholas: 2011 (2015). "A Bactrian Document from Southern Afghanistan". *BAI* 25: 39–53. (With an Appendix by Étienne de la Vaissière).

Sims-Williams, Nicholas: 2012a. "Bactrian historical inscriptions of the Kushan period". *The Silk Road* 10: 76–80.

Sims-Williams, Nicholas: 2012b. *Bactrian documents from Northern Afghanistan, Vol. 1: Legal and economic documents*. Revised edition. London: Nour Foundation.

Sims-Williams, Nicholas: 2012c. *Bactrian documents from Northern Afghanistan, Vol. 3: Plates*. London: Nour Foundation.

Sims-Williams, Nicholas: 2015a. "A new Bactrian inscription from the time of Kanishka". In: *Kushan histories literary sources and selected papers from a symposium in Berlin, December 5 to 7, 2013*. Edited by Harry Falk, 255–64. Bremen: Hempen Verlag.

Sims-Williams, Nicholas: 2015b. "Excursus: The Inscriptions on Four Silver Vessels from Ancient Elymais". In: *Arts of the Hellenized east: precious metalwork and gems of the pre-Islamic era*. Edited by Martha L. Carter, 288–89. New York: Thames & Hudson.

Sims-Williams, Nicholas: 2016. "Bactria – Balkh: variations on a place-name". In: *Études de linguistique iranienne in memoriam Xavier Tremblay*. Edited by Eric Pirart, 273–281. Leuven: Peeters.

Sims-Williams, Nicholas and J. Cribb: 1995(1996). "A new Bactrian inscription of Kanishka the Great". *SRAA* 4: 75–142.

Sims-Williams, Nicholas and F. de Blois: 1996 (1998). "The Bactrian calendar". *BAI* 10: 149–65.

Sims-Williams, Nicholas and F. de Blois: 2005. "The Bactrian calendar: new material and new suggestions". In: *Languages of Iran: Past and Present. Iranian studies in memoriam David Neil MacKenzie*. Edited by Dieter Weber, 185–96. Wiesbaden: Harrassowitz.

Sims-Williams, Nicholas and François de Blois: 2018. *Studies in the chronology of the Bactrian documents from Northern Afghanistan*. Vienna: Verlag der Österreichischen Akademie der Wissenschaften.

Sims-Williams, Nicholas and D. Durkin-Meisterernst: 2012. *Dictionary of Manichaean Sogdian and Bactrian*. Turnhout: Brepols.

Sims-Williams, Nicholas and J. Lee: 2003. "The antiquities and inscription of Tang-I Safedak". *SRAA* 9: 159–84.

Sirat, Colette and Cauderlier, Patrice: 1985. "Un contrat de mariage juif au Ve siècle". *Comptes rendus des séances de l'Académie des Inscriptions et Belles-Lettres* 129: 348–360.

Skaist, Aaron: 1980. “The Background of the Talmudic Formula והכל שריר וקים”. In: Sarfatti et al., 1980, xl–liv.

Skaist, Aaron: 1983. “The Clasula salvatoria in the Elephantine and Neo-Assyrian Conveyance Documents”. In: *Arameans, Aramaic and the Aramaic Literary Tradition*. Edited by Michael Sokoloff, 31–41. Ramat-Gan: Bar-Ilan University Press.

Skaist, Aaron: 1990. “The Sale Contracts from Khafajah”. In: *Bar-Ilan studies in Assyriology: dedicated to Pinḥas Artzi*. Edited by Jacob Klein and Aaron Skaist, 255–276. Ramat Gan: Bar-Ilan University Press.

Skaist, Aaron: 1995. “Šīmu gamru: Its Function and History”. In: *Solving riddles and untying knots: biblical, epigraphic, and Semitic studies in honor of Jonas C. Greenfield*. Edited by Ziony Zevit, Seymour Gitin and Michael Sokoloff, 619–26. Winona Lake: Eisenbrauns.

Skaist, Aaron: 2008. “Precursors of the Emar Conveyance Deeds”. In: *City of Emar*. Edited by Lorenzo d’Alfonso, Yoram Cohen and Dietrich Sürenhagen. 219–29. Münster: Ugarit.

Skaist, Aaron: 2015. “Dees of sale and transfer”. In: *The Oxford encyclopedia of the Bible and law*. Edited by Brent A. Strawn, 172–77. Oxford: Oxford University Press.

Skjaervo, Prods O.: 2002. *Khotanese manuscripts from Chinese Turkestan in the British Library*. London: The British Library.

Skjaervo, Prods O.: 2017. “Khotanese land purchase deeds”. In: *Studia Philologica Iranica: Gherardo Gnoli memorial volume*, edited by Enrico Morano, Elio Provasi and Adriano V. Rossi, 455–67. Roma: Scienze e Lettere.

Slanski, Kathryn E.: 2003. *The Babylonian entitlement narûs* (*kudurrus*). Boston: American Schools of Oriental Research.

Sokoloff, Michael: 2002. *Dictionary of Jewish Palestinian Aramaic of the Byzantine Period*. 2nd edition. Dictionaries of Talmud, Midrash, and Targum. Ramat-Gan: Bar Ilan University Press and Baltimore: Johns Hopkins University Press.

Sokoloff, Michael: 2003. *A Dictionary of Judean Aramaic*. Ramat-Gan: Bar Ilan University Press.

Sokoloff, Michael: 2009. *A Syriac lexicon*. Winona Lake, IN: Eisenbrauns.

Sonnenschein, Ephraim: 1925 (1927). “Beiträge zu den neubabylonischen Urkunden über Kauf”. *Rocznik Orientalistyczny* 3: 180–215.

Spada, Gabriella: 2018. *Sumerian Model Contracts from the Old Babylonian Period in the Hilprecht Collection Jena*. Wiesbaden: Harrassowitz.

Spieckermann Hermann: 2014. “Eternity: I. Ancient Near East and Hebrew Bible/Old Testament”. In: Encyclopedia of the Bible and its reception. Edited by Dale C. Allison and Heinrich Assel, 8: col. 73–5. Berlin: De Gruyter.

Steingass, Francis Joseph: 1963. *A Comprehensive Persian-English dictionary, including the Arabic words and phrases to be met with in Persian literature*. London: Routledge and Kegan Paul.

Steinkeller, Piotr: 1989. *Sale Documents of the Ur-III-Period.* Stuttgart: Franz Steiner Verlag Wiesbaden.

Stemberger, Günter: 2011. *Einleitung in Talmud und Midrasch.* München: C.H.Beck.

Stolper, Matthew: 1990. "Late Achaemenid legal texts from Uruk". *BaM* 21: 559–622.

Streck, Michael P.: 2014. *Altbabylonisches Lehrbuch (Zweite, überarbeitete Auflage).* Wiesbaden: Harrassowitz.

Szubin, H. Z. and Porten, Bezalel: 1983. "Testamentary Succession at Elephantine". *Bulletin of the American Schools of Oriental Research* 252: 35–46.

Takeuchi, Tsuguhito: 1995. *Old Tibetan Contracts from Central Asia.* Tokyo: Daizo Shuppan.

Taubenschlag, Rafal: 1934. "Die Geschäftsmängel im Rechte der Papyri". *ZSSR* 54: 137–46.

Taubenschlag, Rafal: 1949. "Papyri and Parchments from the Eastern Provinces of the Roman Empire outside Egypt". *JJP* III: 48–61.

Taubenschlag, Rafal: 1955. *The Law of Greco-Roman Egypt in the light of the papyri.* Warszawa: Panstwowe Wydawn.

Teissier, Beatrice: 1998. "Sealing and Seals: Seal-Impressions from the Reign of Hammurabi on Tablets from Sippar in the British Museum". *Iraq* 60: 109–86.

Teixidor, Javier, Denis Feissel and Jean Gascou: 1997. "Documents d'archives romains inédits du Moyen Euphrate (IIIe siècle après J-C)" *Journal des savants* 1: 3–57.

Thommen, Lukas: 2010. "Griechische und lateinische Texte" In: Hackl et al., 2010, 2: 1–490.

Tolstov, S.P. and V.H. Livshits:1964. "Decipherment and interpretation of the Khwarezmian inscriptions from Tok-Kala". *Acta Antiqlla Academiae Scientiarum Hungaricae* 12: 231–251.

Tsukimoto, Akio: 1990. "Akkadian Tablets in the Hirayama Collection (I)". *ASJ* 12: 177–259.

Tsukimoto, Akio: 1991. "Akkadian Tablets in the Hirayama Collection (II)". *ASJ* 13: 275–333.

Tsukimoto, Akio: 2011. "Ein neuester Text im Ḫana-Stil in mittelassyrischer Schrift". *RA* 105: 85–94.

Tucker, Gene M.: 1965. "Witnesses and 'dates' in Israelite contracts". *The catholic biblical quarterly* 28: 42–5.

Turner, Eric: 1978. *The terms recto and verso: the anatomy of the papyrus roll.* Bruxelles: Fondation Égyptolog.

San Nicolò, Mariano and Arthur Ungnad: 1929–1937. *Neubabylonische Rechts- und Verwaltungsurkunden.* Leipzig: Hinrichs.

Van der Mieroop, Mark: 2002. "A History of Near Eastern Debt?". In: *Debt and economic renewal in the ancient Near East.* Edited by Michael Hudsonand and Marc Van de Mieroop, 59–94. Bethesda: CDL Press.

Van der Spek, Robartus J.:1995. "Land Ownership in Babylonian Cuneiform Documents". In: Geller and Maehler, 1995, 173–245.

Van Soldt, Wilfred: 1994. *Letters in the British Museum* (*Altbabylonische Briefe in Umschrift und Übersetzung Hefte 13*). Leiden: Brill.

Van Soldt, Wilfred: 2010. "The Akkadian legal texts from Ugarit". In: Démare-Lafont and Lemaire, 2010, 85–124.

Vandorpe, Katelijn: 1996. "Seals in and on the papyri of Greco-Roman and Byzantine Egypt". In: Boussac and Invernizzi, 1996, 231–91.

Veenhof, Klaas R.: 1996 (1993–1994). "C. Old Babylonian and Old Assyian Tablets (Nos. 16–17)". *Jaarbericht van het Vooraziatisch-Egyptisch Genootschap "Ex Oriente Lux"* 33: 133–42.

Veenhof, Klaas R.: 2003. "Old Assyrian Period". In: Westbrook, 2003a, 431–84.

Veenhof, Klaas R.: 2005. *Letters in the Louvre* (*Altbabylonische Briefe in Umschrift und Übersetzung Hefte 14*). Leiden: Brill.

Verger, Alessandro: 1965. *Ricerche giuridiche sui papiri aramaici di Elefantina*. Roma: Centro di studi semitic. Istituto di studi del Vicino oriente.

Vita, Joan Pablo: 2018. "Defining the Corpus of Legal Documents in Ugaritic". *ZAR* 24: 25–35.

Vleeming, S.P. 1981. "La phase initiale du démotique ancien". *Chronique d'Egypte* 56: 31–48.

Vogelsang, Willem J.: 1992. *The rise and organisation of the Achaemenid Empire*. Leiden: Brill.

Vogelsang, Willem J.: 2000. "The sixteen lands of Videvdat 1". *Persica* 16: 49–66.

Von Dassow, Eva: 1999. "Introducing the Witnesses in Neo-Babylonian Documents" in *Ki Baruch hu: ancient Near Eastern, biblical, and Judaic studies in honor of Baruch A. Levine*. Edited by Robert Chazan, William W. Hallo and Lawrence H. Schiffman, 3–22. Winona Lake: Eisenbrauns.

Von Soden, Heiko: 1973. *Untersuchungen zur Homologie in den griechischen Papyri Ägyptens bis Diokletian*. Köln: Böhlau.

Waetzoldt, H. et al.: 2009–11. "Schreiber". *RlA* 12: 250–80.

Waghmar, Burzine: 2010. "Preliminary Remarks on Bactrian Diplomatics". In: Macuch et al., 2010, 245–54.

Wallenfels, Ronald: 1998. *Seleucid archival texts in the Harvard Semitic Museum*. Groningen: STYX Publications.

Watanabe, Kazuko: 1985. "Die Siegelung der Vasallenverträge Asarhaddons' durch den Gott Assur". *BaM* 16: 377–92.

Weber, Dieter: 1997. "Pahlavi Phonology". In: *Phonologies of Asia and Africa*. Edited by Alan S. Kaye, 601–36. Winona Lake: Eisenbrauns.

Weber, Dieter: 2008 (2012). "New Arguments for Dating the Documents from the 'Pahlavi Archiven'". *BAI* 22: 215–22.

Weber, Dieter: 2008. *Berliner Pahlavi-Dokumente*. Wisbaden: Harrassowitz.

Weber, Dieter: 2010. "Parthische Texte". In: Hackl et al., 2010, 2: 492–588.

Weinfeld, Moshe: 1976. "The Loyalty Oath in the Ancient near East". *UF* 8: 379–414.

Weisberg, David B.: 2003. *Neo-Babylonian texts in the Oriental Institute collection*. Chicago: Oriental Institute of the University of Chicago.

Welles, Charles Bradford, Robert O. Fink, and J. Frank Gilliam: 1959. *The Excavations at Dura-Europos, Final Report V, Part I: The Parchments and Papyri*. New Haven: Yale University Press.

Wells, Bruce: 2004. *The law of testimony in the Pentateuchal codes*. Wiesbaden: Harrassowitz.

Wells, Bruce: 2012. Review of "Gross, 2008". *JAOS* 132: 125–7.

Wenger, Leopold: 1923. "Signum". In: *PW II2*, col. 2361–448.

Westbrook, Raymond: 1971. "Purchase of the Cave of Machpelah". *Israel Law Review* 6: 29–38.

Westbrook, Raymond: 1991. "The Phrase "His Heart Is Satisfied" in Ancient Near Eastern Legal Sources". *JAOS* 111: 219–24.

Westbrook, Raymond (Ed): 2003a. *A history of ancient Near Eastern law*. Leiden: Brill.

Westbrook, Raymond: 2003b. "Introduction: The Character of Ancient Near Eastern Law". In: Westbrook, 2003a, 1–90.

Westbrook, Raymond: 2003c. "Old Babylonian Period". In: Westbrook, 2003a, 361–430.

Westbrook, Raymond: 2003d. "Emar and Vicinity". In: Westbrook, 2003a, 657–91.

Westbrook, Raymond and Jasnow, Richard (ed.): 2001. *Security for debt in ancient near eastern Law*. Leiden. Brill.

Westbrook, Raymond and Wells, Bruce: 2009. *Everyday Law in Biblical Israel*. Louisville: Westminster John Knox Press.

Westenholz, Joan Goodnick: 2000. *Cuneiform inscriptions in the collection of the Bible Lands Museum Jerusalem: the Emar tablets*. Groningen: Styx.

Wilcke, Claus: 1982. "Zwei spät-altbabylonische Kaufverträge aus Kiš (Exkurse: a. nudunnûm und nišītum; b. Quasi-Hüllentafeln und kanikāt/tuppāt ummatim)". In: *Zikir Šumim: assyriological studies presented to F.R. Kraus on the occasion of his seventieth birthday*. Edited by G. Van Driel, Th. J.H. Krispijn, M. Stol, and K.R. Veenhof, 426–83. Leiden: Brill.

Wilcke, Claus: 2007. *Early ancient Near Eastern law*. Winona Lake: Eisenbrauns.

Wilcken, Urlich: 1920. "Die Lederhandschrifton aus Kurdistan". *AP* 6: 369–70.

Windfuhr, Gernot (Ed): 2009. *The Iranian languages*. London: Routledge.

Witzel, Michael: 1980. "Early Eastern Iran and the Atharveda". *Persica* 9: 86–128.

Witzel, Michael: 2000. "The home of the Aryans". In: *Anusantatyai: Festschrift für Johanna Narten zum 70. Geburtstag*. Edited by Almut Hintze and Eva Tichy, 283–338. Dettelbach: Röll.

Wolff, Hans Julius: 1957. "Die Grundlagen des griechischen Vertragsrechts". *ZSSR* 74: 26–72.

Wolff, Hans Julius: 1974. "Zur Geschichite der Sechszeugendoppelurkunde". In: *Akten des XIII. Internationalen Papyrologenkongresses*. Edited by Emil Kießling und Hans-Albert Rupprecht, 469–79. München: Beck.

Wolff, Hans Julius: 1978. *Das Recht der griechischen Papyri Ägyptens in der Zeit der Ptolemaeer und des Prinzipats*. München: Beck.

Wunsch, Cornelia: 2021. "Fingernail Marks on Neo-Babylonian Tablets: Their Placement, Shape, and Captions as Means to Classify and Date Tablets". *AfO* 54: 159–96.

Yadin, Yigael, Jonas C. Greenfield, Ada Yardeni, and Baruch A. Levine: 2002. *The documents from the Bar Kokhba period in the cave of letters: Hebrew, Aramaic and Nabatean-Aramaic papyri*. Jerusalem: Israel Exploration Society.

Yakubovich, Ilya: 2006. "Marriage Sogdian Style." in: *Iranistik in Europa: gestern, heute, morgen*. Edited by Heiner Eichner, Bert G. Fragner, Velizar Sadovski und Rüdiger Schmitt, 307–344. Vienna: Verlag der Österreichischen Akademie der Wissenschaften.

Yakubovich, Ilya: 2013. *Novoe v sogdijskoj ėtimologii*. Moscow: Jazyki Slavjanskoj Kul'tury.

Yamada, Nobuo: 1964. "Uigur Documents of Sale and Loan Contracts Brought by Otani Expeditions. Appendix: The Forms of the Uigur Documents of Sale Contracts". *Memoirs of the Research Department of the Toyo Bunko* 23: 71–118.

Yamada, Nobuo: 1981. "A Uighur Document for the Emancipation of a Slave, Revised". *JA* 269: 373–83.

Yamada, Nobuo: 1993. *Sammlung uigurischer Kontrakte*. Edited by Juten Oda, Peter Zieme, Hiroshi Umemura and Taltao Moriyasu. *Band 2: Textband*. Osaka: Osaka University Press.

Yardeni, Ada: 1997. "Aramaic and Hebrew Documentary Texts". In: Cotton and Yardeni, 1997, 9–129.

Yardeni, Ada: 2000. *Textbook of Aramaic, Hebrew and Nabataean Texts for the Judaean Desert*. 2 vols. Jerusalem: Hebrew University, Ben-Zion Dinur Center for Research in Jewish History.

Yaron, Reuven: 1957. "The Schema of the Aramaic Legal Documents". *Journal of Semitic Studies* 2: 33–61.

Yaron, Reuven: 1958. "On Defension Clauses of Some Oriental Deeds of Sale and Lease from Mesopotamia and Egypt". *BiOr* 15: 15–22.

Yaron, Reuven: 1960a. "Aramaic Deeds of Conveyance". *Biblica* 41: 248–74.

Yaron, Reuven: 1960a. "Aramaic Deeds of Conveyance". *Biblica* 41: 379–94.

Yaron, Reuven: 1960c. "The Murabba'at Documents". *JJS* XI: 157–71.

Yaron, Reuven: 1961. *Introduction to the Law of the Aramaic Papyri*. Oxford: Oxford University Press.

Yaron, Reuven: 1970. "Review of Muffs 1969". *Revue Biblique* 77: 408–16.

Yarshater, Ehsan (ed.): 1982–. *Encyclopaedia Iranica*. London: Routledge.

Yiftach-Firanko, Uri: 2008. "Who Killed the Double Document in Ptolemaic Egypt?". AP 54: 203–18.

Yiftach-Firanko, Uri: 2013. "Doppelurkunde" in: *The Encyclopedia of Ancient History*. Edited by Roger S. Bagnall, Kai Brodersen, Craige B. Champion, Andrew Erskine and Sabine R. Huebner, 2209–2210. Chichester: Wiley-Blackwell.

Yon, Jean-Baptiste: 2013. "Palmyrene epigraphy after PAT, 1996–2011". *Studia Palmyreńskie* 12: 333–79.

Yoshida, Yutaka: 2003. "'Translation of the Contract for the Purchase of a Slave Girl found at Turfan and dated 639'. As Appendix In: 'New work on the Sogdians, the most important traders on the Silk Road, AD 500–1000' by Valerie Hansen". 159–161. *T'oung Pao* 89: 149–61.

Yoshida, Yutaka: 2013. "Review of Sims-Williams, 2012c and 2012d". BSOAS 76: 156–159.

Young, Gordon D., Mark W. Chavalas and Richard E. Averbeck: 1997. *Crossing boundaries and linking horizons: studies in honor of Michael C. Astour on his 80th birthday*. Bethesda: CDL Press

Younger, K. Lawson: 2014. "War and Peace in the Origins of the Arameans". In: *Krieg und Frieden im Alten Vorderasien*. Edited by Hans Neumann, Reinhard Dittmann, Susanne Paulus, Georg Neumann and Anais Schuster-Brandis, 861–874. Münster: Ugarit.

Zaccagnini, Carlo: 1979. *The rural Landscape of the land of Arrapḫe*. Roma: Universitg di Roma – Istituto di Studi del Vicino Oriente.

Zilliacus, Henrik: 1956. "Zum Stil und Wortschatz der byzantinischen Urkunden und Briefe". In: *Akten des VIII. Internationalen Kongresses für Papyrologie, Wien 1955*. Edited by Hans Gerstinger, 157–65. Vienna: Rudolf M. Rohrer.

Zilliacus, Henrik: 1967. *Zur Abundanz der spätgriechischen Gebrauchssprache*. Helsinki: Helsingfors.

Online Sources

Encyclopedia Iranica http://www.iranicaonline.org/.

Gāndhārī Language and Literature https://gandhari.org/.

The Comprehensive Aramaic Lexicon http://cal1.cn.huc.edu/.

Thesaurus Indogermanischer Text- und Sprachmaterialien TITUS http://titus.uni-frankfurt.de/indexd.htm.

Whitting, Robert, *Catalog of Tell Hadidi Tablets* http://www.helsinki.fiji/~whiting/hadidcat.html.H.

Index of Legal Terms and Related Terminology

Iranian

Bactrian

Pahlavi

Sogdian

Khotanese

Persian

Semitic

Akkadian